JAMES EDWARD KEOGH is a private security consultant and the author of *Burglarproof: A Complete Guide to Home Security*.

THE SMALL BUSINESS
SECURITY HANDBOOK

James Edward Keogh

A SPECTRUM BOOK

PRENTICE-HALL, INC., Englewood Cliffs, New Jersey 07632

Library of Congress Cataloging in Publication Data

Keogh, James Edward, 1948–
   The small business security handbook.

  (A Spectrum Book)
  Includes index.
  1. Small business—Security measures. I. Title.
HV8290.K46   658.4′73   80-23813
ISBN 0-13-814293-9
ISBN 0-13-814285-8 (pbk.)

© 1981 by Prentice-Hall, Inc., Englewood Cliffs, New Jersey 07632

A SPECTRUM BOOK

10 9 8 7 6 5 4 3 2 1

Printed in the United States of America

Editorial/production supervision and interior design by Frank Moorman
Manufacturing buyer: Barbara A. Frick

PRENTICE-HALL INTERNATIONAL, INC., *London*
PRENTICE-HALL OF AUSTRALIA PTY. LIMITED, *Sydney*
PRENTICE-HALL OF CANADA, LTD., *Toronto*
PRENTICE-HALL OF INDIA PRIVATE LIMITED, *New Delhi*
PRENTICE-HALL OF JAPAN, INC., *Tokyo*
PRENTICE-HALL OF SOUTHEAST ASIA PTE. LTD., *Singapore*
WHITEHALL BOOKS LIMITED, *Wellington, New Zealand*

Contents

CONTENTS

With love and thanks to Anne Keogh, Sandra Keogh, and Joanne Keogh
without whose cooperation this publication would not have been possible.

What this book will do for you

Operators of small businesses are in a difficult position compared to others in the economic community. On the one hand, the business is not small enough to be totally directed by one person. On the other hand, the business is not large enough to support a staff of experts who will answer the most complex business questions. This book will not solve all your problems, but it will act as your personal advisor when you must deal with business security problems.

Many business decisions can be made by the "seat-of-the-pants" direction given by the small business manager. Decisions involving marketing strategy, for example, can be made and then corrected after the results are in without having too much effect on the overall business operation. If the wrong product is purchased, for example, the manager will probably simply not reorder the merchandise, but his or her business will continue to operate.

One cannot, however, use the same method in making decisions when those decisions involve the security of business. The wrong decision could lead to a very costly mistake. The business operator may have only one chance to make the proper decision when it comes to security. The business may not be able to afford nor to survive a mistake in this area.

This book will give you the professional and technical knowledge you need to make the right business security decision the first time. Everything you need to know about security is contained in this book. After reading this book, you will know how to select the most secure business location, and you will be able to conduct a professional survey of the security of the neighborhood, the community, the building, and even the local police department. You will also be able to conduct a security survey of your own business. Without incurring the additional expense of a security consultant, you will know how to pinpoint potential thefts, how to spot cash security problems, and how to spot the risk of embezzlement.

One of the most risky areas of a small business is employees. Your investment and business depend on the employees not only performing their tasks with as few mistakes as possible but also performing them honestly. This book will show you how to interview a prospective employee, what to do if you find a dishonest employee, and what security devices to acquire in order to keep your employees honest.

After reading this book, you may find a need to hire either security guards or an outside consultant. How do you hire persons and firms to whom you are going to trust your business? This book will show you how. You will learn how to interview security guards and how to investigate security consultants and alarm installers. Most important, you will learn how much you should spend for outside security help.

Every business today is involved with handling checks and credit transactions. Since nothing is more secure than cash, there is always the possibility that checks and credit are bad. This book will show you how to prevent accepting bad checks and giving credit to uncredit-worthy customers. This book will show you how con artists overcome normal check and credit security procedures and, most important, what alternatives are available in check and credit security.

This book will give you important information about how to prevent shoplifting, burglary, and robbery. In each case, you will learn how to identify the criminal and how the criminal intends to attack you and your business. A good offense is the first line in defense, and this holds true in security. This book will show you what security devices you can acquire that will protect you against shoplifting, burglary, and robbery.

More and more small businesses are turning over many functions to computers, but are these functions safe? This book tells you how computer security is violated and how to identify a computer thief. You will learn what security devices to acquire to combat computer crime and what to do if your computer security is violated.

There have been many newspaper stories and even movies dealing with how organized crime has taken hold on some parts of the business community. You are in the business community. Do you know the threat of organized crime to your business? Most business managers cannot answer that question affirmatively. This book will tell you what threats exist to you and your business. But that is not all. This book will show you what alternatives are open to the small business manager when confronted by organized crime and what legal recourse is open.

Many small business operators have seen movies depicting police operations. A crime occurs; the police hunt down the criminal; and before the movie is over, the criminal is in jail. In real life, this is not as simple as it is in the movies. There are long court proceedings and many important requirements that must be met before the suspect is found guilty. Most citizens do not become aware of the real life courtroom proceedings until they have become the victim of a crime.

This book will tell you what to do if you become a crime victim and how you can help the police find the suspect. You will learn what evidence is required by the police before an arrest can be made. You will also see how both the police and the courts operate in real life—before you become a crime victim.

Security means protection for your business. Although you can attempt to keep out criminals through the use of security devices, even the best security device can be defeated by a professional thief. To have true protection for your business, you need insurance against the financial impact of crime on your business. This book will show you what protection you will need and what information you will need in order to make a successful insurance claim. You will also learn about self-insurance.

Business security should not be taken lightly. With this book, you will be able to deal with your security problems in a professional manner.

SECURING YOUR LOCATION AND YOUR EMPLOYEES

I

Professional tips on finding a secure business location **1**

HOW TO CHECK THE LOCATION'S CRIME RATE

Over the years, members of the law enforcement community and government officials have told small business managers that crime against the small business operator is on the upswing and that, no matter where a small business is located in the country, the hands of the criminal are not far away. Statements such as these are misleading, since the number of criminals and the incidence of crime differ in each area of the country. A small business owner from New York City will have a different interpretation of this statement than the manager of the same type of business in a suburban community. The crime rate of the location of the business is just as important as the marketing considerations of the site selected. In business, the small business person can sell milk anywhere in the country. Of course, the most important question to be answered by the business person is, "How much milk will be sold?" The answer will determine whether the

3

business will succeed. The same logic must also be considered when looking at the security of a location. The small business person will be a victim of crime; the question is, how much crime? The higher the crime rate, the more uneconomical the location is for doing business. Just like market potential, crime can also be estimated for a desired business location.

Crime is measured by various governmental organizations. The more common agencies involved in the compiling of crime data are the Federal Bureau of Investigation (FBI) and the municipal police department. Other agencies, such as the state police, the county police, the court system, and a host of smaller government departments all play a role in establishing a crime pattern for the particular area of criminal justice that is of interest to them.

Data, as most business people know, can be less than truthful. When looking at any crime data, be sure to understand who compiled the information and how the data filtered through the system. Before proceeding further, let us take a closer look at the typical system of policing a community. Almost everything filters through the local police department. Officers are involved in rendering first aid; catching dogs; and, most importantly, investigating crimes and making arrests. The center of the activity at police headquarters is usually at the operations desk. This is where the crime data collection begins.

As members of the public present their problems to the desk officer, among other duties, that officer must log the complaints on the record book under one of many listings. For example, a complaint from an elderly woman who thinks someone stole her pocketbook could be listed as a snatched purse or as a lost property. A complaint from a home owner who reported that his or her house was broken into and that property was found missing could be recorded as a break and entry. On the other hand, the home owner could have made the house appear that a crime had occurred in order to allow an insurance claim to be filed. But even if the latter is true, the police report would still show that a crime of break and entry had occurred.

These are two brief examples of the kinds of labeling that may be reflected in a crime data report. In one case, the decision about how to label the crime was left up to the officer at the desk. Based on his or her discussion with the elderly woman, the officer's decision could reflect a higher incidence of crime than might actually exist. In the second example, the crime statistic would also be misleading. The possibility of errors in labeling is especially important to consider when dealing with more serious crimes.

4

Further possibilities of misleading information also exist within the system. Once the crime data are collected by the desk officer, an activity report listing the alleged crimes is filed with the higher officers in the police department. Eventually, these figures are reported to the governing body, to the federal government, and to the public. As in business, many individuals' jobs are graded. After the statistics are reviewed by the superiors, the lower-ranking employee is then graded, a procedure that also takes place in the police department as well as in government. If crime based on the actual complaints received by the desk officer had increased over a manageable amount, some management action would be expected against the patrol. The same review of statistics takes place throughout the ranks, on up to the elected officials who are judged by the voters. In some police departments, the decision as to which classification to place a crime in is influenced to some degree by the grading of the officer. If the officer has some control over the recording of crime, human instinct will normally dictate steering the results to the more favorable trend.

When looking at crime numbers, keep in mind that the statistics are supplied by the people whose job it is to keep the numbers low. Most police departments try to project an honest picture in their crime data; however, always consider the human factor—both possible mistakes and possible deliberate misinterpretations—when judging crime information about a location.

Methods of Reporting Crime Data

Crime data is reported in several forms, each attempting either to illustrate a point or to render a clear picture of the situation. One of the most common methods employed by law enforcement agencies is the trend. A trend in crime will be reported as in increase or decrease from a previous period (See Figure 1–1). The trend must be defined in terms of the same set of circumstances that occur each year. To illustrate, let us look at burglary. In the first month of the year, burglary was up 10% over the previous month. As long as the same definition of burglary was used in both months, the information is meaningful. If the definition was altered in any way, the statistic becomes worthless. Some departments have been known to alter the definition of a certain crime, which would later be misleading, in that it would show a sharp decline, presumably because of increased efforts by the police.

Crime reports are also reported on a population basis—listing a certain number of crimes per thousand persons (see Figure 1–2). Such a method of measurement permits the reader to compare different locations

5

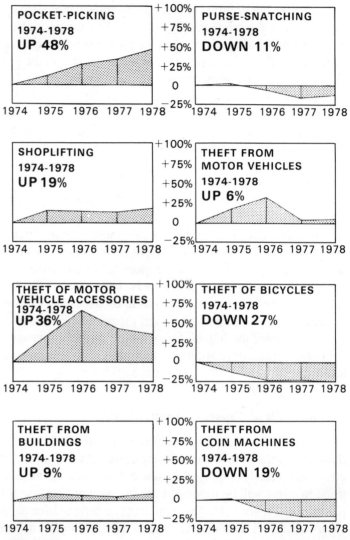

Figure 1-1
Sample of crime trend (*The Uniform Crime Report*, Washington: Federal Bureau of Investigation, 1979).

of the country as well as to compare communities. Another common method is a measurement of crime per population area. This method allows comparison between two or more similarly populated areas. Cities can be compared to cities of the same size, whereas suburban communities can be compared to their counterparts in other locations. The list of ways to compute crime is almost endless; however, the more common methods

Table 1.—Index of Crime, United States, 1978

Area	Population[1]	Crime Index total	Violent crime[2]	Property crime[2]	Murder and non-negligent man-slaughter	Forci-ble rape	Robbery	Aggra-vated assault	Burglary	Larceny-theft	Motor vehicle theft
United States Total	**218,059,000**	11,141,334	1,061,826	10,079,508	19,555	67,131	417,038	558,102	3,104,496	5,983,401	991,611
Rate per 100,000 inhabitants		**5,109.3**	**486.9**	**4,622.4**	**9.0**	**30.8**	**191.3**	**255.9**	**1,423.7**	**2,743.9**	**454.7**
Standard Metropolitan Statistical Area	**159,388,199**										
Area actually reporting[3]	99.0%	9,282,753	925,984	8,356,769	15,683	58,168	395,892	456,241	2,573,406	4,900,044	883,319
Estimated total	100.0%	9,356,438	930,629	8,425,809	15,740	58,468	397,219	459,202	2,592,698	4,942,712	890,399
Rate per 100,000 inhabitants		5,870.2	583.9	5,286.3	9.9	36.7	249.2	288.1	1,626.7	3,101.1	558.6
Other cities	**25,890,583**										
Area actually reporting[3]	96.3%	1,085,750	71,060	1,014,690	1,299	3,901	12,490	53,370	256,604	699,591	58,495
Estimated total	100.0%	1,129,850	73,882	1,055,968	1,347	4,059	12,963	55,513	267,110	728,152	60,706
Rate per 100,000 inhabitants		4,363.9	285.4	4,078.6	5.2	15.7	50.1	214.4	1,031.7	2,812.4	234.5
Rural	**32,786,218**										
Area actually reporting[3]	93.8%	627,488	54,255	573,233	2,302	4,332	6,394	41,227	233,778	300,828	38,627
Estimated total	100.0%	655,046	57,315	597,731	2,468	4,604	6,856	43,387	244,688	312,537	40,506
Rate per 100,000 inhabitants		1,997.9	174.8	1,823.1	7.5	14.0	20.9	132.3	746.3	953.3	123.5

[1]Populations are Bureau of the Census provisional estimates as of July 1, 1978.
[2]Violent crimes are offenses of murder, forcible rape, robbery, and aggravated assault. Property crimes are offenses of burglary, larceny–theft, and motor vehicle theft.
[3]The percentage representing area actually reporting will not coincide with the ratio between reported and estimated crime totals, since these data represent the sum of the calculations for individual states which have varying populations, portions reporting, and crime rates.

Figure 1-2
Sample of crime density (*The Uniform Crime Report*, Washington: Federal Bureau of Investigation, 1979).

have been identified. Each method is important to the small business person who is left with the decision of establishing a new business location.

Criteria for Establishing Locations

One of the first criteria for the small business manager to satisfy is that of density of the population. Depending upon the nature of the business, a certain population base is required in order to support the business venture. This is seen most often in retail outlets. Market decisions will determine the nature and numbers of people required to support the business activity. Once the population has been isolated, areas of either the country or state can be considered as possible new business locations. Before settling on a site, the small business manager should consult *The Uniform Crime Report,* published every year by the Federal Bureau of Investigation, which contains crime statistics as well as population areas on most communities in the United States (see Figure 1–3).

Police departments from all over the country send the FBI local incidents of crime broken down into several categories. Check all the potential sites for your business against the crime statistics found in the FBI's report. The primary items of information to use in comparing locations are the crimes per population size and the crime rate per thousand residents. The latter statistic is particularly useful, but both listings will give you an idea of the probabilities of becoming a victim of a certain type of crime.

Once you have established several likely locations that have less crime, according to the FBI report, than other sites, additional investigation is required. The next step is to check with the police departments at each of the locations. When discussing the location with the desk officer, ask to see the annual crime report for the community for the past three or four years. In most communities, this information is on public record or is part of the minutes of a public meeting. If this record cannot be obtained, check with the libraries for back issues of *The Uniform Crime Report* that contain this information. Then develop a trend line for each crime category that might affect your business. Using this trend line as a basis, again establish a ranking system for the remaining site locations. You should be able to spot several desirable locations that show less crime than others. But this is just the beginning of our investigation into the security of the site.

As we have seen, crime statistics can tell untruths. Therefore, when looking at the crime data in the FBI report, remember that the data is

Table 6.—Number of Offenses Known to the Police, Cities and Towns 10,000 and over in Population, 1978—Continued

City by State	Popula-tion group	Crime Index total	Murder and non-negligent man-slaughter	Forcible rape	Robbery	Aggra-vated assault	Burglary	Larceny-theft	Motor vehicle theft
UTAH—Continued									
Orem	4	1,744	1	5	4	19	222	1,420	73
Provo	3	2,151	1	4	12	85	382	1,520	147
Roy	5	850	....	1	7	30	148	628	36
Saint George	5	421	....	....	4	4	57	316	40
Salt Lake City	2	16,103	21	131	451	459	4,499	9,130	1,412
South Ogden	5	611	....	....	5	23	89	466	28
Springville	5	451	....	2	4	14	87	316	28
VERMONT									
Brattleboro	5	986	....	2	1	104	207	627	45
Colchester	5	526	....	....	....	17	219	271	19
South Burlington	5	901	....	1	6	6	175	673	40
VIRGINIA									
Alexandria	2	8,251	11	41	405	270	2,356	4,677	491
Alexandria State Police	9	23	....	....	....	....	1	20	2
Arlington	2	9,222	3	54	256	219	1,554	6,535	601
Arlington State Police	9	27	....	....	....	4	....	19	4
Blacksburg	4	828	....	5	8	19	141	625	30
Bristol	5	686	2	1	8	29	166	433	47
Bristol State Police	9	2	....	....	....	....	....	2	....
Charlottesville	4	2,883	1	9	37	161	415	2,137	123
Charlottesville State Police	8	11	....	....	....	....	3	8	....
Chesapeake	2	4,010	6	31	126	169	1,293	2,191	194
Chesapeake State Police	9	28	....	....	1	....	1	25	1
Colonial Heights	5	441	1	2	3	9	58	359	9
Danville	4	1,802	3	8	19	79	345	1,289	59
Danville State Police	8	4	....	....	....	....	....	4	....
Fairfax City	5	1,449	1	4	15	38	166	1,110	115
Fairfax City State Police	9	5	....	....	....	....	....	5	....
Fredericksburg	5	1,114	....	4	26	31	319	681	53
Fredericksburg State Police	8	6	2	....	....	....	....	4	....
Front Royal	5	634	....	....	7	14	133	450	30
Hampton	2	6,458	9	51	140	192	1,557	4,291	218
Hampton State Police	9	23	....	1	3	1	2	15	1
Harrisonburg	5	520	1	1	7	19	106	365	21
Hopewell	5	1,354	5	6	21	73	321	864	64
Lynchburg	3	4,029	6	16	36	266	677	2,858	170
Lynchburg State Police	9	8	....	....	....	1	....	6	1
Manassas	5	533	1	1	8	13	154	322	34
Manassas Park	5	404	....	....	1	16	70	294	23
Martinsville	5	1,234	6	1	14	83	177	886	67
Martinsville State Police	8	5	....	....	....	....	....	5	....
Newport News	2	7,350	11	67	218	344	2,111	4,096	503
Newport News State Police	9	21	....	....	....	3	....	16	2
Norfolk	1	19,472	45	138	794	1,189	4,346	11,800	1,160
Norfolk State Police	9	28	....	....	1	2	....	21	4
Petersburg	4	3,252	8	14	112	110	717	2,148	143
Petersburg State Police	9	15	....	....	....	....	....	14	1
Portsmouth	2	5,869	14	71	263	352	1,337	3,388	444
Portsmouth State Police	9	18	....	....	....	....	....	18	....
Pulaski	5	544	3	1	5	26	101	367	41
Radford	5	280	1	....	....	6	57	194	22
Radford State Police	8	5	....	....	....	....	1	2	2

Figure 1-3
Sample of *The Uniform Crime Report* (Washington: Federal Bureau of Investigation, 1979).

supplied by the local police and that the statistics are thus within the control of the police department. Areas of similar size should have similar crime patterns: This is a law in statistics. If an area you are looking at falls beyond the reasonable limits of communities of a similar size, be ready to have serious doubts about the information.

Besides drastic differences from the norm for similar communities, two other methods are used to try to flush out the safer community. Police have reported that high crime areas are usually located in low economic-based communities. Many studies have proven this to be true. If the crime statistics show a very low occurrence of crime in a poor community, you should question the information. Local police departments in such areas have been known to make attempts to hide a high incidence of crime. The second method is to read the newspapers. Although the police usually have total control over crime reports, they have little control over the news media. Although you will not be able to quantify the crime problem through newspaper reports, you will be able to get a feeling for the situation; when comparing this feeling to the police crime report, you will be able to know whether or not to have faith in the crime information.

HOW TO CHECK THE SECURITY OF THE NEIGHBORHOOD

A study of the location's crime statistics can assist the small business manager in isolating various possible sites for a business. Besides the limitations of crime statistics, another obstacle that the small business operator must overcome still remains. *The Uniform Crime Report,* as well as local police crime reports, will give an indication of crime on a community by community basis, usually by municipalities. The knowledge of a municipality's rate of crime may suit the needs of a business whose prime dealings are with market areas larger than those of a small town. Other businesses, mainly in the retail sector, must also consider the rate of crime within sections of the selected town. Even a municipality of one square mile will have varying crime rates throughout neighborhoods within the square mile.

The Uniform Crime Report and local police reports will rarely give the reader any indication as to where crime patterns exist within the municipality. Therefore, once the small business operator has used these reports to narrow his or her selection of a possible business site, further considerations need to be satisfied before signing the lease or purchase agreement. There are two types of small business managers who should be considered at this point. The first is the retail store manager, who usually depends heavily on the immediate neighborhood for most sales. These managers usually consider the economic conditions of the area of the municipality very carefully before opening up shop, but few small business people actually take time to consider the neighborhood in terms of crime and safety.

The second type of small business operator is the manager of a business whose prime market lies outside the municipality. This category is usually associated with service industries, where a service for a business client is performed on the premises and then delivered to the client. Such businesses are usually located in small office buildings and in the industrial areas of a municipality. Although managers of such businesses are usually least concerned about the neighborhood, these small business operators should consider the neighborhood as part of the requirements in selecting a new location. Crime in industrial areas and office buildings can be costly and inconvenient, a hazard to the smooth management of a plant operation. An incident that occurred in Michigan will illustrate this concern. A manager of a typesetting service was relocating his plant site. He had decided on a relatively quiet community that reserved several areas for light industrial use. The manager had toured the site during the day. He saw no signs of a security problem outside of the average security risks faced by all small businessmen. He had moved in and set up shop. Three months later, when he and the other staff members reported for work one morning, all the typesetting equipment had been stolen. There wasn't a single machine left in the shop. Apparently, late the night before, a group of professional thieves had entered the building, moved all the equipment onto a truck, and left. Without equipment, the manager was out of business. There was a three-to four-month lead time required to replace the typesetting machines. Although his business insurance handled the loss of equipment, he had lost his clientele.

A good rule of thumb to follow is to inspect the prospective location both during the day and at night. In the day, most industrial and business locations are busy and appear secure; however, in isolated business areas where few houses exist, there is a good chance that no one would be around a three-to four-square block area in the center of the site late at night. The ideal business neighborhood should be lively by day and at night; if it is not, alternative security systems must be employed.

Therefore, the question that both types of small business managers must answer is this: How can the businessman be sure that the neighborhood is safe and has a low incidence of crime? To answer this question, the businessman must imagine himself a thief. What conditions will look attractive to a thief? Before proceeding, let us take a look at who the thief is. There are two basic types of thieves. The first is the professional thief who is out to steal items of known value that can easily be sold within a few hours after the crime has occurred. In fact, many professionals will steal to order. The professional thief will usually prey on businessmen rather than the average home owner. The second type of thief is the youngster. Teenagers ranging in age from 12 to 19 are prime suspects as thieves and are the more common participants in small business crime.

Police Patrols

In general, the thief will look for areas of a community that are not frequently patrolled by the police. Several lonely blocks in a business neighborhood would obviously attract thieves, either professionals or youngsters. Police in many communities will be more concerned about patrolling residential streets than about patrolling the industrial portion of the municipality unless pressure for such patrols is mounted by local business interests. This is not to say that police patrols do not patrol business districts: The point of interest is the frequency and quality of the patrol. During the inspection of the potential site of your business, visit the neighborhood late at night or very early in the morning. Stand on the corner or wait in a parked car. Notice the frequency of the police patrols. Many times, police patrols will speed by the location without physically determining whether the neighborhood is secure. The ideal condition during a police patrol of the business district is at least to have the patrol car drive ever so slowly through the streets while shining a spot light at the businesses.

For the business manager selecting a site in an industrial area of a municipality, the frequency of police patrols provides sure warning of potential security problems. If, during your survey, you notice no police patrols, a red flag should be raised in your mind. The reverse is also true. Numerous, heavy police patrols in the neighborhood are an indicator of a high crime area. Lastly, if police patrols do not give even a brief look at the buildings, there is a potential security problem in the neighborhood.

With regard to police patrols, the retail small business operator is in a situation similar to those of businesses located in industrial areas. Police, however, usually keep a closer eye on retail stores because both lives and property are at stake, as compared to property only being at stake in an industrial area. But overall, police patrols will vary from community to community and from neighborhood to neighborhood.

Other Areas to Check

Besides looking into police patrols, there are a few other things small business managers can do to determine the security of a neighborhood. Since youthful offenders are responsible for a large portion of small business crimes, determine the make-up of the teenage population in the neighborhood and in neighboring portions of the municipality. If youngsters and young adults congregate in the neighbrohood every night, a security problem may exist. Not all members of this age group will cause trouble; however, the more kids gather in groups on the street, the greater the chance that small businesses in the area will be troubled by a security problem. A group of youngsters hanging around late at night is one of the first signs of trouble.

The accessibility of the neighborhood to major roadways is another important security consideration. Unfortunately, this is one of those criteria where the business manager will be damned no matter what decision he or she makes, since many businesses depend on a location near major highways and thoroughfares as part of their marketing make-up. Yet police in many states have noticed that crime seems to follow major roadways. If you again think of yourself as a thief, you can understand the nature of this statement. A thief who is not of local up-bringing will try to place miles between himself and the site of the crime. The farther away he or she gets from the crime scene, the better his or her chances of not being caught. Therefore, locations near major roadways also increase the risk of crime.

One of the best ways to determine the security of a neighborhood is to ask other small businessmen their views on crime in their community. Most people are willing to discuss this topic without much prompting. Don't just stop with other small business managers but continue to question others in the community, including potential customers and, most important, the local police department. When approaching the police, two techniques are particularly useful. Your initial discussion should be held with the police chief, asking for details about crime in various parts of the municipality. Later on, ask the same questions of a patrolman who frequently patrols the neighborhood that interests you. Many times, the patrolman will be closer to the actual conditions of the neighbrohood— more so than the chief, who does not patrol the area for hours each day.

13

The final items to check when looking at a neighborhood are the buildings surrounding the site of your potential business location. Businessmen will usually take security precautions by having various security devices installed at their businesses. To illustrate this, let us look at three candy store operators, one in the rural area, the next in the suburban community, and the last in the inner city. The small businessman in the rural part of the country may not have any security devices installed. He may even leave the store open when going to lunch, trusting that his customers will be honest. The same type of store in the suburban town may have a small security system installed. The inner city store operator may have bars across all the windows and doors, even during business hours. The kind of security system found on neighborhood stores is a good sign of the incidence of crime in the neighborhood. Usually, the more security devices, the higher the crime problem in the neighborhood. Once you have developed a feeling for neighborhood crime, you can decide which neighborhood will give you the lesser risk of becoming the victim of a crime.

Seven Steps to Selecting a Secure Neighborhood

1. Inspect the location of the business at night, after hours.
2. The location of the business should be lively, day and night.
3. Check police patrols.
4. Check for youth groups "hanging around" the neighborhood.
5. Check with other business operators about security.
6. Check with the police about security.
7. Check existing security devices on neighborhood buildings.

HOW TO CHECK THE SECURITY OF THE BUILDING

By following the advice described above, the small business manager will be able to narrow the site selection for the new home of his or her business down to only a few candidates. Many times, the investigation will limit the selection to two or three neighborhoods, and then the process of final selection is determined by the availability of the property and by economic factors. But business managers should not stop with those two variables in reaching a final decision. The security of the building must also be taken into consideration. Even though the municipality and neighborhood may

14

meet acceptable standards during the initial search, the building itself may not lend itself to being properly secured from a thief.

If a building appears desirable, continue to investigate the situation from a security viewpoint. The small business operator should conduct his or her own security check of the building regardless of whether the property is to be rented or purchased. For most small businesses, the location is their bread and butter. Any condition affecting the business location usually has immediate repercussions on the business and, eventually, on the financial statement.

Exterior Security

A do-it-yourself security check is not difficult to perform: It can be accomplished within an hour, depending on the size of the building that is being inspected. An initial starting point is the outside of the building. All sides of the building should be clearly visible from the street. Careful attention must be paid to any entrance to the building, especially doors and windows. All entrances must be seen from the street and must be well lighted. The primary reason for this requirement is that it forces anyone seeking to break into the building to work in a bright area and in full view of anyone who is passing the building. As you have found out during your neighborhood search, police patrols will, on the average, make only a quick pass in front of the business location. If all the entrances are hidden from the street, there will be little chance that the police officer will notice someone breaking into the building.

While checking the exterior of the building, be sure not to overlook fire escapes and entrances to basements. These, too, must be in plain view of the passing patrol car. To continue the exterior security check, compare the proposed site location with neighboring buildings. Buildings too close together offer an unpreventable obstruction of side entrances from the street. Remember that entrances are not only on the street level: Many buildings can be entered from the roof. Police officers are taught that few people ever consider problems with anything above the street level. This is why most police surveillances are conducted from atop buildings rather than from parked cars. Thieves tend to look in every direction except up for the police.

Buildings that are close together offer a thief almost total freedom to break into the building from the roof, completely out of the sight of passers-by. If the building is in such a location, check that other security precautions have been taken before making a final decision on the site.

15

Free-standing buildings that are out of jumping range from other structures are the safer of the two types of structures.

Access to the roof is also an important item to check. Besides gaining access to the roof from another building, entrance can be made using other items around the building, such as a high fence that is close to the side of the building. Other items to look for include boxes or garbage stored close to the building or even a tall tree located within climbing range of the roof. If a building has such a security problem, the condition should be improved before moving your business to that location.

Windows and doors are designed to keep honest people out. A dishonest person will usually try to find the weakness in these structures in order to gain entrance to the building. Although entrances may be well lighted, special attention must also be given to the structure of windows and doors. An incident at a county school illustrates how even a professional security consultant overlooked a basic security consideration—the door. The school building contained automotive equipment and was therefore well protected with a security system. The system consisted of bars on all the windows, which had shatter-proof glass. The windows were taped with alarm sensors, and the locks on the door were pick-resistant. One morning when the maintenance crew showed up for work, they noticed that the front door of the school building had been opened. On further inspection, the men soon realized that a few pieces of expensive equipment were missing. The security consultant who designed the system to protect the building from thieves overlooked a design problem with the door. The door hinges were constructed in such a way that they faced the outside rather than the inside of the building. The thieves realized this security fault and carefully removed the door from its hinges. All the security devices designed to protect the property became useless.

With the example of the school in mind, examine the quality of design in the door of the building. Hinges should be facing the inside of the building. The door itself should be constructed of thick, strong material, such as metal or wood. Make sure that the construction of the door is completely uniform. Older structures frequently have thick, heavy wooden doors with thin quarter-inch wooden panels placed for design purposes in the center of the door. Such a door will not give the premises adequate protection. Thieves have been known to break the thin wooden panels in order to gain entrance to the building. In modern buildings, doors are usually constructed out of metal, an excellent security device. The condition of the door frame is another item to inspect. A door is only as good as the parts connecting the door to the building. If the door frame appears worn or of poor quality, beware that a security problem could exist.

Windows, like doors, must also be made of the proper materials. Weak window frames or unprotected glass will not deter a thief. Windows must be completely secured in the side of the building. Glass panes should be shatter-proof, containing thin strands of wire throughout the glass. If a thief attempted to gain entrance to the building by breaking the glass, he or she would have to spend hours removing glass splinters from the frame and then would have to cut the thin strands of wire. The additional time required to accomplish this task will usually deter a thief. Still another area of the window to check is the molding around the edges of the glass panes. A thief can remove the glass in the same manner as a maintenance person would use to install the glass. The molding around the glass panes must be designed in a way that prevents the removal of the glass pane from the outside of the building.

Before leaving our discussion about the exterior security survey of the building there is one more area of the security check that must be mentioned—the search for signs of a previous crime. For a moment, the small business operator must play detective. Doors and windows must be examined for signs of attempted forced entry. Such signs are pry marks around the molding of the windows or the door frame. Any marks on or near any locks should be suspect. Broken glass, either in a window or as particles found on the floor, should be questioned. It is better to know what security risks might be present in the building before you select the site. Checking for these telltale signs of past trouble will give you an insight into the historical security situation of the building.

Interior Security

The exterior security of a building is of prime importance to the small business operator who is not involved with off-the-street retail trade. Interior security is of less concern, since the addition of security devices will reinforce any security faults in this area of the business. The retail operator, on the other hand, must concern him- or herself to some extent with both the external and internal security of the premises.

First of all, carry out an inspection of the entrances similar to that performed during the exterior security inspection. Any new repairs of the entrance should be questioned. If the property is to be rented, the owner of the property is likely to conceal previous attempts to break into the building by hiding or covering up signs of the attempt. While inside the building, examine the existing security system or signs of a previous security system. If the system appears to be extensive, beware! Only two types of businesses require such a security system: those that have been victims of a crime and those that have highly valuable property in the building. Ascertain which of the two pertains to the site you are considering.

The retail business person must also consider the path of customers through the building. Besides the construction of the entrances, the retail manager must consider the location of the entrances as he or she plans the store layout. The property that is either leased or purchased must be flexible enough to permit the business manager the opportunity to design a store layout that will minimize the security risk of the operation.

When conducting the interior security investigation, you should compare the existing condition with an ideal security layout. If the present interior design of the building allows the manager to approximate an ideal layout in his or her plans, the location may be considered desirable for the business. In the ideal situation, the path of the customer into and out of the building must be controlled by the small business manager. There should be only one entrance to the building, usually located by the check-out counter. Customers must enter and leave in complete view of store personnel. The doors should be offset from the actual location of the cashier. This position will lengthen the customer's exit while still controlling the site of the exit. All other doors must be locked and equipped with an emergency alarm that will permit exits in emergencies, such as fires. The open door also sounds an alarm to the store manager that a potential emergency condition exists.

The entrance to any storeroom should be completely closed off from personnel inside the store as well as from the normal path of customers. Products should be delivered from the storage area to the floor by conveyor belt, and the entrance to the storage area should be located apart from the main entrance to the store. If there is an entrance to the storage area from inside the store, this door should be locked at all times.

The store manager will find this list of do's and don't's helpful; however, understanding the reasoning behind these rules is more important. In the retail business, the most risky security areas are the theft of money and the theft of products through shoplifting. Store management has a better chance of deterring and spotting a shoplifter if all customers are required to pass through a single location, usually one that is visible by store employees. The control of cash is also an important security consideration. If cash is kept in a single location, such a situation is more secure than if cash is deposited at varous check-out locations throughout the store. Cash collection can be made periodically within a matter of minutes by management personnel walking down a short single aisle of check-out counters. If the check-outs are located throughout the store, the time may increase to an hour, and the distance to be traveled by the manager will be greater. Usually, the longer times and distances required to collect cash increase the security risk. Requiring stocking help to be located either in the storage room or in a place where they can receive goods from the conveyor belt limits the chance that a customer may remove goods from the storeroom. Not all locations will provide for such a design; however, the more this design is incorporated into the interior of the store, the better the security of the business will be.

Six Ways to Check Exterior Security

1. All sides of the building should be clearly visible from the street.
2. All entrances must be able to be seen from the street.
3. All entrances must be well lighted.
4. All fire escapes must be visible from the street.
5. All roof exits must be locked, able to be opened only from the inside.
6. All boxes and garbage cans must be away from the building.

Important Checkpoints for Interior Security

1. Check for new repairs around the windows and doors.
2. Check the existing security system.
3. Check for an interior that will offer the best security layout for the business.

HOW TO DETERMINE THE QUALITY OF THE LOCAL POLICE DEPARTMENT

During the discussion on how to conduct a security check of potential locations for a small business, we looked at crime reports, crime rates, and police patrols. All are good indications as to the security of the municipality. But we also noted that the accuracy of crime statistics—reports and rates—depended on the honesty of the police officials. Therefore, in assessing the security of a location, the small business operator must examine the quality as well as the abilities of the local police force.

19

The only contact the majority of the public has with the police is through television drama. Almost every night, the viewer is presented with police stories depicting how the police act in fighting crime. This image, unfortunately, is misleading. There are few police departments that operate on such a professional level as those shown on television dramas. During the brief encounters that do occur with real police officers, the public may not be able to gain the proper image of what a top quality police officer and police department should be. For the small business manager who must check the quality of the police department in several municipalities, he or she needs to have an idea of what characteristics a good police department should have.

When reviewing a police department, the first item to ascertain is the size of the police force. There is really no ideal number of men and women that will keep a community completely safe from crime. However, government officials have developed a guide in establishing manning requirements for police departments who seek governmental financial support and grants. *The Uniform Crime Report,* which reports statistics on crime for almost every community in the country, also contains the size of local police departments by municipality and a correlation between the size of the police force and the population of the community. *The Uniform Crime Report* lists the minimum, maximum, and average number of police officers per thousand residents, broken down according to the size of the community. For example, this report indicates that cities over 250,000 will have an average of 3.6 officers per thousand residents, with a maximum of 7.5 officers and a minimum of 1.6 officers (see Figure 1–4).

The initial step is to consult *The Uniform Crime Report* for a reading of the average number of police officers for a municipality the size of the location or locations that you are considering. The *Report* should also tell you the number of police officers there are on the local police force at these locations. By comparing these two sets of data, you will be able to find out if the police department is properly manned. To confirm this information, the small business manager should contact the local police department and confirm the number of police officers on the force. Since *The Uniform Crime Report* is usually a year behind the actual condition, any security investigation should use the latest available data. After you have checked the information, called the department, and made a comparison, rank the remaining locations according to the results you obtained.

Contact the police again and try to find out how the police officers are distributed. The small business manager should be concerned about the numbers of men on patrol rather than the total manpower of the police

POLICE EMPLOYEE DATA

AVERAGE NUMBER OF POLICE DEPARTMENT EMPLOYEES, AND RANGE IN NUMBER OF EMPLOYEES, PER 1,000 INHABITANTS

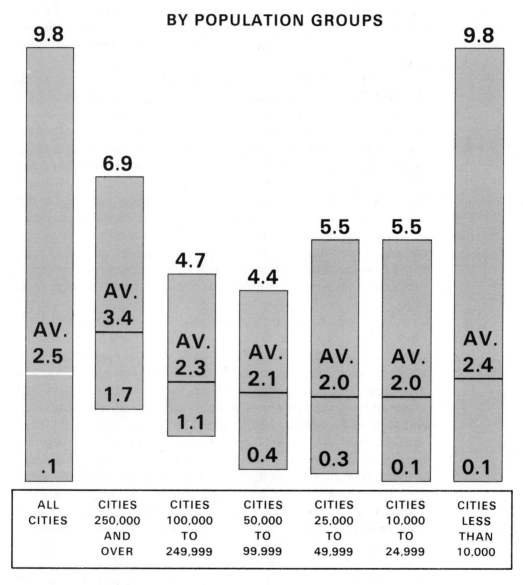

BY POPULATION GROUPS

ALL CITIES	CITIES 250,000 AND OVER	CITIES 100,000 TO 249,999	CITIES 50,000 TO 99,999	CITIES 25,000 TO 49,999	CITIES 10,000 TO 24,999	CITIES LESS THAN 10,000
9.8	6.9	4.7	4.4	5.5	5.5	9.8
AV. 2.5	AV. 3.4	AV. 2.3	AV. 2.1	AV. 2.0	AV. 2.0	AV. 2.4
.1	1.7	1.1	0.4	0.3	0.1	0.1

Figure 1-4
Size of police force (*The Uniform Crime Report*, Washington: Federal Bureau of Investigation, 1979).

force. For small business operators considering locations in large cities, instead of going to the central police headquarters for city-wide data, more meaningful information can be obtained from the local precinct. Therefore, when determining the size and disbursement of the police force in the city, concern yourself only with those officers operating from the local station house nearest your proposed location. Comparing the averages given in *The Uniform Crime Report* will still be valid for your local station house.

The distribution of police officers is important. In a town in Texas, the police force protected a community of about 25,000 residents. According to *The Uniform Crime Report,* the department had about 30 officers. On the surface, the community appeared properly protected. However, upon closer examination a small business operator who was considering the town as a location for his business discovered that there were 16 ranking officers and 14 patrol officers—more chiefs than Indians. The situation in the example typifies a problem faced by local police departments. Usually, there are few ranking officer positions available, given the normal course of activity, in a smaller police department. The police activity simply does not require more than a handful of superiors. The turnover in the smaller police department is almost nonexistent. Unless someone dies or retires, there is little chance of being promoted from patrolman for upwards of ten years.

Those who govern small towns are, of course, politicians. Many times, the influence of the 30 men on the police can be the key to winning an election. Therefore, political leaders in small towns usually try to return favors to police officers in the way of promotions—even when there may be no need for another superior officer. Some departments have been expanded into areas that were not really required, such as a drug squad. Although small towns may have drug problems, most of the real investigations are handled by outside agencies or by the detective division. The implications here are that a town having a police department of all chiefs and no patrolmen will give the small business person little protection.

While reviewing the distribution of the police department, take careful consideration of the number of police officers available for patrol. Patrol officers are the first line of police protection. The more frequent the police patrols are in an area, the more the risk involved in committing a crime in the area. When looking at the number of available patrol officers, keep in mind that each officer works eight hours a day, five days a week. There are usually three shifts of officers per day. During the vacation period, each officer will have about two weeks off the job. Using this typical schedule for a police department and knowing the number of available patrol officers, the small business operator can easily determine how many police officers are on patrol for a given shift. Even for a small town, there should be at least three patrol officers in cars checking the community.

The importance of this information can be seen from a case in a New England community. The town consisted of a one square mile area. On numerous occasions, there were only two police officers on duty for a late night shift, with others on call. However, with only two men on duty, one officer was patrolling the area in the car while the other officer handled matters at the police desk. As luck would have it, a relatively minor traffic accident occurred. Although no one was injured, the accident scene and the paperwork that followed took the patrolling officer off patrol for almost two hours. For two hours there was no one patrolling the streets. A careful examination of the work force was later made by the chief. The result of his investigation mandated an increase in patrol officers.

The number of police officers on a force, therefore, is not as important to a small business person as the actual number of officers on patrol during an average shift. After completing this calculation, again rank the remaining communities and locations accordingly.

Besides the manpower requirements and proper deployment of the police force, members of the department must be well motivated in order to perform their duties to the full extent of their abilities. Management studies have found that two types of officers are ideal for the patrol function of a police department—the new, young police officer who has been on the force no longer than three or four years and those officers who are rotated to other duties every two to three years. According to management theory, the officer will need about a year to learn the patrol function and two years or so to practice his or her skills so that he or she reaches peak performance. After three or four years in the same position, most officers will begin to slack off and will not perform at ideal levels. It is at this time that well-managed police departments will rotate the police officer to other assignments rather than simply promote the officer.

Therefore, when reviewing police departments, look for a department that has young officers on patrol and a management policy that encourages the officers to move into other areas of law enforcement within a reasonable time. Such a policy will be a motivating factor in how well the police department will protect the public. Such a policy will encourage the police officer to keep the community secure rather than just to put in his or her eight hours and go home. Again, compare the situation in the communities being reviewed and list them according to their quality.

Five Steps on Checking the Local Police Force

1. Check the disbursement of police personnel.
2. Check the number of police officers on patrol.
3. Check police management policies.
4. Check the ages of the police officers.
5. Check the physical condition of the police officers.

Finding a secure location is not an easy matter. Hours of investigation are required, both in the library and on the streets. Every aspect of security must be considered, from the condition of the windows and doors to the quality of the police department. Only after all these considerations have been reviewed should a location be chosen.

Key factors in surveying your security faults yourself 2

WHAT SIGNS A THIEF LOOKS FOR IN SELECTING A VICTIM

However well the established business location seems to offer the small business person a solid market for conducting a business, municipalities and neighborhoods change through the years. The old friendly customers may still patronize the stores, but more and more small business people are finding out that they have become open for attack by all sorts of criminals. Times have changed. In some parts of the country, small business operators have more on their minds when opening for the day then whether they will make their sales objectives. In many parts of the country, small business managers are also thinking about whether or not they will become victims of a crime—a statistic on the police record book.

Some of the small business manager's fears are real, and others are more psychological than probable. Most small operators will not have the financial ability nor the desire to relocate the business. Therefore, these managers find themselves in a dilemma. How can they be protected against potential losses? There is no simple and quick answer to this problem; however, there are a few steps that the small business owner can take to reduce the risk of becoming a crime statistic. The manager must take him- or herself out of the role of store manager and imagine that he or she is a thief searching for a victim. In ''becoming'' a thief, you will be able to spot security problems within your own business and to find out how attractive your business is to a thief.

There are a few clues that thieves—both professionals and amateurs—look for in selecting a victim. The professional thief will direct his or her attention to businesses containing large sums of cash or highly valuable goods that can be transferred into cash within a matter of hours. The amateur thieves, usually youngsters, will be looking for what they see as a quick dollar or attractive goods, regardless of value. The amateur will not care if he or she harms anyone and will usually behave unpredictably during the actual crime.

Let us look first at the professional thief. We indicated that he or she will be looking for businesses with large sums of cash: These will include supermarkets, banks, doctors' and dentists' offices, and larger retail stores, especially around the busy times of the year. The professional will also be looking for valuable merchandise, in quantity, designed for resale—the sorts of goods found in quality jewelry shops, trucking operations, and warehouses. The amateur, on the other hand, will be looking for small retail stores, even ones within walking distance from his or her house.

If you look at your own small business operation, you will be able to determine which thief is most likely to seek your business out. For example, a small liquor store will be the target of an amateur thief who is unpredictable and who should not be interfered with. On the other hand, a trucking warehouse firm will have to deal with the professional thief who is out after the valuables and who will try to avoid harming any individual.

Professional Thieves

The professional thief will look for a firm that has a fairly open security system—that is, one that has few checks and security stops on the premises. A building with a padlocked fence and no guard on duty would attract the professional thief; such a thief will usually avoid a building with a guarded fence. The professional will also look for dimly lighted buildings; for goods left unlocked, such as those waiting on a loading dock; and for carelessness throughout the building, such as unlocked windows and doors and no internal alarm system.

The professional thief will usually study the situation for days or even weeks before taking any action. He or she will plan his or her moves down to the letter and will usually plan for quick changes in the "game." When looking at a large retail business, such as a supermarket, the professional will study how the flow of cash moves from the cash register to the office and from the office to the bank. The thief may even be employed at the store, which permits a closer view of both the cash system and the security system.

A large supermarket owner in California discovered how well a thief will plan a crime. The owner had established what he thought was a well thought-out plan to keep the large sums of cash in his store safe. During the busy period, he would make his normal collection of cash from the registers and store the large sums in a safe in the office. Once or sometimes twice a day, an armored car would arrive, and two armed men would carry the money out of the store and to the bank—or at least that is what appeared to happen. At times, more than $10,000 was in the store, with only $1,000 taken out by the armored car service. Around break time, the owner would take his brown bag to his car and leave the parking lot. Although most of the employees and customers believed that he was having a snack that he had brought from home, the owner was really bringing the rest of the money to the bank. He thought that a thief would never believe that a large sum of money was in the brown bag.

However, the trick did not work for long. Apparently, a professional thief had joined the company as a checker and had somehow discovered the owner's trick. One night, the trick did not work, and the thief made off with the money. The owner was doubly surprised over the incident: first, that someone had discovered his trick, and later, when his insurance company only covered the amount of money transported by the armored car. The store owner had apparently violated his insurance contract.

To conclude, the professional will look for easy entrance to the property, time and quiet to commit the crime with some degree of security, and time to make a quick and clean escape.

Amateur Thieves

The amateur thief rarely plans the details of his or her crimes. He or she will walk into the first store on the block and ask for all the money in the register. The amateur may even miss large sums of money contained elsewhere in the store. His or her escape may be on foot through alleys and backyards or even by making a fast run down the main street of town. If police are informed within a few minutes after such a crime has occurred, there is a good chance that the suspect can be arrested. If the theft occurs when the store is closed, the amateur thief will probably look for items of personal use, such as beer and cigarettes. Although the crime may not seem worth the risk, the amateur usually gives little thought to being captured.

A Preliminary Survey

With a feeling for what a thief may look for in your operation, you are now in a position to spot inviting signs in your business. Stand across the street from your operation and examine the front and sides of the building carefully. The thief will be looking for obstruction in areas where he or she could gain access to the building. Check the windows and doors. If you cannot clearly see these entrances, neither can the police who are patroling the area. If at night you cannot clearly see the windows or doors on the sides of the building, you may later decide to install a light.

Check to see if there are any visible signs that a security system is present on the property. Such items as outside alarm boxes and tape around the windows will give the feeling that there is a system in operation. Can you see any indication that a guard is present, or can you see signs of a guard dog? The thief will be looking for such indications. Consider the window displays. Are there any valuables shown that would be attractive to a thief?

While across the street, you should be able to see inside the store, especially if the business is a retail shop. Many a thief will pass up a store where, throughout the course of the crime, he or she will be in plain sight of the street. Also, make sure that the inside of the store is well lighted enough to permit the police to see the interior clearly even while the store is closed.

A general rule of thumb to use when conducting this survey is to look for an easy method of gaining entrance to your shop without notice. If you can fine one, you have a security fault.

What Thieves Look For in a Victim

1. An obstructed view of entrances from the street.
2. Unlighted entrances.
3. Signs that a security system is present.
4. No lights on inside the business.

Many times, small business managers find out what impact a theft would have on their business only after the crime has been committed, too late to take any precautions. Some losses that would have been obvious during a security survey have had drastic effects on the business operation for many small business owners. A few have been forced out of business due to the nature of the theft. But managers do not have to wait until a crime has occurred in order to determine the impact it would have on their operation. The manager can conduct his or her own "theft" of business property or arrange a security service to help in the theft.

The previous survey, during which the small business manager actually pretended to be the thief looking over the business for inviting signs, should have revealed most of the factors that may make a business attractive to a thief. The same kind of role-playing should also take place when trying to pinpoint the impact of a theft on the business. Once again, the manager becomes the thief or has an outsider to the firm play this role. The latter may prove to be more informative than the manager, who will obviously be able to move throughout the property at will and without any question. The outside "thief," on the other hand, will be able to determine how freely a stranger can move within the confines of the business property.

Corporate Service Businesses

Before discussing several techniques that are used by outside "thieves" to help the store manager, let us first take a look at how the manager can conduct the survey without outside help. Since there are two basic types of small businesses (retail and corporate service businesses), let us consider the survey techniques the manager of a corporate service business might use. Daylight crimes to office property, as strange as it may seem, are far less risky than those committed at night. Most thieves working the office small business crime route depend on one basic rule to protect them—that most people assume others are honest as long as they do not look out of place. A case involving a highly rated music school in New York City illustrates this point. Four workmen drove up to the school in a large moving van. Taking their time, they proceeded past two guards and up to a music room where pianos were kept for students who frequently used the instrument for lessons. The workmen disassembled the nine-foot long piano and wheeled the huge instrument down the hallway to a window that faced the front of the building. They then removed the window from the building. After a block and tackle had been attached to the roof of the building, the men stopped and went to lunch. After the lunch hour, one of the men asked the guard to stop people from walking in front of the building long enough for them to lower the piano out the window and into the truck. The guard complied without question. After all, the guard thought that someone must have checked out the workmen and given them permission for such an act. But, as you may have suspected, the workmen were really thieves who had stolen a piano worth more than $10,000.

The thieves played a role that others within the building accepted. Whenever a piano had to be repaired, workmen followed the same procedures that the thieves used. Everyone working in the building knew the role of the workmen and what roles they should play in response. All except the guard left the men alone and stayed out of their way. The guard knew that his role was to help the men and to protect all the others around the building, which he did. All parts of this play seemed to be in place and appeared natural to the surroundings.

With this technique and the case of the missing piano in mind, the small business manager should walk around the building observing how his or her business is operating on a daily basis. Areas that are usually prime targets for a thief are the loading dock and the shipping and receiving area. When surveying these areas of your business, be sure to check for packages left unguarded near the door of the dock or on the dock. Most of the men or women working on the dock will assume that no one would dare to steal the packages in daylight, an assumption that is invalid. If any packages are present on the dock and unguarded, make a note of the contents of the packages, the value of the goods, and the importance of the goods to the business.

The next area of importance when surveying the loading dock is the method in which goods are shipped and received. Since most if not all of this activity depends on truckers, watch the procedures that are followed when a truck arrives. Many times, a trucker will arrive at the dock and have to wait before anyone will question him or her. If the dock's door is opened during that period, the trucker could help him- or herself to any of the cartons standing within a reasonable distance inside the warehouse and could remove these goods without anyone realizing the theft. If this is the case during your survey, estimate the number of boxes that might be taken within ten minutes, the value of the goods in the cartons, and the importance the loss of the goods will have on your business.

Continue surveying the loading dock area, but this time, concern yourself with the receiving function. The normal procedure for many small businesses is for the trucker to pull up to the dock, unload the cartons, present a bill or a list of contents to the clerk, obtain a signature, and leave the building. The clerk then files the paperwork and stores the cartons in the warehouse. As long as the number of boxes matches the number on the bill, the clerk will not question the transaction. What may also have happened is that the clerk has signed an agreement that the goods were received in proper order. Legally, the business has received the goods; however, there is really no knowledge of what goods were actually received.

A case that will point out what problems could occur during such receiving procedures involved an appliance store in Florida. The store handled a high volume of television sets. Because of the store's discount policy, consumers would check the prices there before buying a set elsewhere. Obviously, the store depended greatly on this high volume in order to assure a good financial picture at the end of the year. Right before their big yearly push on television sets, the receiving department signed for several hundred television sets, all enclosed in cartons. It was the store's policy to sell the sets to the customer without opening the cartons. As part of the normal course of work, the trucker delivered the load of television sets, all in tightly secured packages that were clearly marked "television," with a model number shown. The sets were unloaded, counted, signed for by the clerk, and then stored. The trucker left. Soon after the first few sets were sold, the store manager was faced with complaints from his customers. The store had sold the customer a box marked "television" that contained metal fill—not a television set. The trucker had apparently intercepted the delivery, removed the televisions, placed metal fill of equal weight in the boxes, and then resealed the boxes.

Naturally, the store manager was upset over this discovery, and the impact of the theft almost forced the store out of business. The manager complained to the trucking company, but the trucking company had a signed receipt from the store's agent stating that the goods were received in proper condition. The trucking company was not legally responsible. The manager complained to the manufacturer, but the manufacturer, who had received a similar receipt from the trucking company, was not responsible for the theft either. The store had to pay for the stolen television sets. The manager of the store did, however, file a claim with his insurance company, which agreed to pay for the wholesale value of the television sets in an amount above the store's $250,000 deductible policy. Financially, the business received only a very small amount of the dollar loss. But there is more to this story. The store had accepted money from customers without giving them the goods. Although the store refunded the amounts customers paid, the state's consumer agency filed charges against the store, and several customers filed criminal charges of fraud against the store owner. The store later paid a $2,500 fine resulting from the consumer agency's charges. The criminal charges were dropped; however, legal fees amounted to $10,000. Also, the store had received so much bad press that sales dropped by almost 50% in the next few months. And to make matters worse, the store could not order any more television sets in time to take advantage of the period of high demand, which caused the store's year-end picture to be in the red.

Although the repercussions of the theft were out of the control of the small business manager, the business nevertheless had to weather through what transpired after the crime had been committed. The lesson is quite clear. When reviewing your own receiving procedures, determine what the impact would be to your business if cartons of an important shipment turned out to be something less than was expected. Remember to note both the dollar value and the impact value. Chances are that if the receiving clerk randomly opens several boxes during a delivery, what happened to the appliance company in Florida will not happen to your business.

Understand that when a small business person undertakes the survey him- or herself, a true picture may not occur, since workers will perform in one fashion when the boss is around and in another, perhaps less attentive, manner when he or she is not present. Therefore, a security survey may be better accomplished by using outside help, such as a very close friend or a security service. Before reviewing how to use outside help, let us look at other parts of the business. The office is another place where the business could come almost to a halt if certain machinery were stolen. When conducting the survey of your office, try to discover the normal employee patterns of movement during the day. As with the loading dock procedures, determine how freely a visitor or service person can move throughout the office. If a visitor stands in an office area waiting for assistance while there is no one in sight, then note the small business items and other items found in an office that could be removed within three or four minutes. Be sure to include typewriters, tape recorders, radios, cash, pocketbooks, and so on. Also note the estimated value of such items and their impact on the business.

Retail Business

The same type of survey can be conducted by managers of small retail stores. When conducting the survey, the manager must take himself out of the picture and determine what items are left open and unguarded in the shop. During slow periods, for example, the cash register may be unattended, or the door to the store may be out of sight. If you find these factors in your store, make a list of the items around the door that can be taken within a matter of minutes and determine the dollar value of these goods. Do the same with all the money normally kept in the cash drawer during the day, for this is the amount that could be lost in a theft.

Both types of small business managers can closely approximate what could be taken by a thief if an outside ''thief'' is employed. If the manager uses an outside helper in conducting this form of security check, the manager must make sure that the person is trustworthy. A relative, a close friend, or an employee of an established security service are the best persons for this technique. But be sure to give this outside person written permission to conduct the survey. Such a permission slip will answer many questions if the person is caught and the manager is not around to inform employees and the police about the survey. The hired ''thief'' should try to walk through the security survey recommended above. The only difference is that he or she will, with the permission and assistance of the manager, try to ''steal'' a sample of the goods that might be stolen. For example, instead of simply noting the cartons left unguarded on the loading dock, the ''thief'' will try to walk away with a carton. Or, in an office situation, the ''thief'' may attempt to walk off with a typewriter. And in a retail store, the ''thief'' may attempt to remove cash from the register. The ideal situation is for everyone in the business to go about his or her normal routine. In fact, this kind of security survey should be conducted with as few employees as possible knowing about it.

The employed ''thief'' should also test the honesty of the employees by offering money to an employee for turning his or her back while the crime is taking place. A report should be made on the outcome of the ''thief's'' offer. Three results may occur from this part of the security survey. The employee may accept the offer, reject the offer and not say anything to his or her supervisor, or reject the offer and tell his or her supervisor. The first two will not be in the best interest of the small business manager; both prohibit the manager from knowing that his or her business is being selected as the target for a crime. Upon hearing the results, the manager should not confront the employee with the report or inform him or her of the security survey. The manager should find other reasons for either transferring the employee or discharging him or her.

After the security survey has been completed, the small business manager will have some very important information to review. The manager will be able to calculate the total dollar loss that could actually occur in

33

a theft. He or she will also know whether the loss will have an important impact on the operation of the business. Most important, the manager will know some of the sites where a new security procedure should be instituted. Such a security survey costs the small business person little or no money and reveals startling facts about his or her business.

HOW TO CHECK GUARD SERVICES ON YOUR PROPERTY

Small business managers sometimes find the concept of security less important than other business matters. Although the manager may take care in selecting what products to sell or what services to offer, he or she will usually accept the security risk without a second thought or try to answer the potential problem quickly by hiring a security service or guard. Managers justify these responses to the security problem by claiming that as long as thefts are kept to a small percentage of gross sales, the thefts can be considered as part of the price of doing business. The second justification is that a professional service or employee can handle matters and keep thefts under control, and the cost of this service or employee is again thought of as part of the cost of doing business.

Having no security and hoping that thefts do not exceed a predetermined limit is one way of responding to the problem. Many businesses take such an approach. However, for many businesses who hire a guard service or provide an employee guard, money spent in this way is almost as good as not doing anything at all to prevent thefts. The small business manager should carefully consider the use of a guard or guard services. On paper, the business may seem to be protected, but even though the manager sees a guard in uniform, few businesses are really protected by security guards.

Hiring a Guard

The security guard gives only as much protection as he or she is trained to give. A guard without any training is nothing more than an employee in uniform. Let us consider for a moment what many businesses receive from a security guard service. Usually, the small business manager, when looking for a security service, will try to accept the least expensive vendor. This is good business practice. However, the manager must realize what he is paying for. The security guard company must pay for various overhead expenses as well as paying the salary of the guard.

Above its normal expenses, the company must also return a profit. If the small business manager pays very little for the guard service, the guard company will obviously be paying very little in the way of salary for the guard. The small business manager should ask the security company how much a security guard is paid. If the salary is extremely low, the manager must ask himself what quality guard would take a job at such a low wage. When dealing with an outside security company, the lowest bidder may not be the firm worth doing business with. Many business managers have been known to hire a guard for $120 a week to watch over two million dollars worth of products.

When hiring an outside guard service, it is important for the manager to ascertain the age and condition of the security guard who will be assigned to the property. Many guard services hire only retired persons or those with low education. A case in New England illustrates this point. A small printing plant owner hired a guard service to watch the building during the off hours. The plant owner took precautions and only allowed the guard to be stationed in a security house at the entrance to the fence that surrounded the plant location. One evening, the owner drove up to the gate and waited for the guard to let him inside. The guard stood at the gate and refused to permit the owner to pass. The owner talked to the guard, but the guard just stood there. It turned out that the guard did not speak or understand English. Soon after, the owner dismissed the guard service.

The printing plant operator saved—or at least he thought he saved—money by accepting the lowest price security service. Unfortunately, he forgot about the old saying, "You get what you pay for." Many times, guard services find it difficult to hire the most desirable candidate for the position. The top- and medium-ranked candidates usually look for some other line of work or join the larger security firms in a management role. What is left of the candidates are those who have had a difficult time finding work—college students, retired police officers, and newcomers to the country who have not been able to move completely into the working ranks. Chances are that the small business manager may have rejected candidates for employment that the guard services have then hired.

Although there are many negative aspects concerning security guards, the small business manager must still determine the quality of a guard service. The age and mental as well as physical condition of the guard, mentioned previously, will have an important impact on the quality of protection the small business manager will receive from the service. A retired police officer would seem to fill the bill as the most likely candidate for the position. He or she is not only well trained but is experienced in

35

handling the public as well as criminals, professionally. As long as the retired officer is recently off the police force, the manager can feel that he or she is benefiting from the full extent of the former officer's background. However, if the officer has been off the force for 10 to 20 years, the performance of the officer as a security guard will probably be seriously diminished. This drop in the quality of performance results from two factors. First, the officer has been away from day-to-day police work for a long period of time. His or her reflexes will usually become untuned because of the lack of the constant stimulus that is found in professional police work. The second factor to cause a drop in quality is age. The officer's prime years have passed. The condition of his or her body may be less than ideal. His or her eyes may not be seeing correctly, and there are cases where mental ability falls off.

On many occasions, small business persons have felt sorry for the retired guard; however, the manager should not be misled by such feelings. The potential risk a guard will face may force the manager to reconsider hiring the retired police officer as a guard. Although 95% of the time the security guard will actually do very little, there is that 5% of the time when he or she may confront a criminal. Will the guard be ready to handle such an occurrence? Most guards cannot. Consider the elderly retired police officer for a moment. If his or her mind is alert, the guard may try to apprehend the criminal—something most persons aged 60 or more could not physically accomplish. In failing to make the citizen's arrest, there is an excellent chance that the guard will be seriously injured—even killed. And the manager who was sympathetic to the elderly guard may well blame him- or herself for the injury.

Another consideration to keep in mind when a security guard service assigns an elderly guard is the legal repercussions that may occur if the guard confronts an alleged criminal. In such a situation, the guard will usually be the only witness to the crime. He or she alone must tell a judge and perhaps a jury that the suspect was the person who committed the crime. This sounds like a simple task; however, the elderly can at times be easily confused when confronted with a defense lawyer asking all sorts of questions designed to trick the key witness. An elderly security guard will usually not be able to convince anyone beyond a reasonable doubt that he or she did not make a mistake in arresting the suspect. Therefore, there are serious doubts as to whether an elderly guard, no matter how bright he or she may appear to be, can protect the small business person's property in the manner he or she expects.

Check Your Protection

Let us now turn our attention to an important method through which the small business operator can determine whether the guard service has protected his or her property. For a few minutes, the manager must again imagine him- or herself a thief. Similar to other security checks, the manager may again care to call upon a trusted friend or relative to assist in the guard service check. From the previous survey techniques, the small business owner should know where the thief will "attack" his or her property. Using this information, the manager must prepare to "attack" his or her own property or enlist the services of a helper who will do so.

The object is to find out how much resistance the guard service is to a thief who has his or her heart set on breaking into your building. During this exercise, try to determine whether the guard is at his or her post and is alert. There have been times when the guard is stationed on duty but is sound asleep. Check on whether the guard has a standard time schedule during the night. Some guards will have to clock in every hour at various locations throughout the building. A professional thief will watch in order to determine the schedule. Then, as soon as the guard is out of sight or is in a particular area of the building, the thief will know where the guard is likely to be and how long it will take the guard to return to the same location. Make a note of how far you will be able to penetrate the building before being detected.

One of the reasons for hiring an outside guard service is that the firm is expected to perform a professional security check on their employees. Some services require every employee to submit to a lie detector test; however, many other firms administer only a very slim examination. Consider the finances for a moment. The security firm is trying to keep its expenses low in order to attract new clients. To do so, the firm must pay low wages and cut costs wherever they can. If the firm carries out a complete security check on every employee, there is a good chance that they will not find enough trustworthy workers willing to take a poorly paid job. In order to make sure that he or she does not have a thief watching the property, the manager should extend his or her security penetration test and try to offer a bribe to the guard to turn his or her back. The results may be interesting.

The same basic approach and series of checks indicated for a manager investigating an outside security guard service can be used to select and check an employee guard. Where possible, the guard should be young and able to protect him- or herself in case the situation warrants it. The guard should be checked out through normal credit channels, and if the local police department will assist, ask them to check on the person. Depending upon the state in which the business is located, the manager may want the candidate for the guard's position to undergo a lie detection test. Finally, the manager should seek either a guard who is already trained or one who will undergo training at a local junior college.

The manager should remember that placing a person in uniform and, in rare situations, giving him or her a gun does not make him or her a professional security guard.

How to Check a Security Guard

1. Check the guard's training.
2. Check the guard's salary.
3. Check the age and condition of the guard.
4. Try to penetrate the guard's security service.

HOW TO SPOT CASH SECURITY PROBLEMS

Next to the security of highly valuable merchandise, the most important item is the protection of cash. In the service business where very little cash is handled, the concern is less about cash than it is with checking accounts and other cashlike items such as credit cards. The small retail store, on the other hand, is in a different situation. Almost all the business is cash and carry. A problem with protecting the cash in a retail business could quickly cause loss of profits and, in rare cases, closure of the business. The small business operator must take precautions to find problems with the security of cash in the store before a thief finds the security fault.

Cash Handling Procedures

The person who handles the cash must be completely trustworthy. It is easy for a cashier, for example, to remove three or four dollars each day from the cash drawer. The difference between the register receipt total and the cash in the drawer is usually accepted as an error in transaction; however, if each cashier does this every day of the week, the small amounts of money can quickly increase into a sizable sum. The trustworthiness of a cashier or other person handling funds must increase gradually over a period of time. If the store owner is going to test to see whether the cashier is honest, it is less costly if the cashier handles $50 than $1,000. Banks follow a similar procedure when working with loan officers. The loan officer may at first be permitted to give out car loans of $5,000. Later, if the officer has proven him- or herself, the bank may permit him or her to handle home improvement loans; then mortgages; and finally, large business loans. If the officer is going to make a mistake along the way, the mistake will usually have a minor impact.

A good rule to follow when looking for problems with a store's cash security is to determine the number of people who handle the same flow of cash. If a single person who is not an owner of the store handles the cash register, and if that person totals the day's cash directly and deposits the money in the bank, the manager should question the procedure. Usually, the more people who are involved in the checks and balances procedures of cash management, the less likely it is that there will be a theft. The basis of this is that there is a real likelihood that if only one person is involved in the cash flow, he or she will find it relatively easy to steal some of the money. If two people are involved in the same situation, both of them must agree to steal the money, and there is less of a likelihood of two people agreeing to commit a crime. If more people check the sum, more people would have to be involved in a potential crime. If the manager does not have at least two people handling and checking the cash, then the cash procedure should be changed.

Not all stolen cash is taken by the cashier or by those who handle the money. Criminals who rob stores usually grab whatever cash is in the register. The manager must consider that this possibility exists. In order to test this possibility, the manager should count the amount of cash in the register at any given point in time. If the amount exceeds a reasonable sum required to complete normal transactions, then there is a serious problem with cash security. Frequently, throughout the day, the manager should remove large sums from the register, leaving only enough money to conduct business. Unless the manager is conducting a business information survey, the removal of the cash from the drawer should be made at random periods in order not to attract attention.

The small business manager must store funds removed from the cash register in an area that is totally safe from a thief. When conducting a security check of cash procedures, be sure to investigate where the cash is stored. Businesspersons have been known to keep large sums of money in strange containers until they have an opportunity to deposit the funds in the bank. Some managers, thinking of keeping large amounts of money in places where a thief is least likely to look, have kept large amounts of cash in a brown paper bag on a shelf in the storeroom. Others, with the same idea in mind, have stored money in meat freezers. A recent case illustrates the extremes to which managers will go in order to keep their receipts from the hands of a thief. A manager of a New Jersey restaurant closed late on a Sunday night. Because the banks had been closed since Friday afternoon, the manager had accumulated a rather large sum of money that could not be deposited until Monday morning. The manager figured that not only would her employees know of the money and the bank closing but that a thief would also know. Since the business did not have a safe, the manager decided to place the money in a brown paper bag and store it in a spot where no one would ever look—the garbage outside the building. She knew that the garbage pickup was not due until Tuesday. When Monday morning rolled around, the manager was surprised to find out that the garbage truck had picked up the trash a day early. Fortunately for her, the men who found the brown bag with the money in it were honest. The woman was happy to receive the money, blessed with the aroma of Sunday's leftover cooking, even though the bank employees did not enjoy working on her deposit.

The small business manager must select the storage site of large amounts of cash carefully. If the business does not have a safe, then the manager should consider that a cash security problem exists. Anything less than a safe will be chancey, as we have seen in the case of the New Jersey restaurant owner.

Safe Procedures

While on the subject of safes, the small business operator who has a safe in the store should check out safe procedures. Trips to the safe should be few and far between and should be made at random times. Any business that is operated completely on a time schedule, including the handling of cash, will be leaving itself open to a potential theft. Check to see who in the business has the combination to the safe. If more than two employees or owners can open the safe, a potential security risk is present. To illustrate the problem that could result from many persons having access to the safe, consider what would occur if someone discovered that the contents of the safe had been stolen.

At first, a check would be made in order to determine whether force was used to break into the safe. If no force was used, then the next assumption is that someone who had access to the safe removed the contents. The more people there are who normally have access to the safe, the more suspects there are to be investigated. However, such an investigation should go beyond the initial owners or employees. Many times, even without the owner or employee realizing it, information about various procedures used in the business are relayed to the friends and relatives of owners and employees. There have been several cases where combinations to safes have been given to people friendly with those employees or owners who have access to the safe. But if few persons have the combination, there will be fewer chances that the combination will get into the wrong hands.

Employee Honesty

Several times throughout the discussion of how a small business manager can detect security faults in his or her business, we have suggested that the manager should test the honesty of the employees. Once again, the manager or an aide should attempt to corrupt employees, especially employees who handle large sums of cash. Most employees are honest; however, cash—especially in a small retail business—is so vital to the financial well-being of the operation that the small business operator must be sure that those who handle the cash will be honest.

Two methods can be used to determine whether an employee will resist the temptation to steal money. The first method, outlined before, is to have an aide to the manager approach the employee and try to enlist his or her help in committing a theft. If the employee does not go along with the request, the manager can assume that the employee will not enter into a conspiracy to steal the cash. On the other hand, if the employee does agree, the manager is alerted to a possible problem, but should not do anything until several days have passed. Any action that will result in the employee's dismissal or transfer must be justified, using any excuse except the agreement to join in the suggested theft. In this way, the "problem" is resolved without anyone really getting hurt.

The second method is a less aggressive one. In this case, the manager will only give the employee the opportunity to steal the money—usually a small amount. An honest employee, even if given the opportunity, will not steal the cash.

Periodically, in the ways suggested, the manager should check the security of his or her cash procedures.

Three Steps to Safer Cash Management

1. More than one person should be accountable for cash.
2. Remove excess cash from the registers.
3. A safe must be used for temporary in-store cash storage.

HOW TO SPOT THE RISK
OF EMBEZZLEMENT

Small businesses can be targets for all sorts of crime. Criminals do not always walk through the front door and hold a gun to the manager's head. Crimes also occur from within, and not only with lower ranking employees. It has been estimated that more money has been stolen from businesses by "white-collar" criminals than by all the robbers in a year. The major difference between a "street" criminal and the white-collar criminal is that everyone is on the lookout for the former, whereas very few business managers and owners ever look for the man in the suit and briefcase who is running all or a portion of the operation. White-collar crimes usually fall under the heading of embezzlement.

Every business, unless carefully watched, can become the victim of an embezzler. As long as the owner of the business is not involved in every transaction and does not sign all the checks, an embezzler can work within the accounting systems used in the business to steal money illegally from the business.

A case in West Virginia will illustrate how one type of embezzler operated on a medium-sized manufacturing plant. Like many small businessmen, the owner of the plant had started his operation on a shoestring. Through years of hard work, he had built his plant to a size where almost 150 people were employed. The owner hired a personnel director to take care of staffing the business. The new director appeared to be honest—unfortunately, no one ever caught on to the method he used in order to make a few dollars on the side. A common practice in business is to hire employees through the use of employment agencies. Most times, the company, either directly or indirectly, pays for this service. The owner of the business left hiring to the personnel director, including the selection of the personnel agencies the firm used. The personnel director used two local personnel agencies to screen all the employees who finally found employment at the plant. In fact, no one was hired unless he or she came through one of the two agencies. In reality, the director of personnel owned, under a different name, both agencies. Without the owner or the accounting department knowing the true arrangement between the personnel director and the employment agencies, the director would sign invoices, which were passed down to the accounting department for payment. Each year, the director would make sure to increase the budget for employment agency fees, and, as you might expect, the employment agency fees increased more than the inflation rate each year. When times were right, the personnel director would cause a turnover in personnel at the plant—not enough to cause alarm but enough to increase the flow of employment agency fees. As with any good company, an auditing firm would conduct an audit of his department each year. However, the auditors rarely questioned why the director used only two agencies. Through years of experience, the personnel director knew that if work was given to only one agency, an investigation by the auditors might be started. Two agencies gave the appearance of good business practice. Of course, both agencies were located at the same address and were, in fact, the same office.

There are all kinds of embezzlers. The personnel director is only the tip of an iceberg that even federal law enforcement officials have not been able to measure. Therefore, it is important that the small business owner makes attempts to spot conditions that will enhance the workings of an embezzler in his or her place of business. Although it is obviously difficult to catch an embezzler in the act, the small business owner can look for signs and procedures that invite such an activity.

Suspect Procedures and Signs

When conducting the security survey to spot flaws that would permit an embezzlement activity, there is one good rule to keep in the back of your mind. Every system involving employees should have many checks and balances. No single employee should be able to complete a total transaction without having his or her actions counter-approved by a superior. In order to illustrate this point, let us take a look at a procedure used in many large corporations to control and account for business expenses. When an employee has incurred expenses during the course of business, the company will reimburse the amount spent. However, approval of the amount and of all the necessary paperwork must be given by the employee's superior and the accounting department. Regardless of the employee's position with the company, his or her superior will always have to approve expenses. This includes top executives. For an employee to cheat beyond a reasonable amount on his or her expense report, the employee would have to enlist the cooperation of his or her superior and a member of the accounting department—a task that is difficult, if not impossible.

The small business owner must consider the checks and balances method used in this illustration and compare this procedure to all internal business procedures that involve important transactions. There should be at least three or four persons involved in the approval process before the transaction is final. Another rule to follow is that the more expensive the transaction is, the more approvals should be received. Even transactions of lesser importance to the business operation, such as office cleaning service or office supply purchases, should be passed through the approval mill, if for no other reason than to prevent embezzlement.

When checking the security of internal transactions, look beyond the number of people who are in line to approve the activity. Also take a careful look at the method in which they review the transaction. For example, a procedure may have been established requiring several signatures on an invoice before the accounts payable clerk writes out a check. The number of approvals required to complete the transactions may meet the reasonable number of approvals required by proper security procedures, but the approval is not useful if the person granting permission "rubber stamps" the issue.

A case in New Mexico will illustrate this point. A few local political leaders decided to embezzle money from a town agency. The town's accounting system required that two signatures of approval be required before the vendor could be paid. The two approvers were the town administrator and the director of finance. Both positions were political appointments, and the political leaders were careful about whom they placed in those positions. In the town administrator's post was an elderly man who had very poor eyesight and who was very grateful to the political leaders for the job. Prior to his appointment, he worked on light construction. The financial director was the town's former bookkeeper. She was also thankful for the promotion.

According to the procedures, the local political leaders would ask the administrator to sign invoices quickly, telling the man not to worry about details. He complied. The director of finance was told not to question the invoice except to determine, first, whether the administrator had signed the form and, second, whether there was enough money in the budget to cover the invoice. As might have been expected, the politicians managed to keep sending false invoices through the system. Strange as this may seem, when the law finally caught up with the political leaders, the government could only make a case stick against the administrator and the director of finance. They were the only officials who had signed the invoices.

This case may seem extreme; however, signing a piece of paper and actually approving a transaction are two different things. Check to see that those who are approving the transaction have stopped to take a second or third look at the invoice. Determine the method in which they sign their approval. Some approvers use a rubber stamp or sign blank forms. If you discover such a procedure in your operation, you have left an invitation open to an embezzler. Make sure that the signature is signed so that someone else can read the signature. A careless signature can quickly be duplicated. Periodically, those who approve transactions and who are two or three steps removed from the day-to-day contact with the vendor should spend a few minutes questioning the invoice. Most approvers who are two or three steps removed from the transaction will simply enter into an automatic approving pattern. When this pattern is broken, and when checks are made and questions asked, those closer to the transaction will be kept on their toes and will realize that there is no security in thinking that invoices can be rubber stamped throughout the system.

Three Ways to Prevent Embezzlement

1. Every system should have checks and balances.
2. All approvals on transactions should be made by written signatures.
3. Approvals should be made by personnel not directly involved in the transaction.

A carefully conducted security survey, as outlined in this chapter, will offer the small businessperson an opportunity to look at his or her business in a way few businesspersons ever see. Looking at the business through the eyes and mind of a criminal will awaken the small business manager to serious security problems that he or she may have overlooked. By redesigning procedures, the small business operator will be able to reduce the possibility that he or she will become the victim of a crime.

Simplified steps for hiring employees and keeping them honest 3

HOW TO INTERVIEW A PROSPECTIVE EMPLOYEE

When hiring an employee, the store manager usually follows one basic rule: Most people are honest. This is a true statement; however, there are a few dishonest people who act the way honest people do and who are really out to steal from a small business owner. There is no easy method to use to tell the honest people from the dishonest people. Many store managers simply talk with potential employees and hope that their ability to judge human nature will protect them against hiring the wrong person for the job. Unfortunately, more times than not, the dishonest person will be such a good talker that the manager's ability to make such a judgment is misled.

The manager's initial task in selecting an honest employee is to develop a list of good candidates for the position. Finding people who want to work is not difficult; however, finding the right person for the right job is not an easy task. The manager must first determine the nature of the job that is to be filled. Each type of position will require a different source of potentially honest employees. For example, if a manager is seeking to hire sales help, there are usually three groups of people who make ideal candidates for such a position: housewives looking for extra money, senior high-school and college students, and senior citizens. Unless the sales position pays a substantial wage, other candidates should not be considered, for several reasons. A man or woman who is supporting a family will require a certain amount of money in order to survive. For many small retailers, the amounts required to support a family are beyond the salary range the small businessperson can afford. Those who require supportive financial needs should immediately be eliminated from job consideration.

Financial Condition

When conducting an interview with a prospective employee, try to obtain a clear picture of the person's financial condition. Determine the person's motivation for seeking the position, especially if the candidate requires more income than what is normally paid by other small businesses for the same service. Key questions to ask are the following: Do you own your home or do you rent? Are you married? Do you have any children? If so, what are their ages? Do you own a car? What kind of car is it? How old is the car? If married, is your spouse employed? Do you have any hobbies? Questions along these lines will give the small businessperson enough information to develop the financial picture of the candidate.

A Vermont businessman was trying to fill the position of assistant store manager. The store owner, who operated two dairy stores, was looking for a person who could eventually manage the entire operation when the owner retired. To start, the assistant manager would be completely in charge of one store. One of the candidates was a man, 25 years old, who had allegedly been released from the service. Through questions during the interview, the owner learned that the candidate owned a 1967 automobile, rented an apartment, was married, had two children, and that his wife did not work. The job was only paying about $150 per week, with no additional benefits. With this information, the store owner was able to quickly estimate the cost of rent, car insurance, food, doctor's bills, clothes—everything required to maintain a family of four at a modest standard of living. The store owner's estimate of the candidate's living expenses amounted to more than what the store owner could pay in wages. The candidate was rejected for this reason. Several months later, the store owner learned, through conversations with other small business owners in the area, that the same candidate had been fired from a similar position because he was removing goods from the store without paying, stealing cash from the register, and converting the store into an outlet for accepting bets on horses.

As illustrated in this example, the purpose of asking for financially penetrating information is not to pry into the private affairs of a potential employee but to determine whether the person has a desperate need for cash. All employees, of course, will need money; otherwise, they would not be applying for a position. However, if the small business operator will be supplying the employee with most of the employee's income, that income must be enough to satisfy the employee's immediate financial needs.

Let us return to the three groups of people who would be ideal for a retail sales position and review their probable financial resources. Senior citizen candidates usually have other income in the form of social security, pensions, and the like. Income from the sales position will permit the senior resident to have some financial "breathing room." His or her immediate needs for money have been satisfied. The senior high-school or college students usually have their immediate financial needs satisfied by their families. Income from the sales position will usually be used to offset some of the expenses of education and living, although most will come from other sources, such as student loans, grants, and family assistance. A similar situation exists for the housewife who is looking for spare money: Her major need for money is taken care of through other sources.

During the interview, the small business operator should also look for the hidden reasons that may cause a candidate to have more financial requirements than are readily seen. These include persons who have habits such as drugs, alcohol addiction, gambling; a divorced person who has to pay alimony and child support, a person over his or her head in a house mortgage, and a person who has major medical expenses in the immediate family. Although the small business operator will be able to develop a financial picture using the more obvious clues, finding the hidden expenses will take time and skill in interviewing a candidate.

The Background Check

Once the small business manager has selected a candidate from the population group and has determined that the candidate's financial needs will not cause him or her to steal from the store, the next step in hiring an honest employee is to make a complete check of the person's background. In order to do this, the small businessperson should acquire an employment application form. Most preprinted forms require the employee to sign a statement claiming that all facts presented in the application are true and giving the employer permission to conduct a complete background check. Be sure to use an application form on which this permission is given by the candidate, as well as one that releases the employer from any claims or events that might occur as a result of this check.

When reviewing the application, make sure that all the questions are answered and that the statement is signed. Records of employment should be completely sequential. Any gap in the employment dates should be questioned and the answers noted on the application. The candidate should also be told that everything on the application will be verified. When confronted by this statement, some candidates will begin to back down from some of the information contained on the application. If this occurs, the small business operator should question the candidate's honesty. Almost everyone stretches the truth a little on an employment application, but few persons will actually lie. The manager conducting the interview must decide if the candidate lied or stretched the truth. If the former is the case, don't hire the candidate. There will always be a question of honesty later on.

When conducting the background check, calls should be made to the candidate's supervisor in his or her former positions. The manager will be able to contact the candidate's past supervisors for at least the previous two to three years. Any employment beyond this period can be verified by contacting the former employer's personnel department. In the first case, the manager can usually talk freely with the candidate's former supervisor, the person who knew the candidate the best. In the second, the manager will at least be able to verify employment dates for employers four or more years past. When contacting previous employers, be sure to determine why the employer and the candidate terminated the working relationship.

Where possible, conduct a credit check, using the services of a local credit clearing house. The information obtained here will verify the debt-payment record of the candidate. A candidate with a bad credit check should not be hired, since his or her immediate need for money may be greater than what was originally outlined in the interview.

Following the steps outlined here will not guarantee that the small business operator will hire only honest employees, but it will help the manager to weed out questionable candidates.

Steps in Hiring an Employee

1. Determine the candidate's financial condition.
2. Determine the candidate's financial requirements.
3. Determine whether a candidate has any expensive habits.
4. Make sure that there are no gaps in the candidate's employment record.
5. Conduct a background check of the candidate.
6. Conduct a credit check of the candidate.

WHAT TO DO IF YOU FIND
A DISHONEST EMPLOYEE

Although almost every business, regardless of size, has established interviewing and background checking procedures, in an effort to hire honest employees, mistakes do occur, and the dishonest candidate is sometimes hired. Such a case occurred in Detroit. A medium-sized department store needed to fill the position of warehouse supervisor. The person filling this position would be required to receive and store merchandise as well as to price all the items that came into the store. At times, this person would supervise two helpers. The store manager eventually hired a neatly dressed man in his late twenties. Early in his working life, the candidate had been employed in a shipping and receiving department and had later worked as a foreman at a truck transfer depot. According to his application, his most recent employment, for the past three years, was as an owner/operator truck driver. He was single, rented an apartment, and owned an older car. He had no credit problems, since he had never applied for credit.

The store manager conducted the background check. Everything except the last three years spent as an owner/operator could be verified. The manager found it very difficult to verify the employment of a person who had owned his own business. There was no business to call, nor was there a supervisor to speak to. The manager concluded that since the candidate's previous work history checked out, he would take the candidate's word for his past three years of employment. About six months later, the store manager discovered that whole cartons of merchandise were missing. The police were called in to investigate. After the investigation was completed, the warehouse supervisor was arrested. The store manager learned from the police that the supervisor had not worked as an independent businessman for the past three years but that he had been serving time in prison on charges of hijacking cargo.

51

Ways of Stealing

Since often, through no fault of the small business operator, dishonest employees can be hired, the small businessperson must still deal with the problem. The initial step the business manager must take in coping with the problem of a dishonest employee is to discover who that person is and what methods he or she is using to steal. Stealing by store employees can be accomplished using a variety of methods. For those employees who handle cash, the temptation is the greatest. All they have to do is to slip a few dollars in their pockets when no one is looking. For members of the sales staff, small merchandise can be concealed on their persons or in pockets, pocketbooks, or shopping bags when the employees leave the store. Salespeople have been known to conspire with customers to steal merchandise. The salesperson writes up false sales slips and attaches the slips to packages that the co-conspirator then takes out of the store. Another technique, along the same lines, is for the sales help to reduce the price of the merchandise.

Although there are numerous techniques employees use to steal from their employers, there are usually only three ways in which a small business operator can discover a dishonest employee. They are as follows: the employee is seen stealing the merchandise; the manager is informed by a third party of the employee's activities; or, in the case of cashiers, the money in the cash register drawer frequently does not agree with the tally on the cash register tape. This becomes obvious, especially if the same amount is missing each time, such as a $5 or $10 bill. A store owner, giving his employees a good night at closing time, once said, "I can just feel that half my store is walking out this door right before my eyes, but I can't prove it."

Ways to Discover Employee Theft

1. The employee is seen stealing.
2. The manager is informed of the stealing by a third party.
3. The cash drawer frequently does not balance with tally.

The Burden of Proof and Defamation of Character

Proof is the important part in spotting a dishonest employee. Unless the store manager catches the employee in the act of stealing money or merchandise or has a witness willing to swear to seeing the crime, there is no conclusive proof that the employee is stealing from the business. Just as with customers, employees have the same rights as any citizen. They are innocent until proven guilty beyond a reasonable doubt. The store manager must keep this right in mind whenever he or she suspects an employee of being dishonest.

The employee does not have to permit the store manager or another employee to search his or her person or property. This means that the store manager cannot, without the employee's permission, look into pocket-books, shopping bags, or automobiles or ask the employee to empty his or her pockets. Without such authority, the store manager is usually helpless in apprehending a dishonest employee. The employee also has a right not to have anyone else defame his or her character. A person cannot spread false rumors about another or write lies about another person. These are two other points the store manager must keep in mind when evidence suggests the discovery of a dishonest employee.

A situation in Chicago illustrates the importance of defamation of character. A store manager of a three-store chain of drugstores suspected that a cashier was dipping into the cash register. The manager called her into the office and confronted her with the situation. The cash in the register drawer did not agree with the register receipt, and this had occurred on a regular basis. The cashier claimed that she had made mistakes in counting out the change for some customers. The store manager thought otherwise and decided to let her go. The reason for the dismissal, according to the cashier, was that she had made too many mistakes. The store manager did not disagree or agree. The manager wrote on the cashier's application, "Dismissed from service because the cashier stole money from the cash register." The application was filed. Several months later, another store owner called the manager as a reference for the cashier. Instead of talking to the store manager, he spoke to a clerk in the central office. The clerk, who frequently gave reference checks over the phone, read the reason for dismissal from the application and told the caller that the cashier had stolen money from the store. The drugstore manager never learned about the call until two weeks later when a man appeared in the store and served him with a defamation of character complaint. The cashier had hired a lawyer, presented the attorney with the facts, and filed action against the manager. The manager felt that he had enough evidence to support his claim and brought several cash-register receipts and corresponding bank deposit slips to court. The judge looked at the evidence and found that the plaintiff was, in fact, defamed. The judge claimed that the manager did have suspicion and grounds for dismissing the employee based on incompetence but that the manager did not, in fact, know, nor could he have known, whether the missing money was the result of incompetence or theft. Therefore, the manager had no right to record the dismissal or to transmit the reason for dismissal as being theft related.

Because of similar cases, many large corporations will not give a character reference, either over the phone or in writing. Companies will only give a verification of employment dates and of the position held with the firm. Therefore, the small business manager should be very careful when dealing with a suspected dishonest employee. Anything the manager states or writes can be used against the manager and the store in a court of law.

Some Guidelines

If a small business manager detects a dishonest employee, he or she should react according to the following guidelines. First, determine the nature of the theft and the number of employees involved in the crime. If, for example, an employee walked off with a battery for a flashlight, the manager must consider whether a reprimand will correct the situation without losing a good employee. Since a battery is a small item of little value, and if the theft is an isolated incident, no one would benefit if the employee were fired. Remember: Never accuse an employee of a crime unless you have strong evidence against the employee. Otherwise, present what evidence you have developed and let the employee label the situation as either a crime or mistake.

On the other hand, if there have been many thefts from the store, and if the manager has definite evidence against an employee who stole a small item, such as a battery, the manager should find a reason to dismiss the employee, regardless of the circumstances surrounding the theft. Such action will quickly and informally warn other employees that similar action will be taken with them if they are caught stealing from the store. The value of the theft may be small, but the principle of honesty among employees is critical in keeping a small business financially sound.

A good rule of thumb to use when you discover a dishonest employee is to dismiss the person for grounds other than dishonesty. This rule should be followed even if the manager has strong evidence against the employee. If the manager presses the issue, there will be additional legal cost and time required to resolve the problem away from the store. In many cases, this additional cost is not justified.

Four Don'ts about Handling a Dishonest Employee

1. Don't assume that an employee is dishonest unless there is proof.
2. Don't fire or transfer an employee who is dishonest unless a different reason for the action is given to the employee.
3. Don't accuse a dishonest employee of a crime.
4. Don't inform a third party that an employee or former employee is dishonest.

TIPS ON SPECIAL INVENTORY CONTROL

In previous sections, we have mentioned techniques of employee theft. Employees steal merchandise from storerooms, display cases, and receiving departments. In a small retail business, the employees are in a unique position. They know where the merchandise is stored, they know the security system in the store, and they also know the store's inventory policy. Employees have the opportunity to spend eight hours a day, five days a week, reviewing methods on how to remove goods from the store without being caught. Obviously, not all employees seek to steal merchandise from their employers. However, those who do will usually have every opportunity to do so without being detected.

A situation in Cleveland clearly brings out this point. The store in question was a full-line drugstore that employed 10 clerks on each shift. One of the clerks, who worked in the camera section of the store, devised a method of stealing expensive pocket cameras without being detected. As is done in stores of similar size, one camera was on open display, and the rest of the stock was locked in a glass display case. A clerk had to unlock the case in order to sell a camera to a customer. Twice a year, a private firm was hired to inventory the entire store. Once every two weeks, the manager checked the camera department as well as other slow-moving merchandise departments in order to determine sales volume and the amount of merchandise to reorder. On the surface, this inventory control system would pick up unaccounted-for merchandise either every two weeks or twice a year. The clerk in the camera department found a loophole in the inventory procedures. Every month or so, she managed to walk home with a pocket camera. When the opportunity presented itself, she removed the contents of the camera box and placed the merchandise in her purse. She then returned the empty box to the bottom of the pile. During inventory and reordering procedures, those conducting the check looked only for boxes

55

and merchandise numbers. No one ever looked inside the boxes in order to determine whether the merchandise was, in fact, in the box.

Dishonest employees and, for that matter, almost any thief use one basic trait of human nature to help commit their crime. Dishonest employees know that many managers make decisions based on assumptions rather than fact. There is a box on the shelf; therefore, the box is assumed to be full. But the manager of a small business must not assume everything all of the time. Obviously, the manager who is conducting an inventory in a store that contains thousands of items of merchandise cannot open every single box; however, spot checks should be made in order to be sure that the numbers appearing on the record books actually represent items of merchandise.

Combating Dishonesty in Receiving

One of the prime areas where employee theft can occur if proper procedures are not developed is in the area of the receiving department. Let us take a quick look at what actually occurs in such a typical department. A truck unloads cartons and gives a clerk a receiving slip. A copy of the slip usually remains in the receiving department until the box is stored. Then the slip is sent to the management office. Here, the numbers of the items are logged into the system. The goods are then placed onto the floor, after pricing, and sold. Rarely, throughout the entire process, does anyone ever count the number of items contained in the carton against the receiving order. Employees who price merchandise in the receiving department, a common practice, will have the opportunity to slip merchandise in their personal carrying cases or even intentionally misprice the item. When the goods reach the sales floor, clerks stocking the displays will rarely check to see whether the price of the item is correct. Clerks usually assume that since the price is on the package, someone else checked the accuracy of the price.

To combat dishonesty in the receiving department, the small businessperson must establish inventory control procedures that will monitor the performance of employees and the flow of goods and paperwork through the system. The control procedure should require that several employees be involved in a checks and balances requirement throughout the various stages of product flow. The more people who are involved in handling the product, the more difficult it becomes for a single dishonest employee to steal from the company. The inventory control procedure should require that a conspiracy of several employees be necessary in order for a crime to occur.

For example, when goods are received by the store or even when the receiving door is open, a security guard should be stationed at that location. The guard should not be permanently positioned at the receiving door. He or she should be present during active periods when goods are or could be moved. A guard stationed at the receiving door for the entire work day could develop a close friendship with employees working in that department, a relationship that might compromise the guard or at least place him or her in a difficult position for performing the assigned task. Such a friendship is difficult to foster when the guard is present only for about a half-hour at any given period.

If at all possible, the receiving supervisor should have one or two of the boxes examined by one of the helpers while the truck driver is present and before the receiving receipt is signed. When merchandise has been verified, the receiving supervisor should mark each carton with the price per item. The receiving clerks can then easily price each item. During this process, the receiving supervisor should spot-check each receiving clerk several times during the day in order to determine whether the goods are priced properly.

Small chain stores and those small retailers who belong to buying cooperatives have developed another technique that eliminates the opportunity for receiving personnel to steal goods by mismarking the merchandise. For these stores, goods are received from a manufacturer at a central warehouse. When the goods arrive, the items in each box are counted, and a clerk prints individual price tags for the exact number of items in each box. The carton of merchandise and the preprinted price tags are then sent to each store. The receiving department personnel can then place only the existing price tags on the merchandise. There is no opportunity for the receiving clerk to create a price for an item.

When the goods reach the sales floor, employees stocking the displays should be required to sign off the pricing sheet—that is, each item being stored should also be listed on an order form or on some other sheet, so that the employee can compare the price marked on the package with the price indicated on the sheet. On a regular basis, store management personnel should spot-check the displays to ensure that the prices are marked correctly. Every employee should be informed about each phase of the inventory control procedure. If a system with tight controls is known to exist, there is a good chance that a criminal or a potentially dishonest employee will not attempt to defeat the system.

Employee Control Procedures

In order to control the loss of merchandise from employees walking off with goods when they leave the store, an employee control procedure should be established. Employees should enter and leave the building using a single door. A security guard should be stationed at the door at all times, and when entering the building, employees should be required to leave any packages, such as shopping bags, and their coats in a room set aside near this entrance. Any employee purchases made during the day should be properly tagged and left with the guard in the cloakroom.

If such a method is used, the employee will have a difficult time concealing merchandise on his or her person. At closing, every employee will have to walk in front of the guard several times before actually leaving the building. There is a greater chance for the employee to be caught under these tight control procedures than if the employee is free to walk throughout the store without going through a security checkpoint.

Security personnel and management should keep an eye peeled for employees who frequently wait on friends. Employees should be instructed that if a friend or relative is buying merchandise in the store, a fellow employee should ring up the sale. When the employee is making a purchase, the same procedure should be imposed—another employee must handle the transaction. Spot checks by management personnel should keep employees on their toes. An honest employee will usually not mind the tight controls.

TIPS ON CASH MANAGEMENT

The sight of what appears to be large sums of cash can be tempting to any employee. Employees have been known to use all sorts of justifications for helping themselves to money from the cash register: The excuses range from low wages paid to the employees to the fact that the store will never miss the few dollars that are to be lifted. To an employee making about $150 a week or less, seeing a daily gross sales receipt of $2,000 or more may foster such justifications enough to "force" an honest employee to become dishonest.

Since the handling of cash in any business is extremely important, the small business manager must make sure that tight controls are instituted throughout the cash handling procedure. As with the other areas of the store discussed previously, employees also have time to study existing cash management procedures in an attempt to find loopholes that will permit the removal of cash without being detected. It is up to the store manager to design a cash handling procedure that will not give the employee too many opportunities to remove funds from the business.

How Cash is Stolen

Before designing any system, a manager must know how some employees have successfully stolen cash from small businesses in the past. A typical cash handling system will require the cashier to open the cash register with a $50 drawer. At the end of the day or the end of his or her work shift, the cashier must obtain a tape showing the cash register total. In some stores, the cashier is required to count the money in the drawer and compare the cash amount to the register total. In other stores, the cashier turns over the receipt and cash drawer to the store manager or to an accounting clerk, who counts the cash and compares the totals. Fifty dollars is then returned to the drawer, and the remaining funds are placed in a safe until the proper time to make a deposit. At that time, either the store manager or some other employee makes the deposit in the bank. About 24 hours later, a bank employee counts the cash, compares the total to the deposit slip, and then charges the amount to the store's account.

Thefts of cash by everyone who handles the money have been known to occur. For example, a case in Texas points out a typical problem. The store owner of a chain of hardware stores realized that cashiers normally make some errors in handling transactions. However, throughout the years, the owner noted, when he compared the amounts in cash drawers to the register totals, that a consistent percentage of cash would seem to disappear. Usually, this amounted to about 1% of the total cash receipts. The owner told his store managers that they should investigate and take action in cases where a cashier's difference in totals exceeded 1% of the total amount in the register drawer. One of his managers instituted a tightly controlled procedure of balancing the cash and register receipts at the end of a day or work shift. Only the manager in this one store was permitted to handle the cash and receipts from the time the drawer was delivered by the cashier to the time the bank deposit was made. No one questioned this procedure, since it was ultimately the manager's responsibility that proper cash management procedures were followed. What was not widely known by the owner of the chain was that the manager, who realized that a loss of 1% of the total cash receipts was acceptable, was skimming 1% of the cash. If the owner asked any questions, which he did

59

not except when the accountants raised the issue, the manager claimed that the errors were caused by the cashiers.

Besides the outright stealing of cash from the store, as illustrated in this example, some cashiers have developed a technique of stealing store money without the theft appearing as a difference on the balance sheet. A major fault with most cash control systems is that the system is designed to monitor cash transactions through deposits only after the cash has been recorded on the cash register and the money placed in the register drawer. There is really no control over the situation during the actual transfer of funds from the customer to the cashier.

Cashiers realize that the small business manager must trust the cashier to ring up every sale and to ring up each sale properly. It is this trust that gives the dishonest cashier the opportunity to steal cash from the store. A dishonest cashier will typically accept money from the customer and "mistakenly" ring up the wrong price, usually one lower than the amount of the merchandise. The cashier will pretend to discover the "mistake" before he or she gives the change to the customer. Usually, the cashier will then explain the error to the customer and show the customer the price on the merchandise. The customer will usually agree that a mistake has occurred. The cashier then places the total amount of money for the transaction in the drawer.

The cashier knows that at the end of the shift the register tape's total will show a lower amount than the cash in the drawer. Since the store manager will question the cashier's cash transaction only if there is less cash than indicated on the tape, the cashier can, in fact, slip the difference in cash into his or her pocket without the cash being missing. Many times during the shift, a cashier may pretend to drop two or more bills on the floor behind the register counter. While bending down to pick up the money, the cashier will place one of the bills on his or her person, such as in a shoe or sock, and return the other dropped bill to the register. From all outward appearances, the cashier could be seen dropping the bills, picking them up, and placing them back into the register.

Another technique used by dishonest cashiers is not to record the sale at all on the register. This technique is common in businesses where receipts are not normally given to customers. Customers usually buy one or two small items, such as cigarettes, place the cash on the counter, and walk away. It is left up to the cashier's honesty to log the sale on the register and place the cash in the drawer. Some cashiers will simply place the cash in their pockets.

Checks and Balances

The small business manager, knowing how cash can be stolen from the store by dishonest employees, must devise a system of cash control that will not give a dishonest employee the opportunity to steal cash from the business. A good rule for the small business manager to follow is to program as many checks and balances as possible in the system in order to give the dishonest employee a feeling of insecurity.

In order to assist the small business manager in developing such a system, several important considerations follow. The first step in the cash receiving process involves the cashier. Where possible during the training period for a new cashier, always require two employees to be stationed at the register. The new cashier will operate the register and handle the transactions, whereas the instructor will observe and act as a bagger. The cashier will thus be observed during the complete transaction and will not be given the opportunity to ''drop'' any cash.

Even after the cashier has been trained, a good procedure to follow is to have more than one employee stationed at each register. This is especially important during busy periods when large sums of money will be exchanged during the transactions. At such times, it is difficult for a dishonest employee to enlist the services and approval of another employee quickly when attempting to remove cash from the drawer.

At the end of the day or shift, the cashier should be required to have another supervising employee close out the register. This involves ringing up register totals and locking the drawer. The supervising employee should hand the drawer and the receipt to an accounting clerk, who will tally the cash and compare the amounts to the register slip. There should be at least three or four other employees in the counting room when each register is counted. If the total on the slip does not match the amount in the cash drawer, a report should be made to the store manager. Regardless of what the difference is—whether there is more money than there should be in the drawer or not—the manager should confront the cashier with the situation. If the same cashier continues to make sizable errors, a new cashier should be employed.

The accounting clerk should make out the deposit slip and should then place the slip and the cash in a bank container that can be locked. The clerk should immediately send a report of the tally to a central accounting office, not to the store manager. The cash deposit can then be made by the store manager or by an armored car service.

As can be seen, many people are involved in such a cash accounting system. Even the store manager cannot steal money from the business without being detected, since the accounting clerk independently sends a report to a central accounting office. Where possible, the small business manager should design a system using the elements outlined here.

WHAT SECURITY DEVICES TO ACQUIRE TO KEEP EMPLOYEES HONEST

Instituting tight cash control and tight inventory control, among other procedures, will lessen the chance that a business will become the victim of a dishonest employee. But there are also other more sophisticated methods, using electronic and mechanical security devices, that will enhance existing control procedures and reduce the labor cost involved with a spot checks and balances system.

A major problem with the checks and balances systems outlined in this book is that they are very labor-intensive. The old saying, "You have to hire a guard to watch the guard," is true in tight security control procedures. For example, in the cash control system outlined, there are about six or seven employees involved in the system—from two employees at the cash register to several accounting clerks, both those in the store and those at a central location. For many small businesses, such a labor expense just to keep employees honest may be required but may not be affordable.

The small business manager, therefore, has two options open to him if the business cannot support such a detailed checks and balances system. First, the manager should determine the amount of money or merchandise that is being removed by employees. If there isn't anything being stolen or if the amount is relatively minor, then the business manager should do nothing. Establishing a control system that would only cost more than the amount of money the business operator would be saving should be avoided. The second alternative, if employee thefts are more than seem reasonable, is to acquire security devices that will act as deterrents to employee theft. Initially, the cost of the security devices will probably be more than the initial labor cost; however, once the security devices have been acquired, no long-range, continuing cost is involved.

Purpose of Security Devices

Before discussing which security devices to acquire, let us consider the actual purpose of such security devices—to discourage employee theft.

As suggested previously, the small business manager should not be seeking to apprehend a dishonest employee in the same way that he or she would seek to catch a criminal. Legal repercussions for the manager and the store operators usually do not justify such a confrontation. Therefore, the purpose of such security devices is not to catch the dishonest employee but to place psychological pressure on the dishonest employee that will make the person less comfortable about stealing from the store. There are generally two psychological conditions that inhibit most employees from stealing from their employers. The first is when the employee feels that he or she is stealing money that the store owner needs to feed his or her family. The employee, in this case, must feel as if the store owner is barely making a living from the business and that every dollar that is in the register will have a drastic effect on the business and the owner. In short, the employer appears to be in a worse condition than the employee.

The second psychological condition is the risk that the employee will be caught. The important point to consider is that the employee must have the feeling, after a careful study of the existing security system, that there is a high degree of probability that he or she will be caught stealing from the store. In reality, the chances may be slim; however, the employee is not aware of this fact. Most small businesses are not able to use the first psychological condition to curtail employee theft. Therefore, the second condition must be used. Security devices offer the greatest opportunity for the small business manager to use the fear of being caught in combating employee theft.

A small business owner in Kansas used a simple security system in order to keep his cashiers honest. The business involved local community purchases, as compared with stores located in areas drawing customers from several communities. Although the business actually depended on every dollar in the register, the store owner did not reflect this need to his employees. During any shift, there was the manager and a hired cashier. On occasions, once or twice a week, the manager would employ a stock clerk to display the merchandise. After a while, the manager found that the cashiers had been dipping into the register. When a pattern had developed with one of the cashiers, the cashier was dismissed from employment. The manager then searched for a security device that would help to resolve the problem once and for all. In this particular situation, the store owner rarely stayed near the front of the store. He usually remained at his desk in a back-room office. The owner decided to install a television camera positioned in such a way as to view both the customers as they entered and left the store and the cashier making the transactions. The camera was connected to a television monitor located near his desk. The cashiers were told that the purpose of such a security device was to be prepared in case someone held up the store. Any questionable activity at the cash register would be seen by the owner, who would call the police. For the dishonest cashier, of course, the new security device required her to steal from the register in front of the store owner. In reality, the owner rarely glanced at the television monitor during the day; however, he did find that employee theft was eliminated.

Some Examples

As illustrated in this example, just the presence of a television camera is enough to place sufficient pressure on a dishonest employee to curtail employee theft. A store manager can usually acquire a one-camera surveillance unit with a television monitor for about $1,500. If the store manager has discovered that employee thefts have taken place throughout the store, then several cameras will be required. Cameras should be placed by the cashier, by the cash counting room, by the stockrooms, and at every entrance and exit in the store. A system involving several cameras will, of course, cost more than $1,500; however, if employee theft over the years exceeds the expense of the camera security system, then the cost of such a system is justified.

If a multi-camera system is to be used, be sure to include several television monitors and a camera switching unit. A typical system of six cameras will also have three television monitors and an automatic and manual override switching unit. Obviously, only three cameras can be viewed at a time; however, the automatic switching unit will alternate which camera is viewed every five or ten seconds. The person monitoring the cameras can override the automatic switching system at any point.

Less expensive security devices used by many stores, are mirrors. There are many types of mirrors used for various situations. The more common are flat mirrors, concave mirrors, and convex mirrors. The flat mirrors can be used behind or over cash registers as part of the store display. Concave and convex mirrors can be used for viewing around corners. The purpose of mirrors is to reflect the actions of the employee. Although the store manager or another employee may not be present in front of the cash register or in the stockroom, there is always the possibility that the manager or another employee will still be able to view the actions of a dishonest employee through the use of the mirrors. In reality, the store manager may never look at the mirror; however, the larger the mirror is, the larger the concern in the mind of a dishonest employee that he or she may be watched while committing a theft.

Instituting tight controls on inventory, cash, and employee movement, coupled with the use of one of the simple security devices outlined here, should curtail the majority of employee thefts. But one more point should be mentioned. Small business managers should not hide all of the business security systems and control procedures from the employees. Major department stores that have spent time and money studying this problem have explained the area of security and controls as part of their introduction package for new employees. The larger stores have found that if they show all the employees how difficult the system has made it for employees to steal from the store, the employees usually will not attempt to defeat the system. This technique has proven successful.

In this chapter, we have discussed various methods used to hire honest employees and how to keep them honest during their term of employment with the store. There is no guarantee that, by following the guidelines presented here, a dishonest employee will not be hired; however, by using these suggestions, the store manager will lessen his or her probabilities of hiring a dishonest employee. Many honest employees will steal if given the opportunity. It is up to the store manager to ensure that this opportunity does not exist.

Important tips on hiring security guards and consultants 4

Business managers are frequently called upon to make decisions in situations where they may or may not be well versed on the technical nature of the problem. As good management procedures indicate, when you are in doubt about a solution to a problem, hire someone with the necessary experience and skills who can steer you toward making the proper decision. This procedure holds true when the small business manager has set out to resolve the security problem of his or her business.

Choices

Usually, the initial step, once the manager has determined that such a problem exists and that the solution may be beyond his or her own expertise and experience, is to contact the local police department. Members of the department have been trained in security-related techniques and have the

67

experience to know which techniques will and will not work in a particular situation. This service is provided by the local police free of charge. Of course, the quality of the police department will differ from community to community, as we have seen in previous chapters. In a town where there are few businesses, the police may, in fact, lack the experience required to survey a business and suggest appropriate security devices and procedures. Although the police may accept such a request from a small business manager in earnest, the manager may not be totally satisfied with the results of the police investigation into his or her security problem.

The manager will usually turn next either to a private security consultant or to hiring a person who has a security background as an employee. Many difficult questions can arise out of seeking aid from security specialists who are not connected with any official law enforcement agency. Where do you find such a specialist? How can the manager tell if the person or consultant is honest? How does the manager know if the person is really a specialist? The manager must answer these questions before contracting with a security specialist. At least when he or she invites the assistance of the local police department in making the business more secure, the manager knows that every member of the police department has to pass a strict background check, portions of which are conducted by the Federal Bureau of Investigation. But a security specialist is a completely unknown entity. This chapter deals with several important points that will enable the manager to know how to satisfy many of the doubts normally associated with hiring a security specialist.

The manager's security alternatives usually end up with one of the two choices mentioned—hire an outside security service or hire an employee who is a security specialist. The decision is usually based upon normal business influences, such as a cost comparison of the dollar value of the selections and a host of other determinants. There is no right decision for every business. Many smaller businesses find that hiring an outside security consultant is less expensive in the long run than if another person is placed on the payroll, assuming that the manager can find a candidate who will accept the position. Other business managers have discovered that an in-house security specialist will provide the manager with more for his money. In either case, many managers find themselves in the position of interviewing applicants for a prime component of any security system—the security guard. Even if the manager hires a guard service, he or she should take the same precautions as though he or she was hiring the guard as an employee. A common statement made by security consultants is, "The guard works for us (the security consultants). We will make sure that he is trained and that he performs well on the job." The manager, who frequently deals with vendors, may quickly agree with that statement; after all, the manager is paying the security consultant for this servive. Yet, often, a "don't worry" statement made by a security consultant means nothing more than "Don't look too closely at who we hire to protect you."

The Interview

Although the manager did hire the consultants to worry about and solve the security problem, the manager still has the obligation to be sure that the money for the service is well spent. Therefore, the manager must have a long discussion with the guard who is assigned to protect the business. The manager must determine the background of the guard, regardless of whether the guard is a regular employee or the employee of a consulting firm. The best time to conduct such an investigation is when the guard first meets the manager. This can be when the guard reports for his or her first assignment or when the guard applies for the position.

During the interview, the manager should try to re-create the background of the guard as well as to discover details about the guard's present situation. The manager should determine whether the guard has had any training in either security protection or law enforcement. Training is an important criterion to examine. There are very few formal training programs that instruct candidates in the necessary areas of security protection and law enforcement. Most, if not all, of the formal training is conducted at police academies or junior colleges. Other ways in which guards receive training are through on-the-job training, through training at a private school, or through training by a security firm. Although some of the less than formal training provides worthwhile information for the security guard, there are no uniform standards throughout the profession. Some private training programs are really fronts to defraud the students. Other programs may be taught by faculty members who are neither qualified nor trained in the art of security protection. In essence, the manager, when discussing training with a guard, should suspect the quality of any training other than that given through a junior college or police academy program.

The manager, during the interview or discussion with the guard, must determine what, if any, legal training the guard has had. If the guard does not know the legal rights of customers and of the store, for example, then the guard can be more of a danger than a protection to the store and to him- or herself. If a guard tells the manager that he or she is properly trained, and if he or she furnishes the manager with the names and addresses of the institutions where he or she has studied, the manager must make it a point to contact these schools in order to verify that the guard did, in fact, attend. The manager should also determine the quality of the training given at the institution. Just because a school has the name "institute" provides no guarantee of the quality of the material presented in the classroom.

The manager should look for a guard who is in relatively good physical shape and who has had, in addition to law enforcement training, some field experience. The guard's training should be as recent as possible, since the laws regarding the rights of citizens have changed over recent years. A guard, for example, who received his or her last police training in the early 1950s may or may not be up to date on the latest laws.

As with any employee, the manager must attempt to construct the guard's financial situation. If a guard has expensive habits or is in debt beyond his or her means, such a person could be placed in a compromising situation. The manager should avoid hiring or permitting a security consultant to assign such a guard to protect the business.

The manager should also request that all security personnel undergo a lie detection review. Lie detection is a means by which certain physiological conditions of the body, which react in particular ways when a person is not telling the truth, are measured. There are two forms of lie detection examinations. The traditional lie detector is called a polygraph; through electrodes placed externally on various parts of the body, it will record the slightest changes in the body when a person is not telling the truth. The newer method is called a voice lie detector. This device detects inaudible and uncontrollable changes in a person's voice that usually occur when he or she is not telling the truth. Both kinds of services are usually available locally. But before proceeding with a lie detection test, you should find out whether it is legal in your state. Some states have laws prohibiting an employer from asking that a candidate undergo a lie detector examination as a requirement for employment. Your business attorney will be able to determine the proper legal course to take regarding lie detection.

A careful interview combined with a lie detection examination—if legal—usually provide the manager with enough information to determine the quality of service a guard is likely to render.

HOW TO INVESTIGATE SECURITY CONSULTANTS

Just as in the case of guards, the manager must also determine whether the security consulting service that he or she has hired will actually perform as expected. It is wise to shop around, to conduct an interview with several consulting firms, to make a visit to their offices, and to run a complete background check on the firm and on the principals of the company. The manager should never enter into a contract with a security consulting firm without knowing, in complete detail, whom he or she is actually dealing with.

A case in Michigan illustrates this point. The operator of a small chain of hardware stores realized that the store required security protection. The manager had investigated the choices between hiring an in-house security specialist or employing a security consulting firm. He selected the outside consulting firm. The manager had noticed that the consulting firm had placed a full-page ad in the Yellow Pages, and, knowing what such an ad would cost, he felt that the firm had to be in good financial shape in order to afford the ad. A representative from the firm visited the manager. Dressed in a business suit and vest, the representative conducted himself like a professional salesman and made such a good impression on the manager that he immediately signed a security contract with the company. It wasn't long before the manager found that the incidence of crime in his stores had increased since the firm had been hired. One day, the manager was contacted by federal authorities, who informed the store operator that the security firm was actually a front for a small group of thieves. The group would gain access to a business by posing as security consultants. Once the business manager signed a security protection contract, the thieves could steal whatever—and almost whenever—they wanted.

The Significance of Trust

The relationship between a security consultant and a client is a unqiue bond that is based on trust. The consultant will be providing guidance and advice to the manager based on confidential information about the business. A security consultant's relationship with the small business manager is similar to a doctor–patient or lawyer–client relationship rather than a vendor–client arrangement. For some small businesses, the security consultant will have inside information about a business that, if it fell into the wrong hands, could cause serious hardship on the business manager.

The manager must, therefore, above all, be able to trust the security consultant. Before the consultant, for example, can suggest means of tightening up the security procedures of the business, he or she must know those areas of the business that are most vulnerable to attack. Of course, a thief would also like to have such information about the business. The trustworthiness of a security consultant must be investigated through conversations with the manager and through performing a background check on the consultant. The manager will usually find that honesty filters through a consultant's organization, enabling him or her to have confidence in anyone in the consultant's office.

Many times, the manager will deal only with a representative of the consulting firm. This person is usually well mannered and is briefed on the latest techniques used to protect a small business. The representative is probably also trained as a salesperson—someone who can tell the firm's story, tailor the services to the prospective client, and bring home the signed contract. Many professional security firms hire former state and federal law enforcement officers to represent the firm during sales conversations with future clients. The client, many times, will be impressed by the fact that a professional law enforcement officer will show the manager the ins and outs of how to protect the business from a thief. Frequently, the former police officer may tell old "war" stories, which often gives the manager the feeling that the representative and the firm are truly well versed and experienced in business security.

Unfortunately for many security firms using such a sales technique, the high quality of security protection stops with the sales representative. The actual persons involved in the protection of the business may have little or no formal training in law enforcement or security. It is not uncommon, for example, for a manager to sign a security protection contract with a former Secret Service agent, a man who protected the president, only to find out that a young high-school drop-out is assigned to protect the business.

Very few states have laws that strictly regulate the security consulting industry. Although not everyone can open a private detective agency without a license, anyone can open a security consulting service without any prior requirement other than the time and money it takes to keep an office and sell his or her services. Even the term "security consultant" has a variety of meanings in the marketplace. Those using such a term to describe their service include alarm installers, detective agencies, guard services, and those individuals who offer lie detection services and illegal wire taps and bugging equipment. When the manager checks the Yellow Pages under the term security consultant, he or she can easily become lost among the listings of those offering a security service. Only one thing is certain: Some of those listed under the heading of security consultants will offer very little service to a client. It is up to the manager to wade through all the offers and to select the firm that will be experienced and will give the service that the manager has contracted for.

Further Tips

The task of investigating a security consultant is not easy. Initially, the manager should ask other business managers to recommend a security consultant who has proven satisfactory. Talking with a former or current client about a security firm will give the manager an opportunity to acquire details about the consulting firm without any sales puff. The manager should also seek recommendations from trade associations and business groups, who frequently have a high membership standard. Those business persons in the trade are usually aware of which firms know the security business and which ones are less than professional in their performance.

The small business manager should attempt to assemble a list containing the names of five to ten security consultants that have been recommended by various sources. The initial contact with the consultants should be by phone. Although phone conversations can be misleading at times, they can provide a few pointers that may alert the manager to potential trouble with the security consulting firm. If it is a solidly based consulting firm, normal office procedures should exist. A phone contact by the manager, for example, should not result in a phone-answering machine responding to the manager's call. If the consultant is good and has an established business, a secretary normally answers the phone. The manager should also listen for background noises on the phone. If the manager can hear the voices of children in the background or if he or she can hear a television set, he or she should not proceed with the consulting firm. Another give away of a less than professional consulting firm is the manner in which the phone is answered. If a person answers the phone by saying, ''Hello,'' there is a good chance that the security expert is working out of his or her home. A solid consulting firm should be able to support an office. If the person at the consulting firm tells the manager to hold the phone for a few seconds, the manager should again listen. If the manager is not placed on ''hold,'' there is a good chance that the consultant is using a home phone and not a business phone, since business phones, having multi-lines, will usually have a hold button.

Once the manager has completed calling the list of security consultants and weeded out those who seem not to qualify, he or she must visit the premises of the firm. Never sign a security contract until you have seen the firm's plant. A solid security firm will be more than happy to invite the potential client to the office. Those who are on a less than solid foundation and who do not have a pleasant office will, of course, avoid such contact with the potential client. During the investigation of the consulting firm, the manager must determine for him- or herself the financial structure of the firm. He or she must be able to know approximately how much of the fee is for the actual cost involved with the protection and how much is pure profit. In order to reach such a conclusion, the manager must know how much the firm pays security guards and how much training the guards receive. A poorly trained, low-paid guard, for example, will not give the manager any protection. To conclude the investigation, the manager should perform a credit check on the business and should check with local law enforcement agencies in order to determine if there has ever been any trouble with the firm.

Tips on Investigating Security Consultants

1. Get recommendations from former customers.
2. Do background checks.
3. Be sure that the headquarters facilities of the consultants are professionally maintained.
4. Check the employees of the consultant for proper training.
5. Note the first impression made from the phone conversation with the consultant.

HOW TO INVESTIGATE ALARM INSTALLERS

For most small businesses, there is really no gain in protecting the business by hiring the services of a security consultant. Consultants, for example, will survey the business in order to locate the weak points in the existing security system. Almost without question, the consultant will suggest the use of one or more security systems that the consultant will install. If the manager agrees, the consultant usually subcontracts the actual purchase of the security system and the installation of the system. The consultant receives the contractor's bill, to which he or she adds a slight mark-up plus his or her own consultation fee. The small business manager, in many cases, could save the added-on cost plus the consulting fee by going directly to the alarm installer.

Alarm installers are usually smaller contractors, a one- or two-person shop, which will give a client a free security survey and help in the selection of the security device that the installer will eventually place on the premises. Most times, alarm installers have a less than professional sales pitch and are not as "slick" as some security consultants. Usually, the alarm installer is an experienced technician who knows security systems, how they work, and where the system can help a business manager. The business manager can be sure that a good installer will reach almost the same conclusion as a security consultant would, since basically most small business security problems are solved through installing an alarm system rather than instituting elaborate security procedures that require special professional law enforcement skills. For example, a retail store concerned about being burglarized should call an alarm installer rather than a security consultant. On the other hand, if the business is having a major problem with shoplifting, then a security consultant would be more beneficial to the business than an alarm installer.

The relationship between a client and an alarm installer is similar to the relationship between a security consultant and a client. For the alarm installer to assist the small business manager in finding the weaknesses in the business security system, sensitive information must be released to the installer by the manager. Therefore, the manager must, as with a security consultant, have a great deal of confidence in and trust for the alarm installer.

As mentioned previously, the initial contact the business manager will have with an alarm installer or security consultant is over the telephone. Conditions such as a telephone-answering machine responding to the manager's call or a woman telling the manager that her husband will call back were identified as danger signs when selecting a security consultant. But this is not necessarily the case when the manager deals with an alarm installer, since many honest and solidly based installers work out of their homes. The manager, therefore, cannot usually visit the installer's place of business, as he or she would do when investigating a security consultant. But visiting an installer is not necessary in order to determine the trustworthiness of the installer and the company.

Checking Alarm Installers

There are, however, a few items that the business manager should check before hiring an installer. First, the installer must provide the manager with references, especially if the manager was not referred to the installer through a mutual acquaintance. Most installers are more than willing to permit a prospective client to contact an existing client for a recommendation. Once the installer's present client has been identified, the business manager should visit the client's premises with the permission of the client. During this visit, the manager should ask questions about the manner in which the work was completed. The manager should also, if possible, examine the workmanship of the alarm installation in the client's place of business. If the alarm is currently being installed, the manager should note the way in which the installer is working. The installer, for example, should be concerned about interfering with the client's business as little as possible. If the installer is seen creating a dangerous condition, such as leaving wires exposed in areas frequented by customers, then the manager should halt any further relationship with the installer. Although if an accident occurs, the liability will usually lie with the installer, the manager may well lose the customer.

Once the manager has satisfied him- or herself that the installer can perform quality work without interfering with normal business, the manager must, as with the investigation of a security consultant, try to create a picture of the installer's financial condition. Before signing any contract for the installation of an alarm system, the manager must be aware of how much of the fee is spent on hardware, labor, and overhead for the installer and how much is the profit margin. Most of this information will be available to a manager who contacts a few alarm suppliers. Once the manager knows these details, he or she can then determine whether the price given by the alarm installer is fair or unreasonable.

The manager must also be concerned about the person with whom he or she is signing the contract. Since installers are usually small business people, their financial structure is not designed to support heavy expenses, and they are noted for cutting corners, mainly in the area of overhead. Some installers cut certain expenses that, under prudent business practices, should not be eliminated. The business manager must be sure that the installer has not cut corners in vital areas of his business, areas that normally include the licensing of the business; filing trade name or corporate forms with the proper state authorities; providing insurance coverage for the installer, the workmen, and the client; and so on. The manager must, for example, have documented proof that the installer is covered by insurance and that he or she is in a position to handle all legal actions that may arise out of conditions caused by the installer that injure a second party.

Most small business managers cannot afford simply to accept the word of the installer concerning insurance and other common cost-cutting areas. There are two forms of evidence that will support the installer's claim of being covered. First is the presentation of an insurance contract to the manager, who must then contact the insurance representative to confirm that the policy is in force. The second form of evidence is less desirable but is acceptable: a communication from the installer's attorney. If the installer does have an attorney readily available for the manager to contact, then chances are that the installer has not practiced false economy by cutting back on the essential coverage required by such a business. The manager must contact the attorney and receive a confirmation about the status of the installer, preferably in writing.

The manager should also investigate the installer for signs of professionalism. Although the installer may not have a formal office or shop to work from, he or she should have a vehicle, such as a van, that contains all the necessary tools and equipment required to install security alarms. The vehicle should also have the name of the firm placed on the sides of the truck. Tools and a van, of course, are not indications of the quality or professionalism of the workers; however, such conditions do tell the manager that the installer's business has a sufficient cash flow to support the vehicle and tools. Such a vehicle also informs the manager that the installer is probably earning his or her livelihood from installing alarms, compared with a person who installs alarms as a part-time job. The installer should have a formal estimate sheet and contract in a printed form. The manager must beware of installers who give the appearance of writing contracts and estimates especially for the prospective client. A professional installer will use printed forms for all his clients.

A final note about alarm installers. The manager should make sure that the installer is both capable and willing to complete the job. One of the major problems involved in dealing with small contractors is that, on occasions, a contractor will start a job and then let it go for a few weeks before completing the work. A good contractor will try to complete the job as efficiently as possible. If necessary, the manager should require the contractor to place a performance bond in escrow.

HOW TO DOUBLECHECK YOUR SECURITY SERVICES

Not so long ago, a manager of a three-chain food store business hired what appeared to be a highly skilled and professional security expert. The person, who had claimed to be a former law enforcement agent for the federal government, gave the appearance of knowing everything there is to know about protecting a business, especially a food business. The security expert surveyed the three stores, discovered many weaknesses in the security system and suggested that the manager require all future employees, especially store managers, to undergo a lie detector examination. He also recommended that he be permitted to install a special security alarm connected to police headquarters. His final suggestion was that the business manager hire his firm on a monthly fee to spot-check and continue to find the weaknesses in the system. Unknown to the individual store managers, a representative of his firm would visit the store without warning and observe the condition of the security system.

The manager agreed to the arrangement. Each month, the manager would receive a report indicating where and when the firm made the security checks. For this information, the manager paid the security expert $200 a month. The contract continued for three years until the manager read about the security expert in the newspapers one day. The expert was arrested by authorities on fraud charges. Although the expert did have the alarm installed in the three stores, no one from his firm ever made any kind of security check at the stores. Each month, the expert would write a factitious report and submit it to the manager, who, without question, considered the report a normal business expense, similar to bills from the power company, and paid the expert $200.

Many times, when a business manager hires an expert, the manager assumes that too much information is factual. Typically, the manager will assume that the security expert is in reality an expert and not a con man. In the example above, the manager assumed that security checks were being performed as agreed. It was understandable for the manager to agree that such checks be made without anyone from the three stores being made aware of checks, since a security check would not produce any fruitful information if everyone in the store knew about the investigation. Of course, in the example, the manager required some form of proof that such a check was made. The report submitted by the security expert was again assumed to be true and honest. Rarely, during the three-year period, did the manager ever question the information on the report, nor did he ever ask to witness a security check.

The old saying, ''You have to hire a watchman to watch the watchman,'' is true when a manager is dealing with representatives of the security industry. Some con men become security experts overnight, especially if they see that there are dollars to be handed out by managers who assume that all persons claiming to be security experts are honest.

Regardless of how well established a security firm or an alarm installer may appear to be, it is up to the business manager to determine how well the expert actually performed his or her job. Even larger and more notable security companies have been known to hire less than competent employees to protect a client. Remember that it is the employee of a security company that does the actual protecting, not the sales representative. Larger security companies have been known to go through expensive presentations of security systems for a potential client; however, such attention by the managers of the firm may disappear soon after the security contract is in hand. Once the contract is signed, the manager must turn to the courts if the performance of a firm is not what the sales staff promised it to be.

Even after a security contract has been in effect for some time, the manager must periodically, on a regular schedule, physically check the presence of the security on the premises and reinvestigate the security firm. Very few things stand the test of time without changing, especially in the security industry. Security companies are formed every day, and others are sold or go bankrupt. The manager must, then, besides making sure that the guard from the service shows up for work and that he or she is actually working, determine whether the vendor business remains on a steady course. Although a security firm may have appeared solvent a year ago, only a reinvestigation, which takes only a few moments, can reassure the manager that the firm is still in a similar or better position.

In the case of an alarm installer, the manager must be sure that the installer is available to service the system. There is nothing more upsetting for a manager than to learn that the alarm system installed two years ago has malfunctioned and that the installer has moved away from the area. Every six months or so, the installer should be contacted in order to assure the manager that service to the alarm system is available on 24-hour notice. In order to prepare for all contingencies, the manager may also ask the installer for the name of one or two of his or her colleagues who could step in for him or her in case such a situation arises.

Before the installer begins work on the alarm system, the manager must also think ahead in order to avoid another pitfall common in the security industry—the availability of parts for the system. To begin with, the manager must be just as concerned about the type of equipment the installer will use on the premises as he or she is in the selection of the installer. The manager must ascertain the name and address of the manufacturer and the local supplier of the alarm components that he or she intends to use. Never accept the word of an installer as to the name of the product being installed. Some installers will consciously avoid committing themselves as to the name of the manufacturer of the products being installed, since an independent contractor can occasionally obtain better purchasing arrangements with lesser known alarm products. Many times, the installer will work for clients who do not care which alarm components are installed, and he or she may therefore have a policy of changing manufacturers, depending upon the purchase price arrangement at the time of the buy.

Once the manager has the name and address of the manufacturer of the alarm products, the manager should contact the local supplier of the product as well as the manufacturer in an effort to determine whether or not additional parts can be obtained without too much delay or difficulty. The manager must consider that, although the local supplier may have parts in stock, there is no guarantee that the supplier will be in business and carrying the same line of goods several years after the installation of the alarm system. The same may hold true for the installer. He or she may or may not be in business when the alarm system malfunctions years from the installation. Therefore, it is up to the manager to be sure that the manufacturer of the alarm products has been in business for many years, appears to have a major position in the alarm products market, and will probably continue to manufacture alarm products for years to come.

There is always the risk that either a security consultant, an alarm installer, or one of their employees may be dishonest and use information gained through a security survey to steal from the business. The risk of such an occurrence, assuming that the manager has followed the steps in this book, is rather low. However, there are some small businesses that must be sure that the probability of such an occurrence is nearly nonexistent. A manager who seeks such a tightly secured system for his or her business should pay close attention to the following steps.

The manager must define, in detail, the security problem and the solution. For example, the manager may feel that the problem is that the store can be burglarized without much effort on the part of the burglar. If the manager does not have knowledge or skills in the area of security, he or she will require a security consultant to indicate the solution—say, an alarm installed and a security guard hired. Many times, a manager will simply hire a security consultant who will subcontract various steps in the actual implementation of the security plan. Unfortunately, those close to the security consultant will usually have access to the complete security system. Therefore, the manager should arrange things so that a different vendor performs each step of the solution. For example, if a security consultant informs the manager that he or she needs a silent alarm and a guard, without any additional involvement by the consultant, the manager then hires an installer who may only install the sensors, leaving the actual installation of the control box to the alarm system to be completed by a different installer. Finally, the manager hires a guard or guard service without the guard or guard service having any idea of how the alarm system operates. In this way, no single person, except the manager, has the overview of the complete security plan for the business.

Tips on Keeping Security While Using Outside Vendors

1. Hire a consultant to design the system.
2. Hire an alarm installer to install only the sensors.
3. Hire an alarm installer to install only the alarm.
4. Hire a security guard or service separately from other security devices.

HOW MUCH SHOULD YOU SPEND FOR OUTSIDE SECURITY HELP?

Many books have been written showing small business managers how to cut costs by doing the work themselves. Depending on the size of the business, for example, the manager may be able to save hundreds of dollars a year by spending $50 for a sign-making kit and creating his or her own signs. Although there are many methods small business managers can employ to cut expenses, when the problem of security is confronted, many managers will immediately call in a security expert to solve this almost unsolvable problem. Typically, such managers have never dealt with security consultants or alarm installers before and, after the initial security problem is solved, the manager may never need to contact the security consultant again. The infrequent use of a vendor service, such as alarm installers or consultants, can leave the small business manager open for excess expenses that can be prevented. Many a small business manager in this situation is like the noted ''out-of-towner'' who got into a taxicab at 42nd Street in New York City and asked the taxicab driver to take him to the main branch of the New York Public Library. The cab driver, noting that the passenger was from out of town, drove around town for almost an hour before stopping in front of the library, which is on 41st Street. The fare, according to the meter in the cab, was close to $20. The passenger paid without complaining, since he did not realize that he was a block away from where he had started.

When either a security consultant or an alarm installer first confronts a business manager about a security problem, the vendor realizes that the manager is usually scared by the criminal element and is almost more than willing to pay any price for protection from the criminal. More times than not, the manager has already convinced him- or herself that the solution to his or her security problem will be expensive and will run into the thousands of dollars. The security vendor knows just about what the typical manager is thinking and therefore prices his or her service to meet the manager's expectations.

Steps to Take

There are several steps the manager can and should take in order to avoid paying too high a price for the protection of his or her business. First, the manager should conduct his or her own security survey (see Chapters 1 and 2). Briefly, the manager will want to make sure that there are intrusion sensors on all possible entrances to the premises. This includes doors and windows, especially those on the upper floors that can be accessible from the ground or roof. Once the manager has determined the number and types of entrances, he or she should contact a local supplier of security alarm products. Usually, a brief visit with the supplier will enable the manager to determine the number and kinds of sensors and other alarm components that he or she will require. Most of all, the manager will also have a price for the materials involved in the security system. Rarely will a small business ever require additional electronic security other than the typical silent police alarm and appropriate window and door sensors.

The manager, if possible, should also pay close attention to employment ads in the classified section of the newspaper. The manager should seek ads from companies that are looking for alarm installers. If such an ad is discovered, the manager should call the company in question and determine how much the installer will be paid. The manager will therefore have an idea as to the hourly wage that would be paid to install a security system. The next step is for the manager to estimate the length of time required for the installation. The manager should use workdays rather than hours when determining the actual time. Through the use of a little mathematics, the manager will be able to know how much money is required to pay for the installation as well as for the materials required. The manager must now add, to the total cost of labor and materials, a reasonable percentage that will constitute the profit for such a job. The manager will have then developed information similar to that which a security consultant or alarm installer uses to determine his or her fee for a job.

With this information at hand, the manager should contact several consultants and installers and request that each vendor review the problem and present him or her with a quotation for the work. Remember always to treat each vendor as if that firm were the only one being considered for the job. Never arrange appointments with vendors who are giving a quotation too close together. And when the quotations are received, be sure that the vendor has specified and itemized the fee or price for each step of the process. That is, the quotation should contain items such as the type of sensors and their price, the type of alarm and its price, the consultant's fee, and the like.

All quotations should be submitted in writing. Decisions as to which firm will actually receive the work should be made in the absence of the vendor. The manager must then compare, line for line, each quotation as it stands in relation to the others as well as to the estimated cost figures if he or she were to undertake the project on a do-it-yourself basis.

Using this system, the manager will be in a position to determine whether a security vendor is sincerely giving him or her an honest price or is trying to prey upon his or her naivete. The manager can also be in a good position to negotiate the price. If the vendor's bill is far out of line when compared to the actual dollar expense for the project, the manager's list of alarm parts and the labor cost of installation can be presented to the vendor. Seeing such information, most vendors will realize that the manager is a good business person. If the vendor wants the job, he or she will know that his or her price must come more in line with the one the manager has developed.

Many times, the manager will find that alarm installers will be fairly realistic as well as flexible with their prices. Security consultants, on the other hand, will have to subcontract the actual alarm installation and therefore will have only a very small margin over the subcontracting expense within which to negotiate. The installer, however, will often be one of the actual workers on the job, and therefore, anything above his or her expenses and personal salary is pure profit. His or her margin is usually wider than that of a security consultant, who must not only subcontract the actual work but also pay expensive overhead.

There will be times when the manager will be able to negotiate with the consultant or installer and other times when such a vendor will not seek the job under any terms other than those of the original quotation. The determining factor as to which direction the vendor will take when confronted by a negotiable price will be the demand for that particular vendor's work. If there are only three such reputable security vendors in a large area, for example, and if many homeowners and business operators seek the services of these vendors, the law of supply and demand will take hold over the situation, making it difficult for the manager to negotiate the price.

Since the manager knows the cost of installing the alarm system, he or she may very well consider his or her own skills and those of his or her staff. Many times, either the manager or an employee will have the required electrical talents to install the alarm system. Before such an arrangement is made, the manager must consider the value of the employee's lost time from the job while the installation is taking place. As long as the employee can handle the job either on off hours or during working hours without seriously hurting the business operation, then the manager may well consider this type of do-it-yourself project.

If the manager should undertake the installation him- or herself, he or she should contact the local alarm component supplier. Usually, the supplier will not only be a source for components but will also be available to give the manager small hints on the proper way to install the system. There is one important disadvantage to a do-it-yourself installation that the manager must consider. After the system is installed, the security device must operate without any problems. A person with the proper electrical skills can usually install the system without problems; however, those persons with half the required skills might make mistakes that can cause the system to malfunction at the wrong time. Before starting such a project, consult with the alarm supplier to determine the degree of difficulty involved with the project.

The business manager's relationships with outside security vendors are important to understand, especially because it is easy to be duped by an incompetent or dishonest security service. Remember that a good manager will always prepare him- or herself by knowing the facts before he or she contacts a security vendor.

IDENTIFYING AND PREVENTING SMALL BUSINESS CRIMES II

Professional ways to handle check and credit security **5**

HOW TO PREVENT THE ACCEPTANCE OF BAD CHECKS

There was a time not so long ago when customers were proud to pay in cash for merchandise. A cash transaction showed to everyone concerned that the customer was honest and could afford the goods. Times change, and the use of cash is almost frowned upon by cashiers and store managers. In fact, many state governments specifically request those paying state bills to make the payments in almost anything else but cash. In some stores, cashiers will automatically ask the customer which credit card he or she is using to make a purchase and will rarely assume that the customer may be paying for the merchandise in dirty old pieces of paper called money. To some people, paying in cash does not necessarily mean that the customer is honest and can afford the merchandise but that the customer may not be credit-worthy or does not have enough money to maintain a checking account.

87

Store managers have looked at this cashless society with mixed feelings. On the one hand, checks and credit card slips are not easily transferrable as cash. Accepting anything but cash permits the store manager to know that his or her money is safe, since rarely will a robber or a dishonest employee have any use for checks and credit slips. No real cash in the register means that there can be no major loss of cash funds. On the other hand, the store manager understands that the store has not legally received payment for the merchandise—a third party must actually transfer the funds into the store's account. There is a possibility that the cash is not transferred because of illegal signatures on the check or credit card receipt. Under such conditions, the store's acceptance of payments made in something other than cash can actually cause the business to lose money. If the purchase is for an expensive item and payment is made using illegal checks or credit cards, the impact of such a transaction on the financial structure of the business can be overwhelming.

Alternatives

Small business managers must usually make a tough decision, a "damned if you do, damned if you don't" choice. Should the small business accept checks and credit cards as payment? If the business is operated on a cash and carry basis, the manager will be sure of receiving money for his merchandise; however, he or she may risk having a cash security problem as well as risking the possibility of losing customers. On the other hand, if the business is to be operated on a noncash transaction basis, the manager will have the security of knowing that cash handling will not be a major concern, although there are several deficits to using this policy. Some customers may not have any other means of payment except cash; if so, those customers will be lost. There is also a serious problem for cashiers whose job it is to determine whether the signatures on the check or credit card receipt is genuine. Errors, which frequently occur even under the best screening procedures, can in fact prohibit the manager from collecting the cash.

There is a third possibility that many stores have adopted—that is, to accept any means of payment from the customer as long as certain forms of payment concur with the management guidelines for accepting a check or a credit card receipt as payment. With this alternative, the manager will have the good and some of the bad of each of the first two alternatives. And customers will not be lost, as they may be with the other methods of completing transactions.

The decision of many small business managers as to which transaction policy to use mainly depends on the volume of merchandise sold per customer. Stores selling under $10 in merchandise for a typical transaction will have a strong cash and carry policy. On the other hand, stores having average transactions that amount to sums higher than $20 will accept cash as well as checks and credit cards. The thinking behind these decisions considers the typical situation of the customer. Most customers will have enough cash to purchase merchandise under $10. More expensive merchandise will usually require the customer to pay by some other means, since the customer does not usually carry large sums of cash on his or her person.

For store managers who are required by local custom to accept checks or credit cards, special procedures will be required to weed out those customers who make purchases using checks or credit cards that are not valid. A case involving a store in Michigan illustrates the problems that can occur if proper care is not taken to establish procedures for accepting checks and credit cards. The store handled large quantities of children's merchandise, such as toys, games, and baby furniture. Near Christmas one year, the busiest time for the store, a well-dressed customer selected merchandise that amounted to close to $300, one of the largest single purchases made in the store's history. The customer asked if she could pay by check. The cashier informed the customer that as long as she could provide proper identification and the check was drawn from a local bank, there would be no problem in accepting the check. The customer presented a check from a local bank in the exact amount of the purchase. She also produced a driver's license. The cashier, trying to please the customer, just glanced at the name on the driver's license, which matched the name printed on the check. The cashier was satisfied that the customer had presented proper identification, and the transaction was completed. Before the end of the following week, the bank notified the store manager that the check was drawn against an account that had been closed three years prior to the transaction. The store manager later learned that the identification and the check presented by the customer were actually stolen. The store had lost the merchandise to a dishonest customer.

Determining Whether or Not a Check Is Good

One of the major problems confronting small business managers is how to determine if a check is good or not before the transaction is completed. As illustrated by the Michigan case, proper identification

89

supplied by the customer should be required before the cashier accepts the check. A comparison of names on the licenses and on the check, as previously pointed out, is a good first step if the cashier or store manager actually makes a good comparison check. In the Michigan case, the store manager later learned that if the cashier had compared the description of the customer to the description given on the driver's license, a discrepancy would have been discovered. The description on the license indicated that the holder of the license should have been about five feet tall with brown eyes, whereas the customer who showed the license was closer to six feet tall and had green eyes. And the expiration date of the driver's license showed that the license had expired three years ago. What had taken place was an old scam used by many dishonest customers. They make such a large purchase of merchandise that the store employee becomes overanxious to complete the transaction. As long as the customer is dressed in the style common to people who make such large purchases, the employee does not become suspicious and just glances at the identification, figuring that the customer looks honest.

In an attempt to try to prevent accepting bad checks, the store manager should require that checks be drawn on local banks and that each check have the name and address of the customer printed on it. Two forms of identification should be required—a valid driver's license and a valid credit card. When both are displayed to the cashier, the cashier should take the check and the identification to a supervisor or store manager for approval. There are many small and large businesses that follow the procedure outlined here; however, the store manager must carefully train the employee who is giving check approvals on how to detect false identification.

Signature Validity

The employee who approves checks must consider several points when examining the identification. First, both identifications must be valid. The check should be refused if either form of identification has expired. The signatures must be compared. The signature on the credit card, license, and check must all match. If there is any question as to the authenticity of the signature, the check should be refused. Although identifying a forgery is not an easy task, especially when a fairly professional forger has signed the document, a store employee who takes care when approving a check will be able to develop the technique required to spot the more common forgeries. The employee should not simply take a formal glance at the identification without studying the document for a minute or two.

No two persons have identical signatures. Although few persons realize it, a person will not write in the same way every time he or she writes. Each signature—even valid signatures—will have some variations. When a store employee examines a signature, he or she must first determine which signature he or she is using to determine validity. When a check is being examined, usually the employee is interested only in validating the signature on the check. In order to do this, the employee must compare the signature on the check with a known signature. In this case, the known signature is contained on the credit card or driver's license. Once that sample signature has been identified, the employee must first place the signatures alongside one another in order to examine the gross appearance of each. Check for general style similarities, such as the slant of the letters, and attempt to determine whether each signature ends the last name in a similar fashion. An even closer examination should entail a study of how the customer makes each letter. For example, an "a" on all the signatures should be written in a similar fashion.

Police and the courts have established a general rule of thumb to be used as proof that a signature is false. This rule, of course, may differ from state to state and from court to court. The rule calls for the person examining the signatures to find at least 10 distinct differences in the two signatures before the questionable signature is disallowed and deemed a forgery. This means that if, for example, the slant of the signatures does not match and if several letters are not made in the same style, the document should be suspected of being a forgery.

When hiring a new supervisor or a person whose duties will include approving checks, the store manager should place this new employee through a training program that, among other things, deals with checking signatures. The store manager should obtain signatures from three or four different persons. Each of these persons should be asked to copy a sample signature as closely as possible. The store manager, during the training program, should present these signatures to the new employee and ask him or her to select the correct signature that matches the sample signature. The results should be interesting, both to the store manager and to the new employee. Typically, after this exercise is completed, both the store manager and the employee will find out that comparing a signature to a sample signature cannot be done in haste.

The store manager may ask the local police department to send a representative to the store to address cashiers and other employees on the

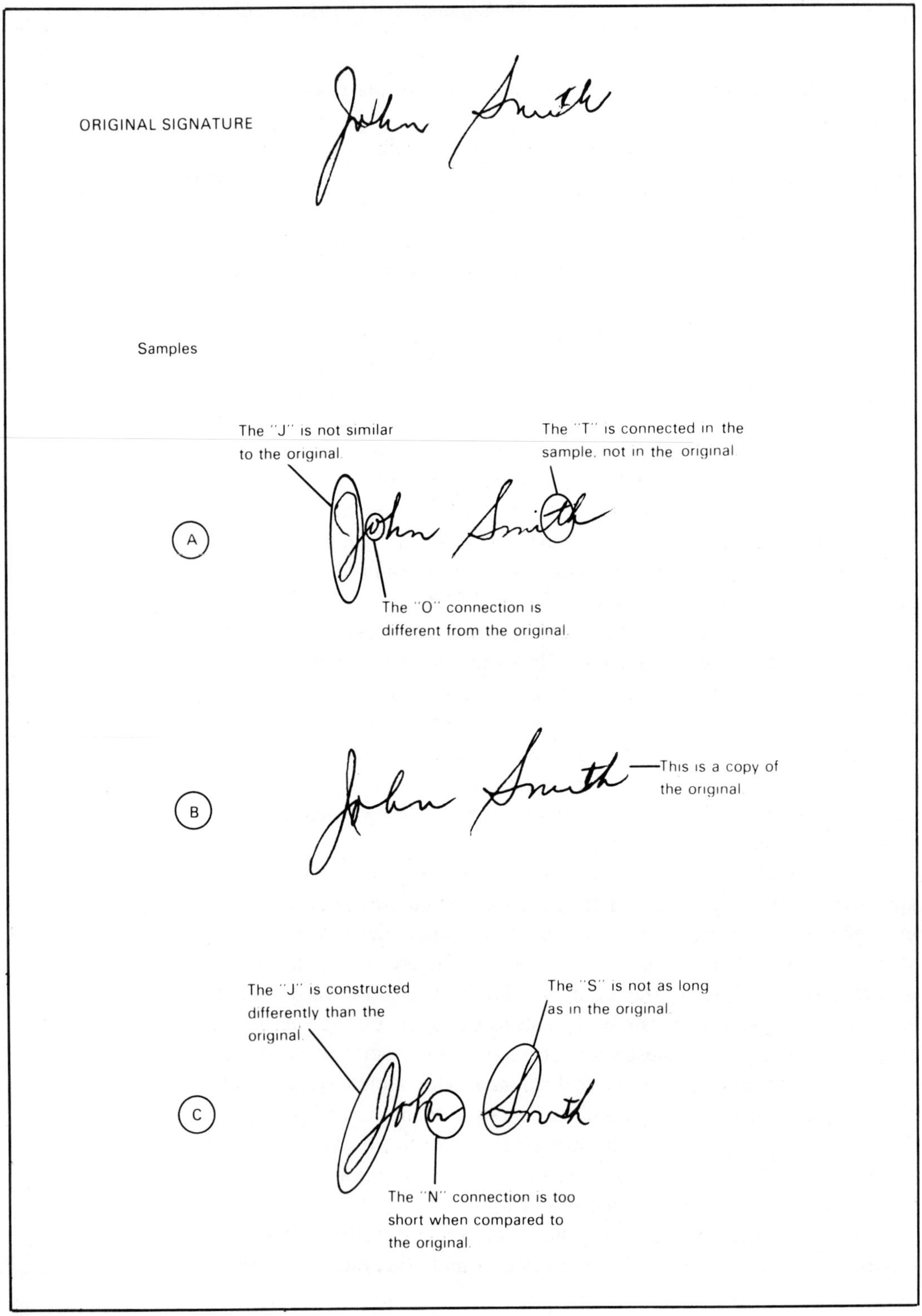

Figure 5-1
Samples of a forged signature.

finer points of comparing signatures. Most local police departments have a trained expert on their staff to assist local small business managers. This advice and instruction by the police department is usually free of charge to the store operator.

As a further part of the recommended check-approving procedure, in addition to the cashier checking the signature and determining the expiration date of the identifying document, the person approving the check should also match the customer's physical description to that on the identification papers, such as a driver's license. Those who approve checks should never assume anything. There may be times when the identification papers (driver's license and credit cards) will not be signed. Usually, once this is pointed out to the customer, the customer signs the document. The store manager should not accept a check if the customer shows documents without signatures. Although the customer may sign the documents in front of the manager, there is a chance that the documents have been stolen. Those persons who deal professionally in stolen identifications, credit cards, and checks can usually obtain such documents from their source, many times either at the government agency or at the printer. Such a document will not have any signature displayed.

If the signature matches on all three documents, the check should be approved. The cashier, before completing the transaction, should write on the back of the check the customer's driver's license number, the account number of the credit card, the name of the card company, and the customer's phone number. The cashier should also ask whether the address that appears on the license and check is a current address, for there have been times when a person moved without leaving a fowarding address and then used old checks and identification to make purchases, knowing that the checking account had been closed out. But once all this information has been ascertained and noted, the cashier can complete the transaction. Before giving the customer the receipt, however, the cashier should mark the receipt with the word "check" and the number of the check. Some customers have been known to make a purchase by check, stop payment on the check, and return the merchandise to the store for cash before the check has cleared. When this technique is employed, the store has possession of the merchandise and the customer has the original funds in the checking account as well as the cash refund made by the store. But if the receipt, which is normally required in making an exchange, is marked "check," the cashier will not allow the exchange to take place until the store receives funds from the bank.

Do's and Don'ts

To conclude, there are a few do's and don'ts for the store manager to follow when handling checks. First, never accept a check that is drawn on a bank outside cities or towns that are a reasonable distance from the store, especially out-of-state banks. The customer displaying such a check may be honest; however, if the customer later proves to be dishonest, the store operator will have a difficult time locating the customer after the check has been declared invalid. Never accept a check on which the customer's name and the name of the bank is not imprinted, particularly if the check does not have a checking account number printed on it. There is little to stop anyone from taking an unprinted check and filling in the required information. At least if the check has the name and address of the customer, the name and address of the bank, and the account number printed on it, the store manager will have additional indications that the check may be of some value. The manager knows that someone had to place money in the bank in order to open the account and receive checks from the bank. Never accept a check when a customer cannot show at least two solid forms of identification that can be checked later if there is any trouble with the check clearing the bank. With a driver's license or credit card, the store manager has a starting point for tracking down the customer who passes a bad check.

Never permit an untrained employee to accept a check as payment for merchandise without having someone trained in the detection of bad checks approve the check. Never cash a check for more than the amount of the merchandise purchased. The purpose of this policy is to minimize the risk involved in accepting a check. For example, the customer who passes a bad check will still have the merchandise, whereas the store has only the invalid piece of paper. If the check is made out for the exact amount of the transaction, the dollar value of the loss is the dollar amount for which the store purchased the goods. This amount is usually less than the full retail price of the merchandise. On the other hand, if the check is made out in an amount over the total amount of the transaction, and if the difference is paid to the customer in cash, then the store's loss is the wholesale price of the merchandise as well as the cash that was paid to the customer. Never cash a check unless the customer purchases merchandise. Unless the business is a bank, the purpose of the business is to sell merchandise. Whenever a store accepts a check, the store is taking a calculated risk—giving up the merchandise before the cash is actually received. The store manager takes this risk as part of the overall risk of selling merchandise. But if the store cashes checks without any purchases being made, the store is taking a risk and not receiving anything in return. Such a decision is poor business sense as well as questionable business security. The small business manager must institute procedures that will strike a balance between protecting him- or herself and the store from bad checks while keeping the customers happy.

Secure Check-cashing Procedures

1. A driver's license and an approved credit card must be shown, and the numbers must be written on the back of the check.
2. The check must be drawn on a local bank.
3. The name and address of the person must be on the check.
4. On all checks of large amounts, the bank should be contacted before the transaction is completed.
5. The signature on the check must be verified with the signature on the driver's license and the credit card by a trained person.

HOW TO HANDLE CREDIT TRANSACTIONS

The store manager now has an idea of some procedures that will permit the store to weed out bad checks before a transaction is completed by the cashier. Another type of transaction that the store manager is taking a risk with is credit purchases where the merchandise has exchanged hands, but the payment is to be made at a later date. Small business operators are typically involved with several kinds of credit transactions. The first is where the store actually gives credit to a customer. Some stores allow customers to charge goods to a store account. After a week or at some predetermined period, the customer comes into the store and pays the bill. This practice is common in smaller communities where the shopkeepers and the customers have more of a neighborly relationship than a strict business environment would have.

The store manager is also involved with credit card transactions. In this situation, the store does not actually extend credit to a customer. Instead, a third party, the credit card company, extends credit. When the credit card receipt is presented to the credit card company by the store manager, the company immediately gives the store the cash equivalent of the receipt. Some card companies only give the store 98% of the total amount of the receipt. The other 2% is a charge to the small store for the services and convenience of using the credit card company. Credit card companies will usually require that the store present them with valid receipts. It is the store's responsibility to compare the signature of the customer to the signature on the card. Beyond such a requirement, the store's risks when accepting a credit card are almost nonexistent.

If the store manager determines that the store should offer credit in some form to its customers, the store manager must first establish several guidelines that will give the cashier and other store employees direction when a credit transaction is about to take place. When the store is issuing credit to a customer, the store manager must remember what is actually happening. Many small business operators who manage neighborhood stores frequently extend credit to customers based on just a handshake rather than on any formal application. When a store operator extends credit to a customer, he or she is really giving the customer money to borrow. The first question that the manager should think of is, "Would I loan money to this customer?" If the answer is, "No," then the same response should be given when the customer seeks credit from the store.

Credit Applications and Checks

Although the neighborly thing to do is to extend credit without asking questions, many small businesses cannot afford to extend credit, especially when doing so may later turn out to be a bad risk. The small business operator should require the customer who is seeking credit to give the manager certain pieces of information that will permit the manager to perform a credit check on the person. Those customers who ask for credit are usually familiar with such commonplace procedures as a credit application and a credit check.

The store manager can obtain a standard credit application form that asks the applicant for his or her name, address, and detailed information about references, such as employers and banks; most forms also contain a credit agreement whereby once the customer has been informed by the store manager that credit has been established, the customer agrees to follow the terms of the credit agreement. After the form is completed, the customer is asked to sign the form. Be sure that the form contains a permission clause that grants the store manager permission to conduct a reference check on the customer. Never attempt such a check without written permission from the customer.

Once the form has been filled out, the store manager should withold granting any credit until the credit check is completed. Some stores will permit the customer who filled out the credit form to make purchases under a predetermined amount during the period when the credit check is being performed. When checking on the credit reference of a customer, one of the first items to check is the customer's employment situation. A call to the customer's employer will usually permit the manager to determine whether the customer is employed and whether the chances of that customer continuing employment during the period of the credit agreement are good. From this call, the store manager is able to determine if the person does have enough income to be able to pay for the merchandise he or she buys on credit. The next step is for the store manager to determine whether the customer has sufficient funds in the bank to pay for merchandise if, for some unknown reason, the person becomes unemployed. In most cases, the store manager will not be able to determine the amount of money the customer has in a bank; however, banks will frequently give creditors some idea of the customer's current balance, such as between $2,500 and $3,500. As long as the monetary range is within a reasonable level, the customer's bank reference should be adequate. The most important consideration when a small business manager is deciding to extend credit to a customer is whether or not the customer has ever defaulted on any similar credit agreement. The manager must determine whether the customer has had credit extended to him or her before, whether the customer paid on time, and whether the customer ever failed to pay a creditor.

Using a Credit Bureau

In order to answer these questions, the business operator should, as a general rule, use the services of a credit clearing-house. Local credit bureaus will usually maintain files on customers, and when a participating business requires information, the manager can call the bureau and give the person at the bureau a special identification number and the name of the customer. Usually, bureaus also require customers' social security numbers. Depending upon the credit bureau, the manager will receive a listing of other companies who have extended credit to the customer as well as a notation of any defaults or late payments made to the participating companies. If the small business manager does not belong to such a credit bureau, the manager should then contact other local businesses and banks to see whether they know the customer and whether they have or had extended credit to him or her. If a customer asks for credit in a local store, there is a good chance that he or she has made a similar request of other store operators in the area.

Warning! Several problems are possible when a store uses a credit bureau. Many credit bureaus will only keep a record of customers if the customer has received credit from one of the participating firms. If credit is extended by a company who does not participate in the credit bureau, there will be no file on that customer. This can also happen if the customer recently moved to the area, since any credit information is usually kept on a local level near the customer's previous residence. Some credit bureaus require that the name, address, and social security number of the customer be exactly similar to the information on their records. For example, a customer may have written the name "Jack Smith," on the credit application. But when the credit bureau receives the credit check request, there is a chance that their record shows the same person not as Jack but as John Smith. The difference is immaterial to a human; but, since the credit bureau uses a cross-reference computer program, to a computer, there is a big difference between Jack and John, and a false reading could result. A similar situation could occur if the person has recently moved and has failed to indicate the change of address on the credit application. The credit bureau will ask the computer, for example, to search for the file marked "Jack Smith, 100 U.S.A. Avenue" (the customer's new address). The computer will have a file marked "Jack Smith, 300 America Avenue" but will reveal no file on "Jack Smith, 100 U.S.A. Avenue."

The final problem with the credit bureau is that the file on a customer may contain incomplete information. It may exist for only a short period of time, anywhere from the past six months to the previous year and a half; or, if the customer was a bad credit risk three years ago, the file may not reflect this past credit problem.

If the business manager does not want to keep track of extending credit himself, the store can offer to accept credit cards. As long as the store cashier and manager maintain a detailed check of credit card signatures and compare the credit card to a book, which is supplied by the credit card companies, listing those cards that have either been stolen or are invalid, the store's security problem regarding credit transactions will be kept to the very minimum. Many credit card companies, however, will charge the store 1 or 2% of the gross receipt for this service.

Problems with Credit Bureaus

1. Only participating firms are allowed to use the service.
2. Files may not be updated.
3. Files reflect only the recent local history of the customer.

HOW CON-ARTISTS OVERCOME
NORMAL CHECK AND CREDIT
SECURITY PROCEDURES

Check and credit security has been a prime concern of major retail stores and federal law enforcement officers. Store managers and managers of large credit card companies have spent millions of dollars studying the security problems involved with checks and credit, yet even after highly technical procedures have been established, professional and amateur criminals alike have managed to outmaneuver the check and credit rules. The old saying, "If man made the security system, man can penetrate the security system," is true when it comes to check and credit security.

A case in point involves an Iowa hardware store. A man drove up to the store in a Mercedes-Benz sports car. The customer was dressed in expensive clothes, or at least that is how it appeared to the cashier and the store manager. The hardware store handled a full line of merchandise, including expensive, large power tools. The customer asked the manager for assistance in locating a certain type of bracket for furniture he was building at home. While walking through the store, the customer stopped in front of an expensive table saw and exclaimed, "That's what I've been looking for!" The store manager was taken aback, since the man was apparently shopping for a bracket. As any good salesperson would, the store manager sized up the customer and determined that the customer could well afford the saw. Since the hardware store only sold one or two a year, the store manager pushed the sale of the merchandise. The customer finally agreed to buy the saw if he could take it with him. The store manager complied. When the customer reached the cashier, he discovered that his wallet was missing, probably left at home. The customer was surprised, embarrassed, and angry at himself, but he explained the situation to the store manager and informed the manager that he had a checking account with a local bank. The manager, wanting to make the sale, decided that the customer was honest, and, from the car he was driving and the clothes he was wearing, there was no question in the manager's mind that the customer could afford the saw. The manager told the customer not to worry and provided him with a blank check. The customer filled in the check, thanked the manager, and left with the merchandise. The manager later explained to the cashier that this transaction was an exception to the store's rules about accepting checks. Two days later, the store manager received a letter from the local police department that alerted the manager that a con artist had been touring the area. The well-dressed criminal drove an expensive Mercedes-Benz and made large purchases of merchandise, using unprinted checks. In the same mail, the manager received the bad check, returned by the bank.

Criminals who usually try to overcome check and credit procedures are called con artists simply because these people have developed a technique of deception that, many times, has the artist's touch. In the Iowa case, the con artist dazzled the store manager by giving the appearance of being wealthy and then by making such a large purchase that the store manager could not refuse, regardless of what rules and regulations he had established. In essence, the con artist's behavior implied to the store manager, "If I can afford a $19,000 car, you can certainly trust me with a $1,500 saw." The store manager fell right into the poor logical sequence set up by the customer. Obviously, the store manager did not really know whether the customer owned the car outright or whether he had stolen the vehicle.

Operating Procedures of Con Artists

Con artists use many different ploys in duping the store manager and employees into making exceptions to the rules. A frequent technique used by these criminals, which was illustrated in the Iowa case, is to select merchandise and, after the cashier has itemized the goods on the register, to realize suddenly that a wallet or money is missing. Some con artists will check pockets, pocketbooks, and the floor around the cash register; they sometimes walk through the store looking for the missing money or wallet. From appearances, the customer is really in a jam and is making an effort to locate the money. A good con artist will not stop his or her performance until there is some terminating response from the store manager. During the period when the customer is searching the store for the lost money, the cashier is usually in doubt as to what he or she ought to do. The transaction is in the register but cannot be completed until the money is transferred from the customer to the cashier. By this time, there is usually a line of customers waiting to pay for their purchases which builds psychological pressures for the cashier. When the store manager arrives, he or she is faced with the same psychological pressures. Two alternatives are open to the manager: first, to complete the transaction by letting the customer take the goods with the promise of returning the following day with the money. The other alternative is to cancel the purchase, letting the customer go home empty-handed. When the customer finds the money, the customer can then make the purchase. If the con artist is a good actor or actress, which most professionals are, the store manager will take the first alternative and permit the customer to leave with the merchandise. As long as the con artist does not use this technique again in the same store, he or she can continue to acquire goods from other stores in the same manner.

Con artists usually use the psychological impact of the situation in order to force the hand of the cashier or store manager. A typical fertile situation for a con artist is a very busy store that has five or six cashiers and a three- or four-employee exchange counter. In many cases, there will be one supervisor or store manager who will resolve conflicts at the registers and the refund counter. During a busy period, the manager is often constantly on the run, trying to settle transactions. With long lines of customers waiting to be taken care of, the manager will usually make decisions very quickly, with little thought.

Most businesses have set procedures governing the acceptance of checks. Con artists also know these procedures. During busy periods, con artists usually seek out the least experienced cashier, often the one who also has the longest line of customers. The long lines of customers and the unfamiliarity with the job usually develop pressures that can force the cashier into making exceptions to the rules. In such a situation, a con artist normally makes a large purchase. After the cashier has tallied the register, the customer writes a check for the amount of the purchase. When asked for identification, the con artist may balk, claiming that he or she does not have a driver's license, only a business card. The cashier, knowing that this type of idenitfication is not exactly the kind normally presented when paying with a check, will seek the advice of the store manager. Many times, during these busy periods, the store manager is tied up handling other matters. If this is so, the con artist can often force the new cashier into making a decision without advice. Other customers in line are usually making all types of impatient gestures and remarks, showing their displeasure to the cashier. The con artist, after waiting a few minutes to let this pressure build, then tells the cashier that he or she has had this problem many times before in this store. "Usually, the store manager will permit me to pay by check without asking for any other identification." The cashier quickly accepts the customer's word and completes the transaction.

When they deal with credit cards, con artists will often acquire the cards from an underground "wholesaler" of stolen credit cards. The stolen card has usually been missing less than a week. This is enough time for the card to be used illegally with the assurance that the card's number has not been placed on the credit card company's hot list and distributed to the stores. Normally, cashiers rarely compare the signature on the credit card to the signature on the receipt. Therefore, the con artist can feel free, for a limited period, to make any purchase without the fear of being caught.

More enterprising con artists have acquired credit cards from the credit card manufacturer. These new, unregistered cards can be used for a slightly longer period of time than a stolen card. Before the card is placed on the credit card company's hot list, the credit card company will have to realize that the receipts submitted by the businesses contain an invalid, nonissued credit card number, which may take some time.

The last ploy a con artist uses involves the assumption of another person's identity. Without too much trouble, the con artist can acquire a person's name, address, phone number, social security number, and bank account number. With this information, the con artist can open up a credit line under the person's name, with all the bills and credit cards being sent directly to the con artist. For example, a con artist can acquire enough information about another person to fill out an application for credit. People frequently move, so that if the con artist, when filling out such an application, uses a different address than that of the actual person from whom he or she is assuming identity, those individuals conducting the credit check will understand the difference in the address.

The credit check would be conducted in the following fashion. The creditor would check with the credit clearing-house under the given name, address, and social security number. The clearing-house would report that there is a file under that name and social security number, but with a different address. The creditor would check the application again, noting that the applicant had indicated a recent move, thus satisfying the discrepancy. The next check would be made by calling the person's employer, who would tell the creditor that a person by the name given by the creditor does, in fact, work there. The final check before approving the credit is made with the bank. The creditor contacts the bank and gives the bank the account number and the name of the person, and the bank confirms that the account exists. The creditor then sends the credit card to the new address contained on the application.

The con artist then proceeds to use the card. When bills are received from the credit card company, they are ignored. This system continues until the credit card company turns the matter over to a collection agency. By this time, bad credit reports have been placed in the file of the person whose identity had been assumed by the con artist. Eventually, a collection agency representative will come to the address, but the con artist simply pleads ignorant, since no one with the name mentioned by the collection agency lives at the address. Credit is usually canceled shortly thereafter.

When to Expect a Professional Con Artist

1. At busy periods.
2. When there are long lines at the register.
3. With an inexperienced cashier.
4. When the customer does not fit into existing check-cashing procedures.

WHAT ALTERNATIVES ARE AVAILABLE IN CHECK AND CREDIT SECURITY?

As we have seen, the small business manager who is trying to please his or her customers while maintaining good check and credit business practices has many obstacles to overcome before he or she can feel totally secure. There are always customers who are trying to steal from the small business person. It is up to the business manager to devise systems to counteract the techniques used by dishonest persons.

In order to assist the store manager in developing alternatives in check and credit security, a few procedures that will help the manager follow. One of the first problems to tackle is that of bad checks—either checks drawn on accounts lacking sufficient funds or stolen checks. On the surface, the store, without cooperation from other local businesses, cannot combat the problem of insufficient funds in a checking account. When the check is presented and identification is checked, there is no procedure available other than establishing some kind of clearing system that will inform the business manager whether funds actually exist in the account.

Some banks, for example, will provide small businesses with a call-in check verification service. When the business manager is presented with a check, he or she calls the verification service. The person at the bank checks the account number against the balance shown on the computer. If the balance is sufficient to cover the amount of the check, the verification service approves the check. The manager is thus assured that there is enough money in the account to cover the transaction.

Many small business organizations will formally or informally compile a list, kept either at the cash register or in the manager's office, of the names and addresses of customers who have issued bad checks. When a check is presented, the cashier or manager checks the list. If the customer's name is on the list, the manager or cashier refuses to accept the check and asks that payment be made in cash. When this technique is used, the store manager must be sure not to inform the customer why the check was

103

refused. Legal problems could begin if the customer discovers that a list of "bad check" customers exists; lawsuits for blacklisting are a possibility. Other reasons should be given for the rejection.

Larger stores may have a central clearing-house for checks. When a cashier or store manager is presented with a check, he or she calls a central phone number, where a list similar to that just described is then checked. The whole transaction and checking procedure takes a matter of minutes. The use of a central check clearing-house or verification service can have a side benefit for the small business manager and the police. If, for example, a customer has been passing bad checks frequently in various local stores, the central clearing-house will be able to track that customer's movements. Each time a check is presented, the manager of the store calls the verification service for approval. If approval is denied, the service can alert other store operators in the area as soon as the verification service has established, through their procedures, a pattern being used by the customer. Once a store has been alerted, the store manager and cashier can be on the lookout for the customer who is attempting to pass a bad check.

In this age of fast communication and computers, some check verification services have established a system whereby the cashier can key the account number on the check and a special code for the bank on which the check is drawn into the register; within seconds, either an approval light or a rejection light will be displayed. There is no need, under this system for the manager or cashier to make a phone call to the verification service. As quickly as the cashier can ring up the sale, the check is approved (see Figure 5–2).

Warning! There are always tricks con artists use to circumvent security systems and procedures. The store manager should not assume that either a verification service or a list of persons passing bad checks can alone take the place of good check identification procedures. The customer should still be asked to present two forms of identification—a driver's license and a major credit card. The driver's license number and the credit card company and number must be written on the back of the check, as well as the customer's telephone number. A combination of check verification and customer identification will usually weed out most of those customers who frequently pass bad checks.

When dealing with credit cards, a similar verification service may exist, depending on the location of the business. If such a service does exist, the same procedure should be followed when a credit card is presented for purchase. Contact the verification service before completing the transaction. If the verification service is not available, be sure that

Figure 5-2
Electronic check clearing machine. Retailers no longer need take a risk in accepting a check or credit card from a customer. As the sale is being rung up on the register, the sales clerk may call up account information, identify a missing credit card or bad check writers, or even check a checking account. (Illustration supplied by and used with permission of NCR Corporation, Dayton, Ohio.)

employees check the credit card company's hot list. Many stores working with the credit card company offer employees a reward for spotting a credit card that is on the hot list. The reward is an excellent motivating factor to encourage cashiers to check the hot list booklet when they are presented with credit cards, for many cashiers will overlook this requirement and simply complete the transaction without delaying the customers waiting in the check-out line.

A procedure that some stores follow in protecting the store during a check or credit transaction is requiring a customer who wishes to pay in such a manner to fill out a credit form prior to his or her purchase. The store manager will then run a credit check on the customer. When the credit check is completed and is favorable to the customer, the store manager issues a store privilege card. When the customer presents a check, for example, the cashier will ask for this privilege card. If the card is shown, the cashier knows that the store has checked the credit-worthiness of the customer and that the check is probably valid. If a store does establish such a procedure, each privilege card should have an expiration date. Although a customer's credit may be excellent on the day of the credit check, that is no indication that the customer is still credit-worthy six months or a year later. By requiring the customer to reapply for the privilege card every year, the store manager is assured that the customer still has a good credit reference.

This chapter outlines some of the problems that small businesses have when dealing with checks and with customer credit. There is obviously no fool-proof system that will prevent a customer or con artist from obtaining credit or from issuing a check illegally. However, the procedures described here should help the small business manager to develop guidelines that will lower the risks involved in such transactions.

Practical ways to combat shoplifters **6**

HOW TO IDENTIFY A SHOPLIFTER

One of the growing crimes in the country is shoplifting. Almost every small retail business has, at some point, become the victim of a shoplifter. Yet many managers realize the impact of shoplifters only when they view the financial results. They know how much merchandise is placed on display, and they also know what profit margins and expected financial gains should result when the goods are sold. However, following an inventory of the store, management soon finds out that merchandise has been "walking out the front door" without cash being deposited in the register. Although larger retail stores have spent thousands of dollars trying to combat shoplifters, for many business managers the effort is wasted.

Types of Shoplifters

There are several types of shoplifters that the retail store manager should be concerned with. First, there are those who shoplift in order to

107

survive. These are usually those customers who look destitute and who frequently are senior residents of the community. Secondly, there are youngsters who shoplift for the excitement rather than out of necessity. The last type of shoplifter is the adult who enjoys the challenge of taking goods without paying for them. Although there are a few professional shoplifters who seek out expensive merchandise that can be sold quickly, with few questions asked, most small business retailers will not come into contact with the professional shoplifter.

The type of clientele a business deals with will usually give the manager an indication of what type of shoplifter to expect. A food store will be victimized by those who need food but cannot afford it, by youngsters, and by a few unneedy adults. A clothing or dry goods store will encounter adult shoplifters who enjoy the adventure the crime gives. A store dealing with high-priced items will find the unneedy adult and the professional seeking to shoplift.

Timing

Timing is important for a shoplifter. There are two circumstances that a shoplifter desires. The first is areas of the store that are obviously unprotected, areas where someone can take an item and place the goods in his or her pocket without anyone seeing the action. The other situation that is ideal for a shoplifter is when the store manager and clerks are busy with other customers. Holiday times are ideal, since, in most larger stores, there are more customers than clerks and fewer eyes on the merchandise.

At holiday times, the busy season for shoplifters, all stores are vulnerable. During this heavy sales period, salespeople are hired in large numbers without any screening beyond a two-minute interview and an hour training period. Although some stores employ security help, the store's first line of defense against shoplifters is usually the salesclerks. During the holiday period, most salespeople are so intent either on satisfying the customer or on ensuring that there are no mistakes during the transaction that very few clerks know how to detect a shoplifter. Shoplifters realize that this confusion exists and use the lack of security to time their activities.

Characteristic Methods

It is up to store employees to keep an eye out for potential shoplifters. Many shoplifters will give themselves away by their actions prior to or after committing the crime. One of the first steps a store employee should take when trying to identify a shoplifter is to establish a norm for customer behavior. Customers tend to behave in predictable ways: They will examine merchandise, look for sales help, ask questions, and then make a buying decision. If he or she does not purchase the goods, the customer will usually proceed to the next counter or area of the store. If he or she makes a decision to purchase the merchandise, the transaction usually takes place without any difficulty.

Once the norm has been established in the mind of the store employee, customers behaving outside the norm should be suspect. For example, if a customer has been seen examining merchandise for a longer than average period without asking for or accepting help from a store employee, then the store employee should become suspicious. The customer may be totally honest and may be having a difficult time reaching a decision. On the other hand, the customer could be a shoplifter waiting for the right opportunity to steal the goods.

Although there is no sure way of identifying a shoplifter, there are clues that store employees can watch for. Those shoplifters who are poor and in need of the merchandise for self-preservation will usually dress accordingly. If a customer who gives such an appearance enters the store, store employees should be placed on alert. Any time youngsters who are not accompanied by an adult are in the store, store employees should watch the movements of these young customers. This is especially important if the youngsters, who may be encouraged to steal because of peer pressure, enter the store as a small group. An adult customer who is overly demanding of the store employee, especially during the transaction stage of the purchase, should also arouse suspicion. The most obvious manner of a shoplifter, especially someone who is new at shoplifting, is nervousness. A shoplifter may spend a long time looking at or touching the merchandise, quickly setting the goods back on display whenever an employee walks past. Or, while standing by the merchandise, the customer may look everywhere else but at the goods. A new shoplifter is concerned about being caught and will try to spot trouble before trouble finds him or her. When the shoplifter is walking out of the store, he or she will try to avoid eye contact with store employees. The shoplifter may also survey everyone around the door when making an exit.

Shoplifters are creative people, especially those in the professional ranks. The techniques used by shoplifters often seem to stretch the imagination. A classic case involving a major department store occurred in New Jersey. A well-dressed shopper walked into the television and radio department and looked at television sets. He wanted to acquire a portable color television. The salesperson was busy and did not notice the customer, who selected a television set from the display, walked over to the sales-clerk, and asked whether the store still repaired television sets. The salesperson informed the customer that the store had discontinued the service several months ago. The customer, with an expression of pain on his face, said, "Do you mean I'll have to carry this television set back out to the car myself?" The salesclerk assured the customer that she would arrange for a stock boy to bring the set "back" to his car. The salesclerk called for the stock boy, who grabbed the portable set from the customer and placed it in the customer's car. Hours later, when the department manager walked by, he noticed that the set was missing. The salesclerk was embarrassed that she had assumed that the customer had brought the television set in for repairs.

Most shoplifters will not be as bold as the customer with the television set. Instead, shoplifters will stand by the merchandise and either create or wait for the opportunity to steal the goods. Some of the more common methods used by shoplifters include the use of overcoats that have false pockets. Such an oversized garment can conceal many large and small items; the false pockets permit the shoplifter to appear to have his or her hands in the pockets while he or she slips a hand through the opening in the coat and removes merchandise. Female shoplifters have been known to wear false compartments, near the lower abdomen, under their coats in which stolen merchandise is stored. From all outward appearances, the shoplifter appears to be pregnant.

Another common method employed by shoplifters is the booster box. This is a neatly wrapped box; usually, it is tied with string and has a handle. One side of the box opens through spring action. The shoplifter will either place the box over the object to be stolen or will put it on a counter where, at the proper time, he or she can quickly push merchandise into the box. From all outward appearances, the box is sealed tight; sometimes it may even be covered with store wrapping. Shoplifters who are less creative will simply wait for the proper time and then place the goods in their pockets.

Conditions that are Ideal for Shoplifting

1. Blind areas in the store.
2. Busy shopping periods.
3. Inexperienced salespeople.
4. Lack of visible security in the store.

Most experienced shoplifters are wise to the legal requirements necessary to arrest and prosecute a shoplifter. Store employees cannot simply walk over to a customer and accuse him or her of shoplifting. There are certain rules of law that must be followed before making such an apprehension. Before we discuss these rules, the reader must understand that each state has specific requirements for proving that a person has committed the crime of shoplifting and that these requirements may be different from those outlined in this book. Therefore, before the small business manager establishes a procedure for apprehending a shoplifter, he or she should consult an attorney.

The Chain of Evidence

Shoplifters must be caught with unpaid-for merchandise in their possession outside the store. Furthermore, the store making such a charge must be able to prove beyond a reasonable doubt that the goods were, in fact, removed from that particular store. To illustrate, if a store employee is walking near the store and notices several youngsters near the store with merchandise that appears to be the store's merchandise, the store employee is *not* in a position to charge the youngsters with shoplifting the merchandise. The store employee did not see the youngsters in the store or see them remove the goods from the shelf.

Most states require that the person making the allegation of shoplifting must see the suspect remove the merchandise from the display and conceal it, notice the suspect's moves throughout the store, notice that the suspect did not pay for the goods, and notice that the suspect left the store. If the person making the charge cannot provide the court with the above information, most courts will rule that the chain of evidence has been broken. Once the chain is broken, legal loopholes may well prohibit successful prosecution of the shoplifter. But one person alone does not have to witness everything a shoplifter does while in the store. As long as there are employees who can continue the chain of evidence where the other employee left off, the chain is not considered broken. For example, if a store employee notices a shoplifter removing and concealing the goods and, without losing sight of the shoplifter, notifies store security, who in turn pick up surveillance, the chain is not broken. The store employee would testify about the removal and concealment of merchandise, and the security person would tell the court about the surveillance and apprehension.

The chain of evidence is part of a long list of rules used by the courts to protect the innocent from mistakenly being accused of a crime that they did not commit. Many stores sell identical merchandise and use the same method to price goods. If a person has a piece of merchandise in his or her possession outside the store, it is up to the store to prove that the goods actually came from that store and not from another shop within the same area. Such a rule can be difficult for the small business manager to prove.

Few customers keep receipts for everything they buy. Therefore, although a customer may have a piece of merchandise in his or her possession outside the store without having a receipt for the merchandise, the courts and the store manager cannot be sure, based on mere possession of the merchandise, that the customer stole the goods from the store. Other possibilities could exist that prohibit prosecution. The store manager, therefore, operates under very strict conditions as to when he or she can charge a person with shoplifting.

Powers of Arrest and Search

Everyone has the power of arrest. A person seeing a crime being committed does have the legal power to apprehend and hold the suspect until police arrive. These are the same powers most store managers and security personnel use when apprehending a shoplifter. The arresting powers of a store manager or security employee do, however, differ from the arresting powers of a police officer, who is always acting on behalf of the community. He or she is allowed to use the force required to take the suspect into custody and has the right to frisk and search the suspect if he or she feels that the suspect may be carrying a weapon.

In most states, the store manager or the security person does not have the right to use force beyond physically holding the suspect. Store employees do not have the right to search the suspect, even if they suspect that he or she may be carrying a concealed weapon. In apprehending the suspect, the store employee cannot use a weapon, such as a gun, a nightstick, or any other device, to threaten the suspect into remaining at the location until police arrive. The only exception to this rule is if the store employee is confronted by a suspect who is obviously carrying some kind of weapon. But even in this extreme case, the store employee is not allowed to confront the suspect unless all other means of escape have been tried.

A person can use equal force to protect him- or herself from attack. For example, if the store employee confronts but does not touch the shoplifter, and if the suspect then turns and punches the employee, the employee can defend him- or herself with his or her fists, but not with a weapon.

When a store employee or a small business owner plans to apprehend a shoplifter, he or she should ask two questions: Am I sure the suspect is shoplifting, according to the chain of evidence? and Is there time to call the police for assistance? If there is doubt in your mind about whether the chain of evidence is intact, do not attempt to apprehend the suspect. If there is any chance of obtaining the help of a police officer before making the apprehension, ask for help. The police officer is well equipped to handle the situation, whereas with a citizen's arrest, difficulties are common.

Always try to have more than one store employee and, if possible, another customer available during the surveillance and apprehension of a shoplifter. This is not always possible, but if such an arrangement can be made, the store will have more than one person's testimony regarding the events. The store employee should follow the shoplifter around the store and then out the door. Immediately after the suspect walks out the door, confront him or her in a quiet and pleasant manner. Above all, do not cause a scene. If a crowd begins to form, try to lead the suspect back into the store. During the confrontation outside the store, do not accuse the suspect of any crime—simply tell him or her that the manager of the store would like to talk with him or her in the office for a minute. Do not try to grab the suspect: Avoid violence and the threat of violence.

As soon as the employee feels that an apprehension is necessary, another employee should notify police headquarters and ask for assistance. The call should be made before the apprehension begins. Therefore, the purpose of the employee in stopping the suspect outside the door is not to make a citizen's arrest but to detain the suspect until police arrive. Many times, the suspected shoplifter will return to the store freely, without violence and without creating a disturbance. Any accusations should take place behind closed doors and in front of the police officer. The shoplifter will usually admit to the crime or will indicate that he or she has made an error and has forgotten to pay for the merchandise.

Any confrontation in the store or on the street will leave the store and the store employee open for all sorts of countercharges if the witnesses cannot provide enough information to convince a judge that the suspected person committed shoplifting. The suspect is innocent until proven guilty *beyond any doubt*. These three words have lost many a case and have set

113

criminals free to commit the same crime again. When the store employee makes an accusation that cannot be supported by evidence, the employee can be found guilty of defamation of character. If an employee physically detains a suspect who later turns out to be innocent, he or she can be found guilty of false arrest. If an employee forces a suspect back into the store and the suspect is found not guilty, the employee can be found guilty of kidnapping. If force is used, assault charges may be brought against the employee.

Besides the criminal liabilities an employee and, possibly, a store may face when making an unsubstantiated shoplifting arrest, both parties may be facing civil action and fines ranging in the thousands of dollars. Many small store owners take no action against shoplifters because of the high risk involved in making a mistake. There are few successful prosecutions of shoplifting arrests because of the difficulty involved in gathering evidence. Many store managers simply turn their backs and raise the prices of their merchandise in order to cover the loss.

Three Steps to Arresting a Shoplifter

1. An employee must see the shoplifter remove merchandise from the shelf and hide the item on his or her person.
2. An employee must have continual sight of the shoplifter while he or she is in the store.
3. An employee must see the shoplifter leave the store without paying for the goods.

WHAT TO DO ONCE A SHOPLIFTER HAS BEEN APPREHENDED

Citizens' Rights

When dealing with the crime of shoplifting, the small business manager must consider the rights of a citizen before making any foolish moves by signing criminal complaints against a suspect. A citizen has the right to move freely without anyone causing his or her detainment without cause. The exceptions to this rule occur when a citizen has probable cause to believe that the person has committed a felony or when a police officer has reason to believe that the person has committed any crime. And even then, detainment, however justified, must be only for a reasonable length of time. At the end of the detainment period, the person must either be charged with a crime or set free.

The citizen also has the right to move freely without the threat of being attacked. If such an attack occurs, the citizen has the right to defend him- or herself. The citizen has the right of privacy and cannot be searched without a court-ordered search warrant. There are two exceptions to this rule: Police officers can search a person for a weapon, and custom officers can search for contraband. A citizen has a right to keep property that he or she has legal title to. The exception to this rule is if the courts order the disposal of the property for legal reasons.

The rights of a citizen may seem very basic, but it is important to keep them in mind, because a store employee trying to enforce or apprehend a shoplifter walks a very fine line between violating these rights and making a legal arrest. But the small business person should also recognize that a shoplifter is, in fact, violating the store owner's basic rights. Although there is a clear-cut line separating the store owner's right to hold title to merchandise and the right of a shoplifter to steal the goods, there is a gray area involved in identifying a shoplifter and proving his or her crime in a court of law.

For a moment, let us take a look at a mistaken identity case involving a store employee in Boston. The store employee noticed a man in a tan raincoat remove merchandise from a shelf and place it in his pocket. The employee followed the man out the door of the store. However, for a brief second, when the man turned the corner, the store employee lost his suspect. The employee quickly turned the corner and noticed a man in a tan raincoat. He ran after the man, yelling, "Stop that man! He's a shoplifter! Stop him!" Everyone on the street turned to look. The employee made a jump and tackled the man in the tan coat. The man resisted. The employee did everything possible, including beating the man, to detain him. By this time, a crowd had gathered around the two people lying on the street. The employee finally grabbed at the man's pockets and then forced him back into the store. When the police arrived at the store, the suspect identified himself as an attorney. He had not been in the store, nor did he have any merchandise from the store in his possession. During that brief second when the employee lost sight of the suspect, the real shoplifter had driven away in a car. Obviously, this case involved mistaken identity.

Let us now take a look at the same case from the attorney's viewpoint. The attorney was shopping when someone ran toward him, waving his hands and yelling. The attorney naturally felt threatened and continued to walk away from the man. Without any warning, the man jumped the attorney and started to beat him up. The lawer struck back in self-defense. The man started to stick his hands in the attorney's pockets, much as a mugger might do. By this time, the attorney, suffering from several cuts, decided that less harm would come to him if he did not resist. He was then dragged into the store and accused of being a criminal.

The same event looks completely different when told from the position of the suspect. In this particular case, the employee, regardless of how justified he thought his actions were, was charged with assault and battery, robbery, illegal search and seizure of property, kidnapping, and defamation of character. The store, since the employee was acting as an agent of the store, was charged with defamation of character and false arrest. And these were only the criminal charges stemming from the case. The attorney sought not only damages but also punitive damages against the employee and the store. The courts agreed with the charges, except in the case of kidnapping. Although the employee did take the attorney into the store against his will, the judge felt that, although the action did meet the letter of the law, it did not meet the spirit of the law. The employee received a suspended one-year jail sentence, was placed on probation for six months, and received a fine of $1,000. The store was also found guilty and was fined $5,000. At the civil hearing, the judge awarded the attorney $20,000 from the store and $1,500 from the employee.

The judges justified the sentencing by pointing out that the nature of the crime and the loss of merchandise, which in this case was a pocket flashlight, did not warrant the flagrant violation of the attorney's rights. The judges stated that the employee, who was not trained in the evidence required to prove shoplifting, should not have been assigned the task or allowed to proceed in apprehending shoplifters.

Some Pointers

In order to avoid the pitfalls of apprehending a suspect, small business managers should compare the value of the goods involved in the shoplifting with the risk the store and the store employee will be exposed to by making a citizen's arrest. If the merchandise is of low value, don't stop the shoplifter unless supportive evidence is available.

As suggested previously, the suspect should be asked to talk with the manager in the office. Once in the office, the manager has two alternatives open for resolving the situation: He or she can immediately confront the suspect with an accusation of shoplifting, or he or she can stall for time and wait for the police to arrive. There are advantages and disadvantages to both alternatives. If the store manager decides to handle the matter without calling the police, he or she will be able to have total control over what information, if any, is placed in the public record. Thus the manager can determine, within reason, the outcome of the confrontation. On the other hand, once accused a shoplifter is under no obligation to remain in the store. In fact, at any time during the entire surveillance, apprehension, and confrontation, the shoplifter can walk out the door. Although, officially, the store employee can make a citizen's arrest and hold the suspect until police arrive, chances are that the store manager will not permit store employees to use any force in such situations. Therefore, the manager must be prepared for almost anything, from the suspect walking out of the store to an assault.

Waiting for the police to arrive will, of course, place the event into public record. Even if no charges are filed, police officers will usually have to log the call on the police blotter, which, in most municipalities, is open for inspection by the public and members of the news media. The police role in the confrontation is twofold. First, the police officer is present to assist the store manager in making a citizen's arrest. In many states, unless the police officer is a witness to the shoplifting, he or she cannot sign the complaint against a suspect but can only assist another citizen in the arrest and criminal complaint processes. The police officer also acts as a peace officer. Although they do arrest criminals, police officers are also required to keep the peace by ensuring that crimes do not occur. Therefore, the police officer acts as a third party to ensure that neither the store manager nor the suspect harms one another.

Many small business managers have developed guidelines on how to handle a shoplifter once he or she has been apprehended. First, the manager attempts to discover whether the suspect is level-headed or whether he or she is inclinded to become physical. If the latter seems to be the case, the confrontation should stop until the police arrive. If the suspect seems less likely to be harmful, the manager should unfold the evidence. Usually, toward the end of such a presentation, the suspect realizes that he or she has been caught. Unless the manager is trying to make a point of a case—an example to other shoplifters—he or she should permit the suspect to return the goods or pay for them. The manager should also request that the suspect sign a release stating that he or she admits committing the crime of shoplifting and releases the store and its employees from any further claim. The shoplifter is then told not to enter the store again. In some com-

117

munities, business people have a central listing of the names and addresses of suspects who have admitted to committing the crime. This list is used as reference material when hiring new employees.

Don'ts

1. Don't use force to detain a shoplifter.
2. Don't search a shoplifter for stolen merchandise.
3. Don't fight with a shoplifter.
4. Don't accuse the shoplifter of shoplifting.

Do's

1. Call the police as soon as a shoplifter is discovered.
2. Detain the shoplifter through normal conversation until the police arrive.
3. Make any accusations of shoplifting after the police arrive.

WHAT SECURITY DEVICES TO ACQUIRE IN ORDER TO COMBAT SHOPLIFTING

Security device manufacturers have devised many machines and sensors to protect small business managers from becoming victims of shoplifting. A manager who wants to ensure that his store will never again be victimized by shoplifters can spend thousands of dollars on all types of devices that will almost guarantee results. However, the manager must be careful not to spend $100 to protect ten cents, which can easily happen when a business begins to invest in costly security systems.

Financial Factors

Before buying a security device to combat shoplifting, the small business manager must consider two financial factors. First, the manager must determine the annual loss in dollars that occurs due to shoplifters. In order to do this, the manager compares the amount of merchandise received, minus damaged goods, with the amount listed on the inventory. This comparison tells the manager the amount of goods on hand and the amount of goods that have been sold. The manager should be able to determine the amount of gross receipts that would have been received if all the goods sold actually were sold. The manager must then compare this estimated gross figure to the actual gross receipts. Any difference can usually be called the cost of shoplifting.

The second factor to consider involves the visibility of the desired security device(s) and its impact on honest customers. If the security device(s) is too imposing to the customer, the store may be losing business because of the security system. The store manager should compare the operations of similar stores using the desired security system before reaching a decision. A talk with another store owner who uses the system will alert the manager to any possible loss in customers.

Inexpensive Security Devices

After considering the factors of lost customers and the current expense of shoplifting, the small business manager is in a position to determine how much money can be allocated to the security system to prevent shoplifting. For example, a store with only a $100-a-year shoplifting expense would lose more money purchasing a $1,500 security system than if the manager did nothing to prevent shoplifting. This is the reason given by many store managers for not instituting a shoplifting security system: The system costs more than the goods that are stolen.

As mentioned in Chapter 3, there are security devices that are affordable and economically feasible for the small business manager to purchase. One of the least costly security devices is a corner mirror. In many stores, there is shelf space that is out of the direct line of sight of the store employees. Shoplifters will usually seek out these areas in the store as prime sites for committing their crimes. A carefully placed corner mirror will expose the shelf space to the eyes of the employees. A shoplifter might think twice before removing merchandise when he or she realizes that a store employee may be watching. Mirrors are usually inexpensive, and they offer a good line of defense for very small stores.

Another security device that does not cost the small store owner money is selecting merchandise that is not easy to shoplift. Although package design is left in the hands of manufacturers, what goods are placed in what areas of the store is determined by the small business manager. The shoplifter, remember, is looking for objects that he or she can conceal easily while walking past store employees. A large bottle of soda is more difficult to hide than a small 16-ounce bottle.

In selecting the merchandise, the store manager must examine the packaging very carefully. There are many blister-packaged goods that, at first glance, appear bulky; however, the item in the blister pouch can often be easily removed from the rest of the package. The packaging must be strong enough to prevent someone from quickly peeling away the cardboard backing and removing the merchandise.

An important security device that is usually overlooked by some managers is the method in which the store marks the prices on the goods. The most common method is to attach printed, gummed labels to the merchandise. Unfortunately, some of the labels are easily removed from the packages by shoplifters as well as by those customers who are inclined to switch prices. When dealing with a shoplifter, the store manager must be in a position to identify his or her own merchandise. The store manager should purchase specially made price labels that will fall apart if a customer tries to remove them (see Figure 6–1). Also, labels should be placed in two positions on the packaging—the first in an obvious location and the second in a location that is not so obvious. An unsuspecting shoplifter who quickly removes the obvious label may not even find the second label. Then, if the shoplifter is caught with the goods, the second label enables the manager to identify the merchandise.

More Expensive Security Devices

The devices mentioned above are the least costly methods of combatting shoplifting. There are expensive devices that will give the small business person better protection. One of these is the hidden or obviously placed television camera. Several cameras are placed throughout the store. Although at first glance, one may expect that the hidden camera would be more effective in fighting shoplifting, the camera placed in full public view outperforms the hidden camera. The concept security firms and store managers use is the theory that the shoplifter will feel self-conscious while committing the crime. The shoplifter, of course, does not want to get caught. A shoplifter may feel reassured once he or she identifies store employees and will then commit the crime when they are not around. However, this reassurance will be shattered when television cameras are installed. The shoplifter can no longer tell whether or not there is someone at a television set watching his or her actions. In fact, there are many large department stores that highlight television security. Cameras are mounted in clear view of customers. What most customers do not know is that there is no television receiver or employee watching the customers who are being

Figure 6-1
Many retailers have been confronted by shoplifters and other criminals who change price tags, thus obtaining an expensive item at a low price. To combat this, some retailers have employed a rip-off price tag. The tag is attached with a special label printer, and it is designed to rip apart if it is removed from the item. (Illustrations supplied by and used with permission of New England Business Services, Inc., Groton, Massachusetts 01450.)

viewed by the television cameras. The cameras are there purely as a psychological deterrent.

Some stores publicize another security device to warn off shoplifters that involves two-way mirrors and peepholes in the walls and ceilings. Two-way mirrors are used as a part of the floor displays. A store employee or guard stationed behind the window will be able to see the movement of a customer without the customer noticing that he or she is being watched. Using a similar method, employees are stationed behind walls and in false ceilings to observe customer actions. Such a system has proved useful in dressing rooms where shoplifters have been known to try on clothes and then hide the garments under their coats when leaving. An employee positioned at an observation point can detect the shoplifter and then cause his or her apprehension. But this system also has a major drawback, in that customers will obviously not patronize stores where they will be observed trying on clothes.

For stores that have lost large amounts of money because of shoplifting, there is an expensive system that will nearly guarantee the elimination of shoplifting. This system involves an alarm detector built into the door of the store. Every item in the store contains a specially fixed label that can only be removed either by damaging the merchandise or by cutting the tag, which is also coded. When a customer makes a purchase, the salesclerk adjusts the tag. Once this adjustment is made, the customer can remove the merchandise from the store without the detector sounding an alarm. If the label is not adjusted, as would be the case with a shoplifter, the detector senses the unadjusted label and sounds the alarm.

There are some disadvantages associated with such a security device. The detector, similar to the metal detectors used at airports, may inhibit honest customers from entering the store. The detector is usually very cumbersome and, in rare cases, can detract from the store's appearance. Another drawback to the system involves human error: The salesclerk may forget to adjust the tag or may adjust it improperly. When the honest customer leaves the store, the detector sounds the alarm, and store employees may well react to the situation as if a shoplifter had been discovered. The store manager would then have to provide an explanation to the customer.

Several kinds of security devices designed to combat shoplifting may be used together. For the small business manager confronted by shoplifting, the main consideration should be justifying the cost of the system. The purchase of the device(s), the potential customer dissatisfaction, the risks involved if the system catches a shoplifter—all of these considerations must be translated into dollars and cents. Then, a business decision can be made.

HOW TO MINIMIZE SHOPLIFTING

The old saying, ''An ounce of prevention is worth a pound of cure,'' holds true when a small business manager tries to protect a store against shoplifting. Shoplifting, as we have seen, is not a crime of violence: Rarely, if ever, does a shoplifter force a store manager into giving him or her the merchandise. Rather, shoplifting is a crime of opportunity and will occur only if the store manager gives the shoplifter opportunities to remove merchandise from the shelves without employees noticing the theft. Shoplifters tend to identify the store's weaknesses not in terms of its security devices but in its concept and layout. Stores should be designed in order to allow the store manager to ''control'' the movement of customers, who should be able to move freely along aisles and yet remain completely visible to employees working in the areas.

Store Design

Store design plays an important role in limiting the opportunities for shoplifters to commit their crimes. In designing the layout of the store, the designer and the store manager must consider several important points that will ease the threat of shoplifting. The focal point of any store should be the check-out counter or cash register. The check-out counter should be located near the main entrance and exit to the store. In designing the check-out counter, the store manager must achieve two objectives: to direct the customer out of the store after the purchase is made and to place the check-out far enough away from the door to prevent an easy escape for a criminal in case of a robbery. A common technique used by shoplifters is to purchase merchandise and then return to the store before leaving the building and place other, unpaid-for merchandise in the bag containing the paid-for merchandise. Employees, seeing the store's bag, usually with a receipt stapled to the top, will assume that the customer has just made a purchase. Little thought is given to the possibility that other merchandise may have been placed in the bag after the initial purchase was completed.

The store should have one active entrance and exit that everyone who goes into the store must pass. Store employees can then easily check to see if anyone is hiding merchandise. Such a checkpoint also lessens the chance that a shoplifter will succeed in committing his or her crime. Such a layout will discourage customers from returning to the display areas immediately following a purchase. In some states, laws require that stores have more than one exit as a safety precaution. Many law enforcement officials, however, will still permit store owners to have only one active entrance and exit as long as the store has one or more locked fire exits that can be opened quickly from the inside of the store during a fire.

Once the focal point has been established, the store manager must give special consideration to the display areas. The store should have aisles that face in the same direction so that employees can walk down the row of check-out counters and see the whole display area by looking down each aisle in turn. Employees will find that such an arrangement makes it easy to spot-check the complete display area in a matter of seconds. Some stores have displays arranged in a maze fashion, which causes blind spots for employees making spot-checks of the selling floor. Where convenient, displays should be constructed in as open an area as possible. The more confined the selling space, the higher the risk will be when confronting a shoplifter. Always try to "force" the customer to make his or her purchase in the open (see Figures 6–2 and 6–3 for examples of store layouts).

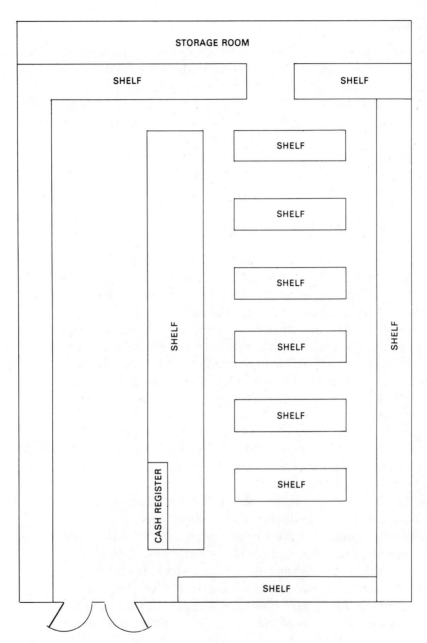

Figure 6-2
A poor store layout.

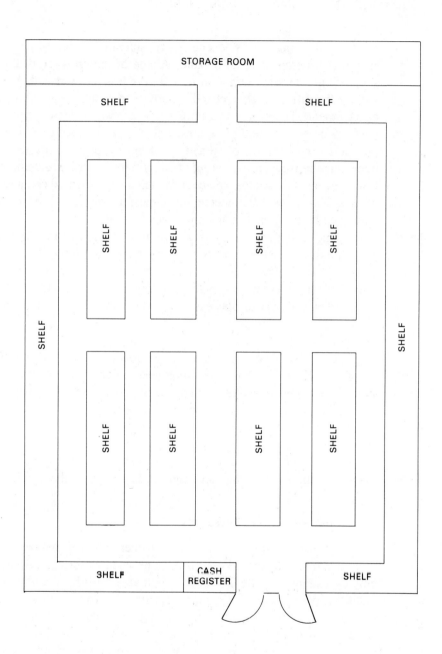

Figure 6-3
A secure store layout.

The store manager's next design consideration involves the value and size of the merchandise to be sold. A rule of thumb when dealing with shoplifting is that the larger an item is, the less likely it is that the item will be shoplifted. All merchandise, however, is not designed to prevent concealment. Therefore, the store manager, when dealing with small, valuable objects, should place these items in secure locations. For example, home repair stores often sell small but expensive drill accessories, items that are frequently a target of shoplifters. In order to combat shoplifters, many of these stores place such merchandise behind counters and in glass display cases. Customers must request the merchandise from a store employee before going to the check-out counter.

Some shoplifters are bold. A case in Los Angeles illustrates how a bold shoplifter found a security fault in a store that placed valuable small items in glass display cases. A man had walked into a home repair store and discovered that there were very few employees on the sales floor. The man, a shoplifter, noticed a display case filled with expensive drill bits. Unfortunately for the store owner, the display case was located out of sight of the cashiers. The shoplifter removed his sweater and walked behind the display counter. To his surprise, the case was locked, but that did not stop this shoplifter. He noticed a store employee walking past the counter. He stopped the young man and asked him if he had the key to the display case. The employee said, "No," but he showed the shoplifter where the key was hidden. The employee thought that the shoplifter was either a store manager or employee. The shoplifter helped himself to the merchandise.

The point of this tale is to illustrate the importance of placing display cases near the front of the store and in clear view of the cashier.

Establishing Set Procedures

The case also illustrates another consideration store managers have in minimizing shoplifting: to establish set procedures for operations that all employees must know and follow. Employees must be identified clearly, and those perons without such identification should be called to the attention of the store manager. It is important to understand that all employees, including management personnel and the owner of the store, should wear some kind of identification. Employees frequently assume that those without identification entering restricted areas are management personnel who are exempt from the identification rule.

Procedures should also be established for handling returns, which is another technique shoplifters use to make a few dollars without removing the merchandise from the store. A medium-sized department store in New Jersey learned about this technique the hard way. The store placed the returns counter in a location that could be reached before the customer passed the check-out counter. The store's policy stated that returns would be made for cash or exchange only if the customer returned the merchandise in good order and if the receipt was present. In many cases, however, the store would accept returns if the clerk could identify the merchandise as items sold by the store. The price tag was used for this identification. During the Christmas rush one year, the store was hit by a series of shoplifters who entered the store, selected merchandise that cost above $20, and removed the merchandise from the display. Immediately, they walked over to the returns counter and asked for refunds. The clerk noticed the price tags and proceeded to make the refunds.

The store manager should institute measures that will prohibit shoplifters from using existing store procedures to commit the crime. One important store procedure includes the identification of goods after the purchase is made. Many stores remove the price tags immediately after the purchase. Special consideration should be given to items that are too large to be taken through the check-out counter. These include such things as large pieces of wood and bicycles. Many times, customers are rarely checked by employees when walking out of the store with oversized merchandise. A case in point involved a department store that sold bicycles. A shoplifter, during a busy period, walked into the store, selected a bike from the display, and proceeded to wheel the bike out the front door of the store. This time, the shoplifter did not succeed. The store manager had just returned from supper. While the manager held the door for the shoplifter, something made the manager ask the shoplifter if he had paid for the bike. The shoplifter said, "No," and the manager called the police.

As we have seen, most shoplifters use the carelessness of store managers and store employees, as well as poorly thought-out store operating procedures, to help prevent them from being caught. As long as the shoplifter can be sure that employees, managers, and customers will assume that anyone acting as if he or she belongs does, in fact, belong, then the shoplifter will succeed in committing his or her crime. Security devices may help to deter some shoplifters; however, there is nothing like strict surveillance and tight operating procedures for combatting shoplifting.

What you need to know about burglary 7

Burglary is a crime that threatens almost everyone in the country (see Figures 7–1, 7–2, and 7–3). Regardless of whether you own a home or a business, the chance of your becoming the victim of a burglar is increasing each year. Burglary is a crime that is committed when no one is in the home or place of business. Burglary, by one legal definition, is the unauthorized entry or surreptitious presence of someone in a building or occupied structure for the purpose of committing the crime. According to the law in some states, burglary is committed when a person enters a building without being authorized; the person does not have to break a window or pick a lock. Such acts are considered breaking and entering. Also, if a person stays behind after closing without permission of the store owner or man-

129

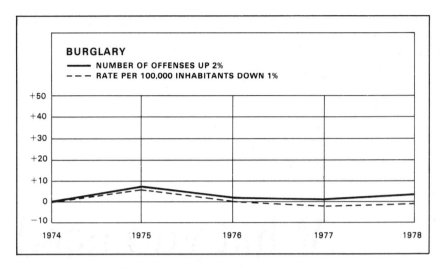

Figure 7-1
Burglary rate (*The Uniform Crime Report,* Washington: Federal Bureau of Investigation, 1979).

ager, he or she can be charged with burglary. Each state has burglary laws; some may differ from the statements made here. Each state has the right to determine its own definition of burglary.

Techniques used by burglars will vary, depending on how professional the criminal has become. The younger, less professional burglars may look for easy victims and for buildings where doors or windows are left open. As the burglar gains experience, he or she will meet the challenge of a locked building or of a possible confrontation with the owner of the business. The professional, on the other hand, will not be scared off by any

Figure 7-2
Burglary by the month (*The Uniform Crime Report,* Washington: Federal Bureau of Investigation, 1979).

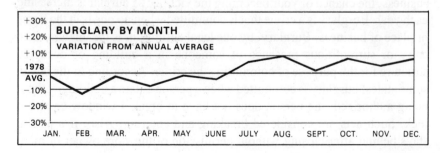

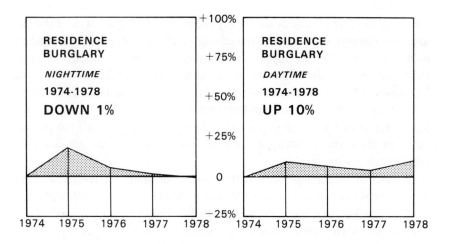

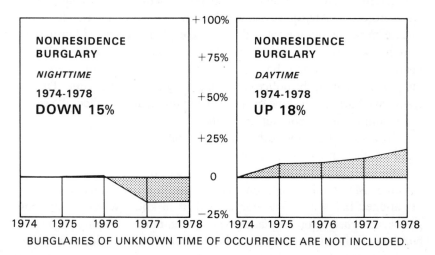

BURGLARIES OF UNKNOWN TIME OF OCCURRENCE ARE NOT INCLUDED.

Figure 7-3
Burglary by time of day (*The Uniform Crime Report,* Washington: Federal Bureau of Investigation, 1979).

security system less than that used to guard gold shipments, and even then, the top professional may take a crack at a gold shipment.

Techniques

Since there is a fine line between burglary and break and entry, we will discuss these crimes as if they are similar. Burglaries are committed in several ways. Initially, the burglar will survey the security system of the building, looking for one or more easy entrances and exits that he or she can use. The passageways must be out of sight and must offer an unobstructed path to safety. For example, the burglar will seek buildings without electronic security devices that have doors and windows that are obstructed by bushes or boxes and are unlighted. Remember that the burglar may have to spend five or ten minutes standing by the door or window trying to make his or her entrance. During this time, the burglar requires all the protection—in the form of entrance obstructions—he or she can get from the small business owner.

Once a target has been selected, the burglar—at least the more professional one—will watch the building for a few minutes, attempting to determine whether anyone is present inside. Usually, burglars will try to avoid contact with anyone during the course of the crime. The burglar will also determine the timing and nature of police patrols. In extreme cases, the more professional burglars will watch the police station parking lot in order to determine the number of officers on patrol. Experienced burglars may also check to see how patrol shifts are handled and how the police will handle a fire call; often, burglars find out the police call numbers so that they can listen in on the police calls while they commit the crime. The more research a burglar has done on a target and on the local police, the easier it is for him or her to commit the crime.

If a burglar discovers that the local police panic when a fire alarm is reported, then the burglar may cover his or her entrance into a building by calling a fire report in to police headquarters before he or she enters the building. Many police departments will assign all available patrol cars to the alleged fire scene. The burglar will then know where all the police patrols are when he or she makes his or her entrance. If highly professional burglars are involved, they may stage a real fire or accident in order to cover the complete burglary.

Many merchants feel that glass on a locked door or window is alone sufficient to keep out a burglar. The thought here is that the burglar must first break the glass in order to gain entrance to the building and that the sound of breaking glass will obviously draw attention. Burglars are, however, wise to this concept and have developed a technique to circumvent this form of security. The burglar tapes the entire window before breaking the glass. Once the tape is in place, a heavy object is thrown against the glass, producing a sound like a low thump. The cracked glass is then removed in pieces by the burglar. The sound associated with glass breaking is caused by glass fragments striking harder objects, not by the actual breaking of the glass.

A skillful burglar will have two other courses open. First, he or she can remove the molding around the glass and then remove the whole glass. After entrance into the building, the glass is replaced. Anyone passing the building will not notice that the glass has been removed and an entrance made. The second method is to use a glass cutter and cut near the location of the window lock. After the burglar removes the smaller piece of glass, the window lock can be easily opened.

Small business operators who rent their stores or offices from a private owner must give careful consideration to the next technique frequently used by burglars. Burglars, like all criminals, look for the fastest way to obtain entrance to a building. The obvious method to use is the door. Some small business managers have been known not to lock doors to the building, thus allowing a burglar to have an easy access to the building. Most managers will, however, have a pick-proof lock on the door, but the size and bulky design of such a lock can give the manager a false sense of security, especially if the building belongs to someone else. The more professional burglar will attempt to obtain the key to the building through various means. Burglars have been known to steal or "rent" keys from office maintenance personnel, building supervisors, building owners, and even from real estate agents. If you rent your business space and have not changed the locks on the door, you should realize that the security of your building may be violated. Consider for a moment the number of persons who would, in the normal course of business, have access to the key of your rented store or office. The owner of the property has access to the key as well as any of his or her close friends and relatives. The property manager for the building has access to the key and so does almost everyone else in both the property manager's and the owner's offices. Maintenance people and their associates have had or will have access to the key; so will any construction crews who modifed the office. The list is almost endless, and there is no telling whether all of the persons mentioned here are totally honest.

Burglary and the Security System

Burglars have been known to defeat a security system before making an attempt to break into a building. One of the easiest security systems to defeat is the outside alarm. A large number of small businesses have such a device located on top of the building. When one or more sensing devices are triggered inside the building, the alarm sounds outside the building. The manager of the business then hopes that someone hearing the alarm

133

will call the police. Businesses usually have one of two types of outside alarms: a simple bell alarm or a bell alarm completely enclosed in a metal box.

When a burglar attempts to defeat such a system, he or she will usually remove the bell of the alarm on a system that is not enclosed in a box. The sensors, after the burglar breaks into the building, will signal the clanger, but without a bell, no sound will be generated. Security manufacturers have considered this possibility and have therefore enclosed the bell in a pick-proof metal box. Unfortunately, the alarm manufacturers are really no match for thieves. Although the box is sealed tightly, there are usually several openings that permit the sound to be relayed to the outside world. Without such openings, little noise would be made. To defeat this system, thieves have been known to use either shaving cream or some other foam material and, carefully, to spray the substance into the metal box through the holes. The box will quickly fill up with foam, preventing the bell from vibrating and, therefore, from sound being produced.

These are just a few tips on how burglars go about their business. Some burglars will simply break a glass window, whereas others will go to the extreme of disconnecting the power to the building.

HOW TO IDENTIFY A BURGLAR

Types of Burglars

There are three categories of burglars that should concern the small business person. The first is the rank amateur, usually young people in their teens. Then there is what some call the experienced amateur or semi-professional burglar. These people usually range in age from their middle to late teens on through to the middle twenties. Finally, there are the professionals, whose ages range from the early twenties on.

Most burglaries are committed by the first two groups. Very rarely are small business persons directly affected by the professional burglar. The only exception to this rule is if the small business person deals with large sums of cash, with top quality jewelry, or with very expensive or rare merchandise. Therefore, our discussion on how to identify a burglar should begin with the amateur burglar, who is usually a local youngster. Several years ago, authors writing a book similar to this one described the amateur burglar as a local high-school student. However, times have changed, and police are finding out that grade-school youngsters have been slowly becoming involved in burglary. The amateur burglar will not usually take time out to select his or her victim or the object to be stolen carefully. Some medical experts state that such a burglar has many motivations for committing the act. They point to the child's upbringing and claim that the child is seeking attention. Other reasons given for a youngster being involved in burglary is that the child is using burglary as a way of "getting back" at the system. Police have found that only on very rare occasions has a youngster committed a burglary because he or she needed food or clothing.

The semi-professional burglar is usually involved with committing the crime every day of his or her life; most, if not all, of his or her income derives from burglary. But the semi-professional burglar's reason for committing the crime is less for personal financial gain than to support some other activity that requires large sums of money, such as drug addiction, liquor addiction, or gambling. Unlike the amateur burglar, who gives little care to who his or her victim is, the semi-professional burglar will usually select his or her victim with some degree of concern for his or her own safety. The semi-professional burglar has probably been committing burglary since early childhood and has developed skills that permit him or her to burglarize a particular type of business with as little risk as possible.

The professional burglar, in contrast, is usually out after financial reward rather than looking for money to feed a habit. Such a person has usually developed his or her burglary and business skills by selling his or her talents either to honest men and women who desire to have objects at a reduced price or to underworld criminals who seek to acquire large amounts of particular merchandise. There are a few professional burglars, for example, who only strike manufacturing corporations that have vital shipments of material in order to keep the assembly line in operation. Once the goods are stolen, the burglar—or an associate—contacts representatives of the business and offers to "sell" the vital merchandise to the firm. Many times, the firm, in such a situation, cannot find replacement material in time to keep the schedule flowing and will therefore pay almost anything, under any conditions, in order to gain control of the material. Such a transaction is usually completed without the knowledge or help of law enforcement agencies.

Tips of Identification

Without a crystal ball, the identification of a burglar may seem next to impossible for police, let alone for a small business manager. But although the identification task may seem difficult at first, it is not impossible to develop the skills necessary to identify a burglar. The small business operator will come in contact with the amateur burglar more than any other type of criminal. The amateur is usually inexperienced in breaking into buildings and even in planning a burglary. He or she may be bold enough to wait outside the business until the building is locked up for the night, but he or she will often be nervous and on the defensive. He or she usually assumes that everyone else is aware of his or her motives, although this may be far from true. Therefore, when closing for the evening, check the area around the building. If you see one or two youngsters hanging around, there is a chance that one or both of them may be planning to burglarize your property. You should, in any case, learn to spot and question people and items that are out of place in a given set of circumstances. Ask yourself, ''Are youngsters usually around the area during late evening hours?'' If the answer is, ''No,'' the store owner should call the police and let these professionals determine whether potential trouble exists.

The semi-professional burglar may not be as easy to identify as the amateur burglar. This type of criminal will try not to stand out in a crowd. He or she may keep a low but friendly profile. From all outward appearances, the semi-professional burglar often looks like the clean-looking ''boy up the block.'' Almost opposite to the amateur burglar, the semi-professional burglar will try overly hard to fit in with his or her surroundings. The burglar will, at times, try to be overly pleasant and will go out of his or her way to help friends and strangers alike. It is this unnatural openness that should alert the small business manager: The burglar will try to be accepted by others to such a degree that his or her actions may seem unsettling and, in fact, may make him or her stand out in a group.

The professional burglar is almost undetectable, even by police. This person will usually find the fine line between nervous and overly friendly behavior. His or her major objective is to fit in as one of the crowd—not as the leader of the group. Telltale signs of a professional burglar are the questions that he or she may ask and the areas within the building that he or she seeks to observe. These signs will usually be obvious. The professional is well trained in acquiring information about the office or store in a subtle manner. The small business manager who might be the target of a professional burglar should be on the alert for seemingly innocent remarks and observations made by vendors, delivery people, salespeople, contractors, maintenance workers, and the like. For example, a new vendor representative may ask the manager if he or she has had any problems with burglary in the neighborhood. The question may seem innocent enough, since most people are concerned about this crime. The representative may justify his or her question by commenting that his or her house has been burglarized recently. When asked such a question, some business managers will continue the conversation either by telling the representative what security measures the business employs or by taking the representative on a tour of the security system.

Before showing or telling anyone about the security system of a business, the manager should ask him- or herself, "Why should a person ask questions about the security system?" Unless the manager can readily answer that question, he or she should say nothing about the system. A good rule of thumb to follow is to trust only those people who are known to you. Never accept appearances as reality. Anyone can purchase or manufacture all imaginable kinds of official-appearing identification. Regardless of how professional an identification appears to be, always question the person, especially if that person is seeking information about the security operation of the business or detailed knowledge about how the shipping and receiving departments operate.

Although we have noted some of the finer points of identifying a burglar, a word of warning is necessary. Each burglar is different, and no burglar wears a badge or sign. There are no set standards one can apply that will fit every burglar in every situation. Therefore, although the identification procedures outlined here point out some of the characteristics employed by burglars, the list is not complete. Burglars of all types have used various techniques to enter a building innocently and illegally, and not one will follow a uniform method of operation.

A good rule of thumb for the small business manager to follow is to become friendly with the local police department and officers. Many times, they can inform the business manager when a series of burglaries is striking the community. The police may even give the manager a description of the burglar(s). By contacting the police for this information and by using some of the basic rules outlined here, a manager should be able to identify a suspect before the burglary is committed.

WHAT TO DO IF YOU HAVE BEEN BURGLARIZED

What Not to Do

Many small business managers have experienced the shock of opening the door to the business in the morning and noticing that a burglary has occurred. During the night, someone has broken into the building and made off with merchandise, machines, cash, or a combination of these. Some managers feel outraged that another party has violated his or her "castle," and one of the first moves some managers make upon discovering burglary is to inspect the building, usually more in amazement than for a purposeful motive. After five to ten minutes, sometimes a half an hour, the manager finally gets around to calling the police. Anyone who discovers such a crime should not do what is described above. A crime scene can be potentially dangerous for the manager and, unknowingly, he or she may disturb vital evidence in the case.

A case in Chicago illustrates this point. One night, a group of teenagers broke into a liquor store. When the store owner arrived to open shop in the morning, the store was a mess. The owner proceeded to survey the damage before calling the police. Finally, when the police arrived at the scene, they informed the store owner that he had destroyed a strong piece of investigative material by walking into the store. Since the local police used police dogs to help track down burglars and other criminals, as long as the burglar was the last person in the building store, the police stood a good chance of trailing the burglar's movements. However, the dogs do not know the difference between a burglar and the store owner. The dogs will only be able to identify the last person who was in the building. By walking into the store, the owner had destroyed the burglar's scent.

There are other reasons why a store owner or anyone should not enter the crime scene. The foremost reason is safety. The small business manager should assume that the crime occurred recently and that the criminal is still present in the building. With this thought in the back of his or her mind, the small business person must think of his or her life before needlessly taking the risk of entering the building. The police, on the other hand, are trained for such investigations and should therefore be the first persons to notify.

Why is not entering the building so important? Remember, for a moment, that there are three types of burglars who could be present in the building: the amateur, the semi-professional, and the professional. The first two types, as we have suggested, are probably more likely to be involved in small business burglaries than the latter, and both types—the amateur and the semi-professional—are unpredictable in their actions. Of course, the first thought that enters the mind of a burglar who confronts a small business manager is that of self-preservation. Although the professional burglar may simply cause a diversion and scamper out a nearby exit, the semi-professional may physically attack the manager in an effort to hinder an apprehension attempt. The amateur may look at a confrontation as a threat to his or her life and may, therefore, try to harm or even kill the manager or anyone else who might get in the way of his or her safety. The risk of serious injury is not worth the few extra minutes necessary for a call to the police.

Guidelines, some have said, are made to be broken, and so will the guidelines set here for a manager confronted with a burglary scene. For those managers who may feel foolish enough to enter a crime scene before the police arrive, a few additional points should be considered. Since a real possibility of a confrontation between the manager and the burglar exists, the manager should have some rule of thumb to follow in such a situation. If such a confrontation occurs, the manager should avoid boxing the burglar into a corner. As long as the burglar feels that an escape route is open, he or she will be more inclined to run than to fight. But if a burglar has his or her back to the wall, he or she can be expected to fight to the end.

How to Handle the Situation

Instead of attempting to apprehend the burglar, the manager should be more concerned about his or her own safety. The manager should also notice anything about the burglar's appearance that may help the police to spot the burglar after he or she has fled the scene. A safe and legal apprehension of a burglar by the police is far more desirable than having the manager injured or killed during the arrest. Usually, goods can be replaced; a life cannot. If the manager does confront a burglar, he or she should step back and let the burglar leave the building. During the brief encounter, the manager should obtain a good detailed description of the suspect. Once the burglar has left the building, the manager should note the direction and manner in which the burglar left and should then notify the police of the situation, giving them the description. Chances are that the police will be able to pick up the suspect before they even arrive at the business location.

Until the police arrive, it is important that the manager not touch anything in the store or office. This includes doors, windows, and any object that appears out of place. If the manager has entered the building, a good rule of thumb is for him or her to turn right around and leave. Police should be called from a phone outside the store. Once the police have been notified, the manager should wait near the front entrance to the building and help to direct the police to the right location.

Some professional burglars use a particularly evasive technique. If the small business is involved with high-priced items and could be the target of a professional burglar, there is a good chance that the burglar will use the quiet approach in removing a particular item. This method requires the burglar to break into the building without leaving any telltale marks. Once in the building, the burglar will select only one or two highly valuable—and, usually, small—items to steal. The burglar will not disturb any displays or other items in the building and will leave the building quietly, making sure to reclose and relock the doors and windows behind him or her. When the manager of the business arrives the next day, there is a good chance that he or she will not realize that the merchandise has been removed. Many times, the burglary will go unnoticed for months, and some have gone undetected for more than a year after the crime has taken place.

If a manager discovers a burglary that may have taken place months ago, he or she should forgo the previous guidelines. The manager should, however, try not to touch the area or display around the missing object. There is a slight chance that the burglar left a clue that may help police to narrow the list of suspects. After notifying the police, the manager should survey the store in an effort to detect the method the burglar may have used to gain access to the building. The manager will be more familiar with the layout of the building than the police and may be able to speed up the police investigation of the crime scene by providing this information.

After the police have arrived, the store manager should begin to prepare an inventory list of the items that have been stolen. This list of stolen property should not be prepared in haste. Although the police will be pressing the manager for the list, an incomplete listing of stolen goods can be more harmful to the small business manager than its helpfulness to the police warrants. Once the list of property has been submitted to the police, that list becomes a part of the public record. Insurance companies frequently check the list of stolen property reported to the police against the list submitted to them by the small business manager. If the lists differ, the insurance company may use the list submitted to the police department as evidence in supporting the manager's claim. It is wise, therefore, not to place a dollar value on the loss until there is sufficient time to examine the complete inventory. Once a dollar value is given to the police, that amount could also be accessible to the insurance company and the news media. Some store managers have found it difficult to explain to the insurance company the difference between the amount of their claim and the listed amount given to the police and the news media.

The guidelines above have been developed by police agencies in an effort to accomplish two objectives: to protect the manager and his or her employees from harm and to ensure, if evidence exists at the crime scene, that the clues are not disturbed. The most important rule of thumb the small business manager should follow when discovering a burglary is, ''Keep your head.'' Think of the guidelines before you act.

WHAT WILL HAPPEN IF YOU HAVE BEEN BURGLARIZED

Most small business managers will not be confronted with a burglary or, in fact, with any crime. But for those who do become victims, the experience is completely new. Managers may not know what to expect after the crime has occurred and the police have been notified. Since such an experience and what follows afterward can be trying at times, the normal routine of the activities following a burglary is important for the small business manager to know. Few civilians have the proper image of a police investigation: The only experience the majority of the public has in dealing with the police is through television and movies, which portray police departments as being totally professional operations. Each police officer on the television police department knows everything there is to know about police work. Rarely does the public ever see a police department that has no scientific methods for investigating crime. On the screen, police officers use vacuum cleaners to pick up every particle around a crime scene, and later, at the police lab, investigators sift through each gram of dust, looking for a possible clue to the crime. Moviegoers frequently see police match suspects to footprints, fingerprints, hair, cloth, buttons, and so on that have been left at the crime scene.

Myths and Realities

Most crime victims will assume that the same techniques of investigation used in the movies will be used by their local police department in tracking down a burglar. Unfortunately, those expecting such actions from the police are likely to be severely disappointed. In fact, most police departments are only trained or experienced enough to handle such investigations as far as getting a description of a suspect, discovering his or her method of entry, and, maybe, taking fingerprints.

Local police departments usually cannot afford the expensive lab equipment and tools necessary to conduct scientific investigations. Municipal departments may not have the funds or manpower to free a few officers to seek further training in investigations. A case that occurred in New

Jersey illustrates the difference between a local police department and those depicted in the movies. Police were called one morning by an elderly man who claimed that his wife had died in her sleep. Since this is a routine case for local departments, only one officer was sent to the scene. The purpose of the police was to determine whether any foul play had taken place. The woman was lying on the floor when the officer arrived. Everything else seemed to be in its natural position. The elderly man, after a few minutes of sadness, asked the officer if he could move the woman to the bed. He felt that she would be more comfortable. The officer complied. The body was later taken to the morgue for an autopsy. Near the end of the official examination of the body, the medical examiner noticed a small object on the table near the body. The object was a bullet. What had really happened was that the woman, who was dying of cancer, had been murdered in her sleep by her husband, who had carefully concealed the blood and the entrance wound. An official investigation was held to determine why the police officer failed to discover the entrance wound. It was later learned that the officer did not examine the body.

If the same case appeared on a television police drama, detectives, lab officers, and the medical examiner would have been present at the scene. In reality, the case drew one poorly trained police officer.

Another myth involves the gathering of evidence. Upon arriving at the scene of a burglary, the police will determine the time of the crime, the method of entrance, and the items that were stolen. Depending on the quality of the police department, some officers may even attempt to discover fingerprints on objects thought to have been touched by the burglar. The officers may search the crime scene briefly, looking for other clues, and may contact neighbors to ask if they have heard any noises or if they have seen the burglar. Beyond this brief investigation, the police will simply type up the report and file the case. If any traceable items, such as a gun, were stolen, the details of the item are sent to the National Crime Information Center in Washington, D.C., where the data is listed on a computer and distributed throughout the country. If the gun is found, the police will contact this center and trace the gun back to the burglary. Rarely will police ever use a vacuum cleaner to gather evidence, nor will they make a cast of a footprint.

In the movies, crime labs are usually the focal point in cracking a puzzling case. In reality, this is far from the truth. There are very few crime labs in operation throughout the country, and most existing labs are operated by large city police departments or by county and state police departments. In addition, a recent study by the FBI revealed that tests performed by the labs often do not provide conclusive evidence in an investigation. For example, labs were given several pieces of hair and asked to identify them. More than half of the labs could not tell the difference between a human hair and a dog hair. Knowing that there is a quality problem in the police labs, many departments find that sending evidence to the labs for investigation is worthless. It is also expensive, since in many states, crime labs charge local police departments for their services.

Crime victims, as we have pointed out, can become very disillusioned by the local police department's seeming lack of performance during a burglary investigation. Crime victims, however, should not place the total blame for such a lack on the police department. The police are just part of a legal system that requires evidence against a suspect to be overwhelming before a court can find that suspect guilty of burglary. It is up to the police to find the required evidence. Anything less than a witness telling the court that he or she saw the suspect break into the building and leave with merchandise or than the police catching the burglar in the act, and the courts will usually let the suspect go free. There are over three million burglaries a year in the United States, and only 18% of those burglaries are solved (see Figure 7–4). The odds are obviously against the police in apprehending a burglar. Police departments, therefore, conduct a burglary investigation in a less than aggressive fashion and as part of their normal routine.

Procedures to Follow

The store manager, after calling the police about the burglary, will have to answer questions that the police will pose. The officers will investigate for about an hour and then leave. The manager must then begin the task of taking an inventory of the store or office. If the manager has had an inventory list prepared for accounting purposes, he or she will find preparing this second inventory list easier. Every item in the store or office must be accounted for. If the item is not present, consider it part of the goods that were stolen. A word of warning: Don't try to take advantage of the situation and include items on the list that were not, in fact, stolen. As you are making the list, be sure that all the items you include could have been removed during the burglary. For example, if a burglar gained entrance to the building through a very small window, all the items stolen in the burglary must have been able to fit through that window. Also, consider the manner in which the insurance company will review the claim.

143

CRIMES CLEARED BY ARREST

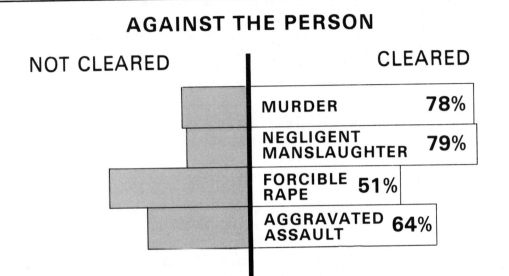

AGAINST THE PERSON

NOT CLEARED | CLEARED

MURDER 78%

NEGLIGENT MANSLAUGHTER 79%

FORCIBLE RAPE 51%

AGGRAVATED ASSAULT 64%

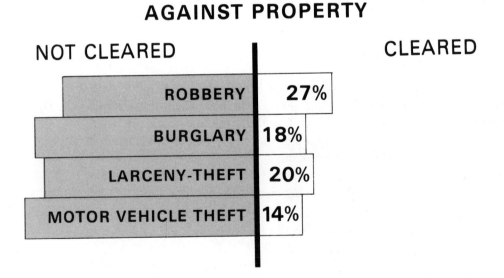

AGAINST PROPERTY

NOT CLEARED | CLEARED

ROBBERY 27%

BURGLARY 18%

LARCENY-THEFT 20%

MOTOR VEHICLE THEFT 14%

Figure 7-4
From *The Uniform Crime Report* (Washington: Federal Bureau of Investigation, 1979).

Not only will they check to see that the goods could have been stolen but also that the items were acquired and that they were contained in the building at the time of the burglary. To illustrate, consider an office burglary where a case of expensive liquor, among other items, was stolen. Since the liquor was to be used as gifts to special clients, it was purchased as part of normal business routine. However, the insurance company, knowing that the business was not a liquor business, required that the small business owner show proof of purchase and proof that the liquor was in the building at the time of the burglary before they paid the claim.

Many things will happen to the store owner after the burglary has been committed. Dealing with police investigations, conducting an emergency inventory, filing insurance claims, and finding proof that stolen goods actually existed are activities most small business managers are not prepared for when they open the doors in the morning. But if the manager has some idea of what procedures he or she should follow when a burglary occurs, coping with the investigation will be easier.

WHAT SECURITY DEVICES TO ACQUIRE IN ORDER TO COMBAT BURGLARY

By now, the small business manager is aware of the seriousness of a burglary and of the chances that a burglar will not be caught. Yet the knowledge that a problem exists in a small business is of no comfort to the manager unless he or she has a solution to the problem. Burglary cannot be prevented, but through the use of security devices, the manager can reduce the probability that his or her store will fall victim to a burglar. Remember that the burglar is looking for a victim who is easy to attack. For example, a burglar having the choice between what appears to be a heavily secured building and one with just an outside alarm bell will, of course, select the latter over the former.

Alarm Systems

With this thought in mind, we will discuss various security devices intended to prevent or to lessen the probability of a burglary. But before going into detail about security devices, let us step back a moment and see what is actually involved in designing a security alarm system. An alarm system is nothing more than a mechanical or electrical device that tells

145

someone that someone else is present in a predetermined area. Every alarm system is composed of the following elements: a sensor, switches, a sounding device, and a receiver. An alarm system without all these components is not a system that will provide adequate protection to a business.

The first element in the system is the sensor, a device that will detect the presence of a person or thing in the secured area. The sensor usually operates on electricity and is like a switch; when the switch is closed by the security violator, current flows through the alarm system to the sounding device, which sends a loud signal to a receiver. In all cases, the receiver is a person—the police, the store manager, a security guard, or even neighbors close to the store. The receiver then takes some action against the intruder.

This sounds fool-proof, but often the so-called human element defeats the security system. For example, there are numerous cases where the sounding device, such as an outside bell, has been activated, but there has been no receiver. Upon hearing the alarm, neighbors have assumed that someone else has called the police when, in fact, no one has notifed them. In any security system, nothing should be left to chance.

Sensors can be purchased in various forms, each designed for sensing a particular part of the secured area. For example, tape is available that will act as a sensor to detect any entrance made by breaking the glass in a window or door. Magnetic sensors are sometimes used to detect the opening of doors and windows. For valuable small items, managers can purchase pressure-sensitive switches that are then placed under an item of merchandise. When the item is removed, the switch closes, and the alarm is sounded. There are sensors called movement detectors, which are designed to pick up movement within a room by transmitting waves and measuring the reflection of the waves (see Figure 7–5). Any change in the reflected waves triggers the sensor. Other sensors used to detect movement are the infrared and visible light beams. When a person walks through the beam, the alarm sounds.

The sounding element usually takes several forms: an outside bell, often contained inside a box near the top of the building; a horn or siren located in a similar area of the building; and a silent alarm that is located either at police headquarters or at the offices of a guard service. Another sounding device that is becoming more popular is the telephone alarm. When the sensor sends the signal to the phone alarm, the sounding device calls a series of numbers and plays a prerecorded message. Calls are usually made to the police, to relatives, or to the small business owner (see Figure 7–6 for a complete alarm system).

The small business manager can also buy a security package that will

Figure 7-5
Movement detectors have been designed to fit all types of business needs. This one is designed for business vehicles. Operating on a twelve-volt supply from the vehicle's battery, it will sound an alarm at the slightest detection of movement in the parked vehicle. (Illustration supplied by and used with permission of Delta Products, Inc., Grand Junction, Colorado.)

prevent burglary. A common package used in stores involves the series lock. Every door in the building contains a lock, which is usually located at the bottom of the door. The manager will have either one master key or a key for each lock. Each door must be locked and unlocked in a predetermined order. If the order is broken or is not completed, the alarm will

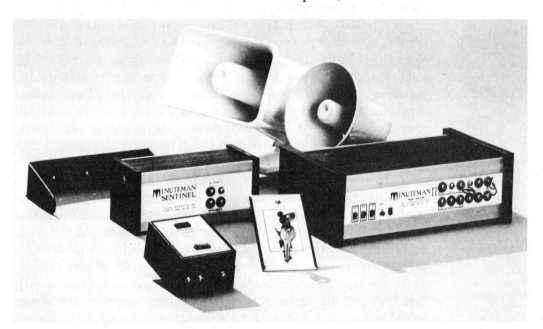

Figure 7-6
Security alarms are manufactured in a variety of sizes and shapes, each designed to serve the needs of a particular situation. The complete alarm system pictured here includes an activation switch, sensors, a sound generating unit, and a loudspeaker system. (Illustration supplied by and used with permission of Delta Products, Inc., Grand Junction, Colorado.)

sound. This sytem also contains a timer that registers when the doors were locked and unlocked. If a burglar uses a key to gain access to the building, he or she has to move quickly in order to discover the locations of the doors and the place each has in the locking sequence; finally, each lock must be opened in the proper order. The time span normal for opening the doors, which is controllable by the manager, is usually too short for a burglar to be able to go through such an investigation.

Faults in Security Systems

Now for some bad news. Every security device mentioned here can be defeated by the professional burglar. There isn't a security device made that will guarantee total security for a business. Even the security around the White House has been violated. However, by knowing the faults with each element in the system, the small business manager will be able to rectify most of the problems associated with each element.

The primary fault in most security devices stems from the power source. If the security system or element is operated through the use of power supplied by a central source, the security system will be inoperative when the source of power is removed. The loss of power can come from repairs made by the power company to feeder lines; from natural elements, such as weather; or from more direct means, through the workings of a burglar. Professional and semi-professional burglars have been known to disconnect the power to a building by cutting down wires, by turning off circuit breakers once they are inside the building, or even by causing a fire in the building. During a working fire, fire officials will request that the power company disconnect the burning house or building from service in an effort to protect firemen working near the wires.

Sensors around windows are also not free from fault. A burglar can carefully cut the window and, using a wire, jump the sensor connection, short-circuiting the sensors. The less technically skilled burglar will simply break the glass and run away. Police and the owner will come to investigate the incident. Usually, the glass cannot be replaced for at least 12 hours. Therefore, since many alarms are wired in series, the whole system must be shut down until the glass is replaced. Although the window will be boarded up and police patrols will check the building visually, a burglar will usually have time between patrols to enter and leave the building.

Sounding devices can also be neutralized in one of two ways. Power can be removed from the system, or a burglar can pack the sounding device with various kinds of sound-absorbing material, such as foam. And the most frequent fault with a sounding device, of course, is that no one is present to listen to the signal. The small business manager cannot be sure that someone will be around to hear and take action if an outside alarm is sounding.

The Ideal System

Reading about the faults in most security systems, a small business manager can feel lost when he or she is trying to protect a business. In order to feel assured that the business is protected, the manager should design a system or have a system designed that is as close to the ideal system as possible. The closer the store's system is to the ideal security system, the less likely it is that a burglar will break into the building.

The building should have all the windows taped with sensor tape. All windows and doors should also be wired with sensors. Movement detectors should be used to protect the interior of the building. Every door in the building should have a sequential lock/alarm device. Every entrance to the building should be well lighted, with the light bulb out of the easy reach of a potential burglar. Sensors should be connected to police headquarters through a silent alarm. Each element in the system should be wired so that the entire system does not have to be shut down if one element is not working properly. Finally, the system should have two power supplies— the first supplied by a normal power source and the back-up supplied by a power generator or battery. The more closely a building's security system resembles the system outlined here, the lower the probability that a burglary will take place.

Any store can become the victim of a burglary. But if the store owner can identify the likely types of burglary, keep calm, and install appropriate security devices, the risks of burglary may be lessened considerably.

What you need to know about robbery 8

Every small business manager must face the fact that crimes against small businesses are increasing every year (see Figures 8–1, 8–2, 8–3, and 8–4). Lately, police officials throughout the United States have seen an increase of violent crime where the victim is either injured or murdered. Robbery is, by definition, a violent crime: It occurs when a person uses or threatens to use any violence when committing a theft. Since many small retail businesses contain relatively large sums of cash and have limited security, the retail business is a prime target for a criminal who is seeking to rob a store.

Robbery of a retail store is a crime that has caused many a store owner to lose his or her life or to be seriously injured, which forces the owner to close down the business. Criminals have used weapons ranging from objects contained in the store to knives and guns in threatening bodily harm against store owners and employees. Usually, the store manager or

151

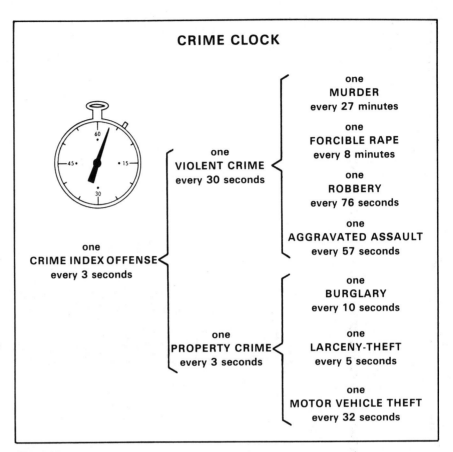

Figure 8-1
From *The Uniform Crime Report* (Washington: Federal Bureau of Investigation, 1979).

employee cannot determine whether the threat is just a threat or whether the robber will, in fact, carry out his or her claim if the manager or employee does not comply with his or her requests. However, many a store owner who has tried to pull a robber's bluff and has not followed the criminal's directions has found him- or herself in the hospital. Those who commit robbery are usually unpredictable in their actions, at least for those directly involved as victims of the crime. When confronted by a robbery, almost anything can happen.

Types of Robbers

In Chapter 7 on burglary, we identified three types of burglars: the professional, the semi-professional, and the amateur. When it comes to robbery, the small business manager is also confronted by robbers of

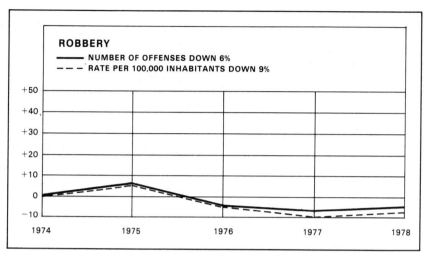

Figure 8-2
The robbery trend (*The Uniform Crime Report,* Washington: Federal Bureau of Investigation, 1979).

different skills. Usually, the store manager has to deal with either the semi-professional or the amateur robber. Just like professional burglars, professional robbers usually attack known places that carry an extremely high volume of money or highly valuable merchandise. Many times, the professional robber will hire out his or her services for a price to underworld connections and, on occasion, to honest citizens.

The small business manager should be aware of how each type of robber operates. The professional, for example, will plan his or her attack with the skill of a general. The timing will be perfect. The professional will not normally attempt to injure anyone during the course of the robbery because he or she realizes that if anyone is injured, the penalty for committing the crime increases beyond the desired risk factor. A professional will usually turn and escape rather than fulfilling any threats.

The semi-professional robber will also plan his or her attack; however, the timing will be less skillful than that of the professional. This kind of robber will usually look for worthwhile victims and times, such as a busy period in a larger retail store. He or she will have a routine—a game plan—from the time he or she enters the store until he or she escapes. The plan may or may not be very detailed, but some organization does exist. There is a chance that the semi-professional robber will injure his or her victims and carry out any threats of violence. Although this criminal may give the appearance of being stable, there are times during the robbery

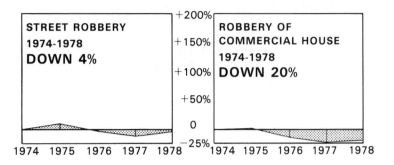

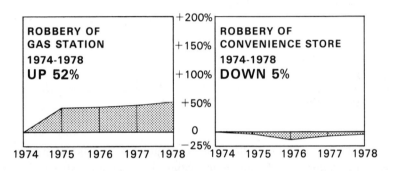

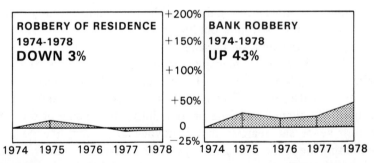

Figure 8-3
Kinds of robberies (*The Uniform Crime Report,* Washington: Federal Bureau of Investigation, 1979).

when the semi-professional could become unstable, especially if the actual robbery does not run as smoothly as the robber had anticipated. This occurs frequently when victims do not comply with the robber's requests, when the robbery takes longer than the robber feels is safe, and when there is either no money or less money than the robber had thought. At these points in the crime, the robber may lose his or her composure and become angry at

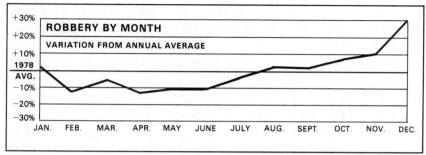

Figure 8-4
From *The Uniform Crime Report* (Washington: Federal Bureau of Investigation, 1979).

the situation. He or she will occasionally take out this frustration on the person or persons who seems to be causing the condition, such as a victim who does not comply with the robber's request or a slow-moving employee who has been asked to turn over the cash to the robber. And in some cases, a robber, after receiving the money or goods, will realize the temporary control he or she has over the others in the store. At this moment, almost anything can happen.

The store manager will also be open to attacks from the amateur robber. This person, many times a neighborhood youngster, is the most frequently encountered robber the store manager is likely to confront. He or she is also the most dangerous and is probably responsible for many of the deaths and injuries that occur during a robbery. The amateur will rarely plan his or her attack. Large sums of money are not required to attract the amateur robber. The knowledge that cash in quantity is contained in a cash register is usually enough to motivate the amateur into robbing a store. For the most part, the amateur will use either a knife or a gun. Many times, the amateur robber will try to imitate television robbers, since this is usually the only role model the robber has in terms of robbery technique. On many television shows, anything goes to bring out the drama and danger involved in a robbery. The same usually holds true when the amateur robber commits the crime. He or she may enter the store waving a knife or gun around. Some amateur robbers have been known to grab a customer immediately and place a knife next to his or her throat while making demands on the store manager or employees. There are two immediate dangers when the amateur robber enters the store. First, the robber is usually highly nervous when committing the crime. Instead of controlling the situation, he or she lets the situation control him or her. The amateur robber is immediately on the defensive rather than on the offensive, like the professional robber. Therefore, the slightest movement could cause the

155

amateur robber to overreact to the situation. Instead of threatening a person who moves during the robbery, the robber may immediately use force and injure the person.

The second danger when the amateur is robbing a store is that he or she is usually not proficient in the use of a weapon. A case in San Francisco illustrates this point. A young teenager entered a drugstore waving a gun. He was highly nervous and told everyone in the store not to move. Customers noticed that the robber was so uneasy that the gun was shaking. When the robber drew his gun and announced the hold-up, he cocked the hammer of the gun. The combination of his condition and the cocked hammer made the situation extremely volatile. Still waving the gun about, the robber instructed the cashier to place all the money from the register in a bag. The robber's eyes were on the cashier when a customer suddenly walked through the front door and startled the robber. Without warning, the robber quickly turned in the direction of the customer and pulled the trigger. Other customers in the store screamed. The cashier fell to the floor. The robber felt as if everything was happening too fast to comprehend. All he could understand was that he was being threatened. Instead of trying to gain control of the situation by using a threat of violence, the amateur robber began firing the gun at other customers. When all of the customers fell to the floor wounded, the robber ran out of the store without the money.

In reality, no customer was attempting to attack the robber. They had, in fact, followed his instructions to the letter. The robber simply became unnerved and reacted in what he thought to be self-defense. When the store owner is confronted by an amateur robber, the owner must realize that anything can happen.

Although the three types of robbers will show various degrees of skill in their crimes, all have the same basic method of committing robbery. Unlike the crime of burglary, where each burglar will usually have his or her own technique for gaining entrance to the building, a robber will simply wait for a time when there is enough money to be stolen, display his weapon, and make his threat. Basically, the robber then grabs the money and runs. A robbery of a small business usually takes less than 10 minutes to commit. For many a robber, the crime is quick and easy to commit, particularly since he or she has the element of surprise on his or her side. Some robbers will survey the store and wait for customers to leave before announcing the robbery. Others will quickly run into the store, grab the money, and leave. In the former technique, the robber tries to reduce the number of witnesses to the crime by letting most of the witnesses—customers—leave before the crime is committed. The latter technique uses the elements of surprise and speed in hopes that the crime will take place so fast that witnesses in the store will not have time to get a good look at the robber.

HOW TO IDENTIFY A POSSIBLE ROBBER

The Probability of Being Robbed

An important question a small business operator must ask is what is the probability that his or her store will become the target of a robber. On the surface, this question may appear to be difficult to answer; however, the store operator can conduct a two-stage survey that will determine the likelihood that a robbery will occur in the store. The first portion of the survey involves *The Uniform Crime Report,* published by the Federal Bureau of Investigation, which lists the number of occurrences of robbery, as well as other types of crime, for the municipality in which the store is located. The report will list robbery in two ways: first, the number of occurrences and second, the number of occurrences per thousand residents. Since, in most communities, robbery usually involves retail stores, the store owner should determine the number of retail stores in the municipality and then divide the number of robberies by the number of stores. The result will give the store operator the number of robberies per store. Although not every store in the municipality will be affected by robbery, the crime per store figure will give the store operator the probability of his or her store being robbed.

The last step in the survey is for the store operator to contact the local police department in order to verify the number of robberies reported in the community over the past several years. The store operator can then determine the trend of robberies for the municipality. For example, if *The Uniform Crime Report* indicates that there are .25 robberies per store in the community, and if the trend developed from the police department indicates a rise in the incidence of robbery, then the store operator will know that his or her chances of being robbed have increased over the previous year.

Spotting Trouble

Once the store operator realizes the probability of being robbed, the next problem that faces him or her is how can he or she lower the chances of being robbed. Unfortunately, there is no sure way of reducing this risk outside of moving the store to an island. However, a prime place to begin in trying to fight back against a robber is for the small business manager to develop his or her skills in spotting trouble before it is too late. Criminals do not wear signs, but certain suspicious traits can alert the small business operator that something is wrong.

Once or twice a month, the store manager should contact the local police department to determine the latest status of robberies in the area. Many times, robbers will "work" a four- or five-town area for a week or so and then move on. Frequently, local police departments quickly identify the pattern and alert neighboring municipalities to the robberies. By keeping in touch with the police on a regular basis, the store manager will be able to know if there has been a series of robberies in the area. This information is helpful, since the manager can then be on the lookout for suspicious individuals in and around the store. Many times, the police will have a description of the suspects and their method of operation. Each piece of information the manager can obtain from the police gives him or her a better edge on detecting a possible robber before the crime is committed.

Another source of information about a spree of robberies is the newspaper. Many times, the newspapers will report such incidents. In reading the news reports, the manager should try to determine how the robberies were committed, the number of robberies involved, and a description of the robbers. The manager should then alert all the store employees and give each employee the description of the suspects.

On many occasions, the store manager will not have advance information about a possible robbery. Therefore, the manager must always keep an eye peeled for suspicious circumstances and individuals. A technique used by a robber in Los Angeles illustrates this point. The store in question served sandwiches to the lunch crowd. During one lunch hour, one of the countermen noticed a customer wearing an oversized windbreaker enter the store. Although the store was crowded, the counterman noticed that the man with the windbreaker had his jacket zippered and that the jacket was bulging. In the man's back pocket was what appeared to be a ski cap. Right away, the counterman became suspicious, since the weather was very warm that day. Quietly, the counterman walked into the back room and called the police. Officers arrived just as the man was removing a gun from his jacket.

Robbers will always have to conceal their weapons until the time is right to announce the robbery. If the weapon is a gun, concealment without arousing any suspicion is very difficult. The robber will also have to survey the store in order to be sure that there are no police officers around. In order to do this, the robber must walk around the store and survey the entire building. The robber may delay longer than other customers in selecting merchandise and heading for the cashier. In warmer climates, concealing a weapon becomes almost impossible, and the robber may have to dress out of style in order to cover up a weapon.

Many times, the amateur robber almost gives him- or herself away by his or her actions prior to the robbery. As mentioned, robbers will usually survey the store before announcing the hold-up. During this period, the amateur robber will be overly concerned about trying to blend in with the other customers in the store. Although a professional or semi-professional robber will dress like the average customer and go about the normal prepurchase actions, the amateur will typically give the appearance that someone on the store's staff is watching him or her. In reality, this may not be the case, but by trying to act normal, the amateur robber usually makes him- or herself stand out among other customers. He or she may be nervous when store personnel come near, or he or she may fumble around with merchandise he or she allegedly intends to purchase. The amateur robber, in essence, will make many simple mistakes. If the store manager and the staff are alert, they will be able to spot the amateur robber before he or she begins to commit the crime.

Attempts to identify a potential robber should begin outside the store. Many amateur robbers will not immediately move in on their targets. The amateur will wait near the target and observe the entrance to the store. The purpose of this move may be less strategic planning than building up nerve to commit the crime. For a youngster, committing a crime can be a nerve-racking task. There is always the danger of not only being caught but of being seriously injured or killed during the robbery. Even semi-professional robbers have been known to get "butterflies" minutes before committing a crime.

Therefore, the small business operator should keep tabs on the activity around the store. The store manager should look for strange faces and for people who are new to the neighborhood or who may not fit in with other customers in terms of clothing style and mannerisms. People sitting in parked cars may be a source of potential trouble. Obviously, not every stranger or person in a parked car will be planning to rob the store; however, noting such persons and making periodic checks will usually give the small business operator an edge over a robber, just in case the suspicious persons actually turn out to be criminals.

If the manager spots a suspicious situation outside the store, he or she should not take any action him- or herself. Instead, the manager should observe the behavior of the suspicious person in order to try to determine whether the person's conduct indicates the overture to a crime. Robbers have been known to make last minute adjustments to their weapons while sitting in a parked car, for example. At times, the store manager may feel threatened by the behavior of a person or persons outside the store. In such cases, always call the police. The suspect may be perfectly innocent of any crime, but the police are the people to determine the motivations of such persons. If the person's intentions are good, no harm will be done if the police arrive. However, if the person has bad intentions, a call to the police will stop a crime before any illegal action is taken.

When trying to identify a potential robber, use one basic rule: Always look for the person or situation that does not fit into the normal course of activity for the store. When noticing such a situation, study the person's behavior very carefully. If his or her behavior appears the least bit threatening, call the police department.

WHAT TO DO DURING A ROBBERY

Robberies usually occur with the same timing as many medical emergencies: They happen when you least expect them. The store manager may be joking with his or her cashier, for example, and the next moment, both of them may be faced with a robber carrying a gun. The actions of the store manager and of others in the store will usually determine the outcome of the robbery. The wrong decision or move during the course of the crime could lead to death and serious injury to occupants of the store.

The Adversary Relationship

Before discussing the do's and don'ts of what to do during a robbery, the role of the store manager in such an event should be understood. During a robbery, an adversary condition exists—the robber against the people in the store. If there is one person in the store at the time of the robbery, such as the manager or a cashier, the relationship is clearly defined: the robber against the manager or cashier. However, the relationship during a robbery can become clouded and confused if there is more than one person in the store during the crime. A robber enters the store and confronts everyone with a gun. Does the adversary relationship exist between each customer and the robber, between the cashier and the robber, or between the store manager and the robber? During such a situation, no one, including the robber, knows the answer.

The identification of the parties in the adversary relationship is highly important in determining the outcome of the crime. Most times, the robber is only after the money in the cash register and in other parts of the store. The actual adversary relationship is between the store manager, who has custody of the cash, and the robber. Anyone else in the store at the time is usually incidental to the actual crime. During any adversary confrontation, there is usually a give and take situation, a form of communication between the adversaries. Without this communication, the situation can become unorganized and uncontrollable. Therefore, before any lines of communication can be established, the adversaries must be identified.

During the first few seconds of a robbery, the situation will be confusing, both for the people in the store and the robber. All parties have to settle down after realizing the initial shock that a crime is being committed. Once the calm has developed, the store manager should take the lead in establishing the identity of the adversaries. Actions during the crime should be made by the store manager and the robber. Once the manager has identified him- or herself to the robber, the adversaries have been identified, and all others in the store then become incidental. The manager must become the leader of all those in the store. Remember that during the first few seconds of the crime, everyone, including the robber, is looking for immediate directions on how to act. Few people have ever experienced a robbery twice; therefore, such an occurrence is completely new ground for everyone in the store.

Handling the Situation

Once the manager takes on the leadership role, others in the store will usually follow his or her directions. Therefore, it is vital that the manager be able to be calm and to concentrate on one objective: letting the robber take the money and escape without harming anyone in the store. Never try to apprehend a robber. Too many store managers and cashiers have been killed trying to be a hero. Remember that money can always be replaced and that it is usually covered under the store's insurance policy. Trying to arrest the robber could cost the manager high medical bills—if not worse.

During the robbery, try to control the situation while talking as little as possible. Any sound can startle a robber, who may, under the pressure of the situation, overreact. Don't try to talk the robber out of committing the crime or to plead with him or her not to injure anyone. Robbers are

161

unpredictable and may be childish at times. Reverse psychology may come into play. Such a case occurred in New York City. A lone robber entered the small branch office of a bank. He announced the hold-up and had all the customers line up near the teller's cage while he waited for the money. During the course of the robbery, an elderly man continually asked the robber not to injure anyone in the bank. The man told the robber to take the money and leave. After the robber received the money, he walked along the line of customers, and when he came to the man who had been pleading with him, he shot him. The man later died at the hospital. Chances are that if the elderly man had kept quiet during the robbery, he would have been alive today.

The manager should comply with every order given by the robber. If he or she asks that the register be opened, open it without hesitation. The more the people in the store comply with the robber's request, the more self-confidence he or she will gain. The robber will know that he or she has complete charge of the situation and that he or she can get whatever he or she wants directly from the store manager. In many cases, the more self-confident a robber is in a particular situation, the less of a chance there is that he or she will overreact or be startled by the movements of those in the store.

While the crime is being committed, the manager and others in the store should remain totally still and quiet, not moving unless instructed to do so by the robber. If someone has to move, it is better if that person announces his or her intentions to the robber before the actual action takes place. The main purpose of this announcement is so that the robber will not be startled by the movement.

Store managers will occasionally keep a gun strategically placed near the location where large sums of money are stored. If a robbery does take place, the manager, pretending to pick up the money, may grab the gun and start a gun fight with the robber. Unfortunately, many a store operator who has tried such a move has lost the gun fight. Such a situation will work in the movies and on television but will rarely be carried out smoothly enough to take the robber off guard. Two things work against the store manager who tries or plans such an action. First, the robber is usually on the lookout for traps and, many times, can spot the gun before the manager can touch the gun butt. The second problem lies with the execution of the plan: Rarely will the store manager ever practice the moves required to take a robber off guard. The gun may be placed in position, but the first time the manager tries to use it occurs under actual robbery conditions. Most store managers who own and have guns in the store rarely fire the weapon, even in practice. The gun, in fact, is hardly every maintained properly, and it may even misfire during the gun fight.

There may be times when the store manager is not directly involved with the robbery but is able to see the action while standing out of sight of the robber. Under such conditions, the manager should not enter the situation. He or she will be of no help if he or she becomes another hostage. Instead, the manager should try to contact the police without causing any suspicion on the part of the robber. Ideally, the call to the police should be made from outside the store. After the police have been notified, be sure to observe the suspect. If the suspect should leave the store before the police arrive, the store manager should notice how the suspect made his or her escape and the direction taken. This information should then be passed along to the police when they arrive at the scene.

Although what we have said thus far instructs the store operator and those inside the store not to take any action during a robbery, now it is time to talk about some things that can and should be done during the robbery. The store operator should try to help the police, not by apprehending the suspect, but by studying the suspect. Chances are that the police will not arrive when the suspect is committing the crime. Usually, the police will have the task of locating the suspect—a person they did not see—after the crime has taken place. To the untrained observer, finding a suspect under such conditions is like finding a needle in a haystack. However, police training has taught professional police officers how to do the near impossible—find the unknown suspect in the middle of tens of thousands of people.

Police must assemble clues that will narrow down the masses to several suspects. In the case of a robbery, the best clues are provided by the persons involved in the crime. The store manager and others in the store at the time of the robbery should begin to develop facts about the suspect that can be turned into clues once those facts are told to the police. The store manager should note the clothes worn by the robber as well as such items as his or her speech pattern, any scars, and any problems with the movement of his or her body. The police should also be told if and where the suspect touched any part of the store. This will enable authorities to lift finger-prints.

What to do in a Robbery

1. The manager should take the lead role in communicating with the robber.
2. Let the robber take the money and escape.

3. Follow all directions given by the robber.
4. Remain totally still during the robbery.

WHAT WILL HAPPEN AFTER A ROBBERY

A robbery can be earth-shattering to those who are directly involved in the incident. Everything happens faster than most people can quickly comprehend. But if the guidelines presented in this book are followed, there is an excellent chance that all those in the store at the time of the robbery will remain unhurt and will be able to assist the police department in recording the crime and in locating the suspect. The period during the crime is confusing, since many robbery victims have never been through such a situation before. For the minutes after the robber has left the store, confusion can also set in, although this is less dangerous than showing lack of direction in the presence of the robber.

Some Common Situations

Three basic conditions are common after the robber has left or is about to leave. (1) The robber will quickly turn and leave after receiving the money. (2) The robber may line the customers up or place the customers in an obscured position and tell them not to move for the next few minutes. Many times, this is coupled with a threat on the life of anyone who moves before the designated time has elapsed. (3) The final condition is that the robber injures someone in the store during the robbery, which may be coupled with one of the previous conditions.

It is rare that a robber will take a hostage when leaving. Such a circumstance will normally not occur unless something went wrong during the robbery. A hostage may be taken if police suddenly enter the situation before the suspect has left the store or if someone in the store tries to apprehend the robber and forces the robber to injure someone. Most robbers are trying to gather as much money as they can and then make a clean, quick, uneventful exit.

The immediate reaction by the store operator following a robbery will depend upon the nature of the conditions that exist when the robber makes his or her escape. For example, if the robber does not give any instructions upon leaving, the store operator should avoid running after the suspect. Instead, the manager should try to position him- or herself at a vantage point where he or she can observe the escaping suspect. The manager should note the direction in which the suspect left and whether the escape was on foot or in a vehicle. If the latter is used, the manager should try to note the description of the vehicle, including its make, model, year, and color, as well as any distinguishing marks, such as a dent or a broken light. The manager's observation should also include the numbers of individuals in the escaping vehicle. Many times, robbers will work in pairs. One commits the robbery while the other drives the "get-away car."

If the robber left instructions not to follow him or her or not to turn around for a given length of time, the store manager and others in the store should follow the robber's directions for a reasonable length of time. For example, if the robber told customers not to move for fifteen minutes, those in the store may wait three or four minutes before moving. Before anyone moves in such a situation, be sure that the robber is out of the store and has left the immediate area. The store manager should not assume that the robber will be gone in a matter of seconds. Give the robber the benefit of the doubt. Usually, five or six minutes is enough time for any robber to leave a store. A few small business managers who have found themselves in such a situation and have moved too soon have ended up injured.

Injuries and Hostages

At times, there are situations where the robber has injured someone in the store. The store manager should always consider the well-being of the injured persons before trying to observe the escaping suspect. If the robber did not leave any instructions, then, upon the escape of the robber, the store manager should notify the police that a robbery has occurred and that someone has been injured. The store manager should then attempt to render first aid to the injured party. When telling the police about the situation over the phone, be sure to inform the officer as to the seriousness of the injury. In such a situation, police have two alternatives: to send both a police officer and an ambulance or to send a police officer and wait for the police officer to confirm the nature of the injury before dispatching the ambulance. But if the store manager informs the officer of the condition of the injured party over the telephone, the officer will have additional information on which to base the selection of an alternative.

If the robber has taken a hostage, the store manager should try to keep everyone else in the store calm. The manager should not attempt to talk the suspect out of taking a hostage. Although at times the manager may be successful in such negotiations, there is a good chance that the manager

165

could make the condition worse than it already is. Always stand back and give the robber plenty of room to move. When police arrive, try to keep yourself and others in the store away from the action. When and where possible, all those in the store should try to protect themselves from any potential violence. Above all, do not do anything that would jeopardize the hostage or anyone else in the store. Police have been trained to handle hostage situations. Remember that the suspect has taken a hostage in an effort to protect him- or herself. Once the suspect feels less threatened and more secure, he or she will usually release the hostage unharmed.

After the immediate threat of danger has dissipated the store manager must continue in his or her leadership role. Everyone in the store should remain in the building until the police arrive. It is up to the store manager to see that this takes place. But remember that the store manager cannot prevent anyone from leaving. If someone does not want to wait until the police arrive, the store manager should try to obtain the name and address of that person and turn the information over to the police. Many people will not want to get involved and will fear retaliation by the suspect if the robber is caught. The store manager cannot force anyone to give information or help to the police, but he or she should try to talk the person into helping. If the person still does not comply, the manager should ask the person for his or her name and address and claim that the information will only be used for insurance purposes. Usually, the person will comply. When the police arrive, this information can be passed along to them. There are times when witnesses and victims require a little ''push'' by the police before they are willing to come forward with information. But if the store manager supplies the name and address of the witness, he or she is giving the police an opportunity to try to convince the witness to come forward.

Once everyone in the store has determined whether to stay or leave, (this is usually decided within seconds after the robber leaves), the police should be called. During this conversation, the manager should, if possible, relay any details about and descriptions of the suspect and the method of escape. Within seconds after the call, this information will be passed along to neighboring police, who may be in a better position to search the area than the local police. There have been numerous times when police three or four towns away from the crime scene have spotted the suspects and made an arrest.

When the police arrive, the manager's leadership role has almost ended. The police officers will instruct the manager and others in the store what to do. They will ask many questions and, at times, may take fingerprints. The store manager's prime task is to determine the amount of money and other merchandise that the robber stole. Such an inventory, as we suggested in Chapter 7, should not be made in haste. Whatever the store manager tells the police will usually be relayed to the store's insurance carrier. If, later, after the report has been made to the police, the manager decides that a larger amount was stolen than he or she reported, he or she may have a difficult time proving the higher claim to the insurance company. Immediately following the robbery, the police only need to know if money was stolen and whether the money was in large or small denominations. A detailed report can probably be made 24 hours after the crime has occurred (see Figures 8–5, 8–6, and 8–7 for arrest statistics).

The final step for the manager, following a robbery, is to contact the store's insurance representative for the proper forms required in order to file a claim. The claim, it should be pointed out, must be reasonable; an unreasonable amount will have to be proven to the insurance company before the claim will be paid.

WHAT SECURITY DEVICES TO ACQUIRE IN ORDER TO COMBAT ROBBERY

When the small business manager reviews the nature of robbery, he or she may throw his or her hands up in the air, feeling that there is little he or she can do to protect the store from a robber. After developing the store's probability of being robbed and establishing employee guidelines in case a robbery should occur, the small business operator may feel that all he or she can do is to wait for his or her turn at becoming the robber's victim.

Insurance Coverage

The small business manager should not give up all hope. There are several types of security devices that will assist the manager in identifying the suspect before the robbery is announced and, if a robbery occurs, in calling the police. As we have seen, there are many kinds of security devices, some using electronically designed circuits and others that are mechanically operated. But strangely enough, the most important security device a small business should have when dealing with robbery does not have any such mechanisms. Although when the idea of security devices is first mentioned, one normally conjures up a mechanism that is installed in the store, the term security device includes anything that maintains the

167

CRIMES CLEARED BY ARREST

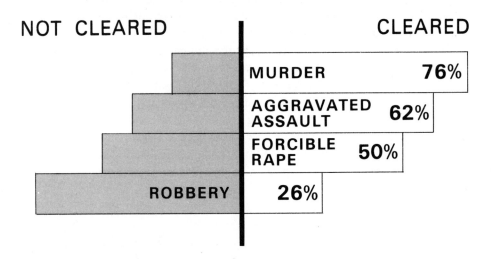

CRIMES OF VIOLENCE

NOT CLEARED   CLEARED

MURDER	76%
AGGRAVATED ASSAULT	62%
FORCIBLE RAPE	50%
ROBBERY	26%

CRIMES AGAINST PROPERTY

NOT CLEARED   CLEARED

BURGLARY	16%
LARCENY-THEFT	20%
MOTOR VEHICLE THEFT	15%

Figure 8-5
From *The Uniform Crime Report* (Washington: Federal Bureau of Investigation, 1979).

PERCENT REPEATERS
BY TYPE OF CRIME
PERSONS RELEASED AND
REARRESTED WITHIN 4 YEARS

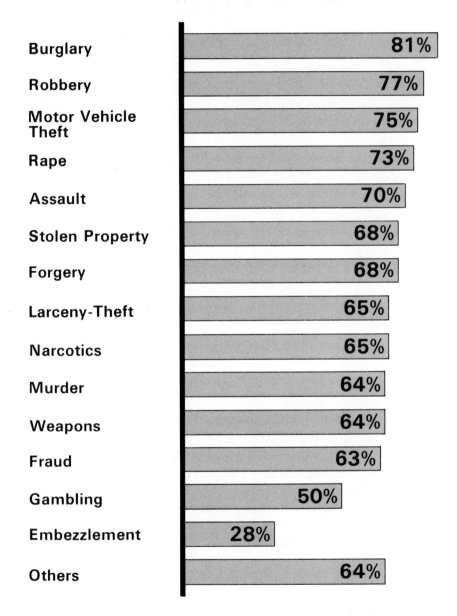

Burglary	81%
Robbery	77%
Motor Vehicle Theft	75%
Rape	73%
Assault	70%
Stolen Property	68%
Forgery	68%
Larceny-Theft	65%
Narcotics	65%
Murder	64%
Weapons	64%
Fraud	63%
Gambling	50%
Embezzlement	28%
Others	64%

Figure 8-6
From *The Uniform Crime Report* (Washington: Federal Bureau of Investigation, 1979).

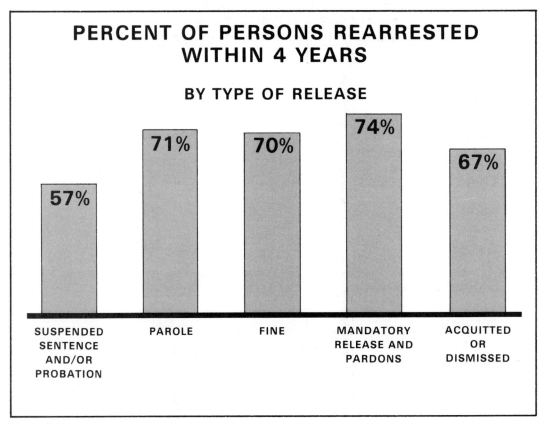

PERCENT OF PERSONS REARRESTED WITHIN 4 YEARS

BY TYPE OF RELEASE

| 57% | 71% | 70% | 74% | 67% |
| SUSPENDED SENTENCE AND/OR PROBATION | PAROLE | FINE | MANDATORY RELEASE AND PARDONS | ACQUITTED OR DISMISSED |

Figure 8-7
From *The Uniform Crime Report* (Washington: Federal Bureau of Investigation, 1979).

protection of a person or a property. The security device that no business can afford to be without is insurance coverage, which protects the financial well-being of the business. For many small businesses, losing a day's or a weekend's receipts can have a drastic effect on the financial balance of the store. Most bills have to be paid within thirty days. If the store is in a poor cash flow situation, the missing funds taken in a robbery can place the store in trouble with its suppliers. A good insurance policy, however, will protect the store against such losses. But there is an important consideration that the store manager must be aware of—the deductible amount of the insurance policy. Although the policy may cost a little more, the store manager should select the policy with the lowest deductible amount available, especially if the business is tight on cash. Although the deductible amount may seem unimportant at the time the policy is acquired, the deductible amount may just equal the total amount taken during a robbery.

A case in Florida illustrates this point. A restaurant owner was unable to make a deposit over a long holiday weekend. The owner had more than $2,000 in receipts on the premises, which was equal to a normal week's receipts. During the last night of the weekend, right before closing, two men who had finished eating placed their check on the cashier's counter and then announced a robbery. The cashier proceeded to give the robbers the money in the register; however, the men figured that more money was stored elsewhere in the building. After they threatened to kill the cashier, the owner of the restaurant decided that the cashier's life was more important than the money. The owner knew that she was covered by insurance and therefore proceeded to give the robbers what they asked for. The robbers left without harming anyone. The following day, the owner filed a claim with her insurance company, showing a loss of $2,800. The owner had selected the company because of their prompt service, which was important to a business that depended on a good cash flow to keep it operating smoothly. Within 48 hours, the insurance company issued a check in the amount of $300. The owner, of course, raised all sorts of complaints, since the business could not survive on what amounted to only three weeks worth of receipts. The complete $2,800 was required to meet the payroll and other forthcoming expenses. The insurance company informed the owner that when she acquired the policy, she had agreed to reduce her premium rate by taking a policy that began with any amount over $2,500. At the time the insurance policy was written, the owner felt that she would save money by taking the policy with the lower premiums and the higher deductible amount. After the robbery, she found out that she had made a poor decision. Special arrangements had to be made with banks and other creditors to float the restaurant during this period of cash deficit.

The small business manager must always be sure that the cash taken in a robbery is replaceable through an insurance policy. The additional expense of higher premiums for lower deductible policies is usually a good investment.

Other Security Devices

Businesses that have frequently been victims of robbery or that have a high probability of robbery should consider sophisticated electronic security devices that will not only alert the store manager to potential trouble but will also notify the police. Since robbery usually involves a suspect entering a store with a gun or knife, the store owner will be able to detect the presence of such heavy metal objects through the use of a metal detector (see Figure 8–8). The detector can be attractively installed on or near the door frame of the entrance. Metal detectors are designed with a sensitivity control that permits the owner to establish which metal objects can pass through the detector without activating the alarm. This control will prevent the alarm from sounding when a person carrying such objects as a set of keys walks through the detector.

Not all weapons will be detected through the use of a metal detector. Depending on the sensitivity control, a knife, for example, may or may not be picked up by the metal detector. In almost all cases, guns will be detected. The metal detector, as the name implies, is only a sensing unit and can only detect the presence of metal. An alarm completes the metal detector security system. A good alarming device is a quiet bell, a buzzer, or a light located either in the back office or at the cash register. The cashier, for example, can be engrossed in a transaction. If a suspect carrying a weapon walks through the detector, the alarm will sound quietly at the cashier's station without alarming the suspect. The cashier's concentration on the transaction will be broken and his or her attention transferred to the suspect.

Knowing that trouble may exist in the store is important for the cashier and the store manager; however, rarely does the knowledge of potential trouble resolve the situation. The store manager and the cashier

Figure 8-8
Metal detectors for businesses (Illustration supplied by and used with permission of Infinetics, Inc., Wilmington, Delaware).

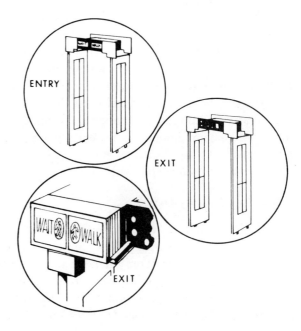

ENTRY

EXIT

WAIT WALK

EXIT

must call for help without alerting the suspect. In order to do this, the small business manager should consider the use of a silent alarm connecting the store to the police station. When the silent alarm is combined with a panic button, the device permits the store manager to call the police without moving from the store. Say, for instance, that a suspect is identified by the metal detector and confirmed either by the store manager or the cashier: One or the other then presses the panic button, which sounds an alarm only at the police department. There will be no indication in the store that an alarm has been sounded. If the suspect actually turns out to be a robber, there is a good chance that the police will arrive just as the robber is about to announce the robbery. If the suspect turns out to be just another customer, the situation can be described to the police; as long as the panic button is not used needlessly on many occasions, no harm will be done.

Other devices that can be used against the crime of robbery include television cameras with a monitor located in the rear of the store or in an office. Cameras can be placed throughout the store and, especially, near the entrance and the cashier. If cameras are used, the store manager must frequently watch the monitor or assign this task to an employee. Such a security system is worthless unless someone is there to watch the monitor. The television camera alone is only sufficient to combat such crimes as employee theft and shoplifting—not robbery.

The store manager can also purchase a capsule-like device, which is placed in a stack of bills. This stack, used only during a robbery, should be one of the first stacks of money given to the robber. Depending on the nature of the device—several are on the market—the capsule will either break under the pressure of handling the stacks or will release a dye after a period of time. In either case, the money becomes marked. There are also similar devices on the market that will release an odor, one so pervasive that the robber cannot easily get rid of it. These devices are designed in order to help police spot the thief after the escape has been made.

Every store, regardless of where it is located, can become the victim of a robber. The store owner should take precautions by purchasing proper insurance, establishing employee procedures, and, if necessary, acquiring security devices. Each item will lessen the risk of a successful attack by a robber.

A step-by-step method for keeping your computer secured 9

HOW COMPUTER SECURITY IS VIOLATED

More and more smaller businesses are using computers to keep track of inventory and accounting. With the onset of the computer age, new thieves have begun to appear. This time, the thief is not a poorly educated neighborhood youngster who always got into trouble; the thief who attacks computers is usually college trained and, in some cases, has a near-genius intelligence. The sure nature of computer accounting challenges the computer criminal's ability to outsmart the machine and the system.

Program Criminals

The computer business system cannot do anything without human instruction, which is called a program. Those who instruct the computer are called programmers. Most computer criminals are also programmers.

175

For most small business managers, there is a technical gap between supplying the computer with raw data and receiving the material organized by the computer in return. Most managers cannot instruct the computer how to organize the material. For such direction, the small business manager must depend upon the computer programmer's skills, abilities, and honesty to instruct the computer in whatever manner the manager sets forth. In essence, the complete computer operation is turned over to a second party who has total control over the information fed into the computer, over how the computer is to organize this information, and, eventually, over the form in which this information is returned to the manager.

When the manager seeks to have the computer keep track of the finances of the business, the complete financial reporting operation is effectively turned over to the computer programmer, who devises a system whereby the computer accounts for the finances of the business. If the programmer cannot be trusted, then the business operator is in for two major problems. First, the dollars and cents of the operation has been turned over to a criminal, and second, the manager and many police agencies are neither equipped nor trained to uncover any illegal manipulations made by the dishonest employee. In short, the manager may know that the programmer is stealing from the business, but he or she does not have the technical ability to show the police or the courts how the programmer is doing it.

Several Examples

A prime illustration of such a theft occurred with a check-writing service company. This relatively small firm used a computer to write and stamp-sign the payroll checks of large corporations. Usually, the corporate clients had thousands upon thousands of employees all over the country who received payment at normal intervals. The programmer instructed the computer to find the average amount of the checks to be issued and then to write 10 checks for that average amount addressed to 10 false names and addresses; these checks were later collected by the programmer. Also in the instruction was a statement that whenever the computer was required to provide a listing giving the recipients' names and the corresponding amounts of each check issued for a company, the computer was to delete the 10 false names.

The computer would print the checks according to the instruction. When the checks came out of the printer, a clerk would place the documents in envelopes. Some checks were individually sent from the check-writing firm, whereas others were bulk-dropped. At the end of the run, the computer issued a list of each check that was written and the corresponding amount. This list was given to the corporate client. Since there is usually a great turnover in a large corporation, especially in clerical employees, rarely did the balance on the list exactly correspond to the amount on the corporate payroll. But as long as both balances were within 10%—which they usually were—the corporate client never raised any question with the check-writing firm.

The computer programmer collected 10 payroll checks every week from 20 companies without the companies or his employer becoming suspicious. The illegal issuance of checks continued for more than 10 years, until the programmer decided to change jobs. To this day, although the programmer is not employed with the check-writing firm, he still receives 10 additional payroll checks each week from about 20 different companies. The check-writing firm would find it difficult to realize that such a condition existed and then to prove it. Every time the firm would request the computer to inventory all the checks written for a given run, the computer, instructed by the programmer, would leave out those 10 checks. Unless a technically trained person managed to ask the computer for a copy of the instructions it was issued for the check-writing program, there would be no way for the check-writing firm to know whether another name or two had been added to the list of checks being written that day.

The most noted case involving computer crime occurred with the Equity Funding Corporation. Unlike the previous illustrations of computer crime, the Equity Funding case did not involve one programmer "stealing" from the company. Instead, the firm and its managers were duping the stockholders and those people and institutions who had purchased the firm's bonds. Equity Funding was basically an insurance company that, according to all its records, was growing at a very rapid pace. The financial condition of the company nearly doubled in a very short time and showed no sign of slowing down. Investors on Wall Street noticed this growth and quickly purchased available corporation stock, a demand for the stock that increased its price.

What really occurred was that the firm was growing by allegedly writing insurance policies for nonexistent people. The task was rather easy for the computer programmers and operators. A supervisor in the computer service department developed a special tape containing a complete list of insurance policies for nonexistent persons. Usually, in modern corporations, the detailed information about insurance policies and other inventory

177

items is contained on a computer tape or disc, whereas the actual doc-umentation—the written insurance contract—is placed in a warehouse location.

Whenever anyone asked for an inventory of insurance policies, the computer would list the real policyholders as well as the fake policies. There would be no way for someone who was not privileged to the scheme to identify the fake policyholders. Only three or four top executives of the firm were knowledgeable about the plan. Whenever the company wanted to show growth, all the computer supervisor did was to add a few more nonexistent policy holders to the computer tape. When this tape was recorded, the computer automatically credited the financial records with the new policies. Whenever an outside firm, such as a bank, wanted to see the financial condition of the company, the bank was presented with a computer print-out that reflected the fake policies.

As required by law, outside auditors spot-checked policies. An auditor would randomly select policies from the computer and ask the company to present the auditor with all the documentation to sup-port the computer's claim. At times, auditors also sent letters to the policyholders asking for written verification that a policy did exist and was, in fact, in force. Equity Funding's plan worked until one of the computer supervisors who was in on the plan mistakenly forgot to remove the tape containing the fake policies from the computer. When the auditors started to select policies from the tape, executives, trying to cover up the crime, began to write policies in nonexistent names to be used as support for the computer's claims. Unfortunately, the executives could not write as fast as the auditors were requesting the information. Before long, the auditors caught on to the scheme and called in the federal government to investi-gate.

Computer criminals, as can be seen by the Equity Funding case, can use computer print-outs to support almost any claim the company would like to make. On the surface, telling such lies to yourself may not seem important; however, when unsupported computer data is fed into such institutions as banks, insurance companies, and other firms who use this data to loan funds to a corporation, fake computer information can be just as serious as a robber holding up the business. This is especially important to consider if the small business is involved in extending credit to corporate clients. Although a client may be housed in a large, expensively decorated office building, that does not necessarily mean that the firm is in stable financial condition. A small business manager must look deeply into a corporate client's finances before lending any credit to the firm.

Another ploy used by computer crooks involves a lesser trained person than a programmer. A case in New Jersey illustrates this point. In a suburban community of New York, a small bank became the victim of a computer thief and almost did not catch on to the technique the criminal was using. In this case, the computer criminal was a college student who had opened an account at the bank. The student was taking several computer courses and had access to a computer coding machine that was commonly used to print such things as account numbers on checking account deposit slips. The student entered the bank and helped himself to a stack of deposit slips that were offered at the bank's courtesy desk. The student coded the slips with his account number and then returned the coded slips to the bottom of the deposit slip pile at the bank. Whenever a customer used one of those deposit slips, the teller would deposit the amount into the account that was listed on the slip. Instead of the money going into the customer's account, the funds were registered in the student's account. The scam did not continue too long before the bank received complaints from customers whose checking and savings accounts were not credited with the proper funds. The bank agreed that a mistake had occurred but could not locate the problem with the system. It was not until a bank officer wanted to deposit funds in his account and used a blank deposit slip that the coded account number was discovered. A quick check of the student's account confirmed that a ''misposting'' had occurred. The bank and law enforcement officials tried to prosecute the student for illegal manipulation of bank funds; however, neither the bank nor the police could prove, beyond a reasonable doubt, that the student had, in fact, placed the coded deposit slips in the bank. The only evidence that the bank had was the transfer of funds that took place, which could have happened without the student's knowledge. The bank also had the blank coded deposit slips, but there was no evidence available that could link the student to the deposit slips. The bank was willing not to continue the investigation as long as the student permitted the bank to remove the ''misposted'' funds from his account, to which the student agreed.

Vulnerability

Computer crime can occur at any point in the computer system. A computer criminal can create fake records, can creatively code computer cards that will give the computer misleading information, and can instruct the computer to ''steal'' funds for the thief. Still another target for the computer thief is the records of businesses. Many businesses, small and large alike, usually have their payroll, inventory, sales, and other important marketing information about the business in a computer file. Some businesses are able to support a complete in-house computer system, whereas others use the services of a time-sharing company. On the surface, detailed information about a business may seem worthless to an outsider to the company, especially if the business is a private corporation. However, this is a misleading assumption. All business exists within a competitive climate. Whether it is the local liquor store or a company servicing corporate clients, there are many business managers trying to acquire the same dollar. There are many facets affecting a business, from cash flow to the number of items sold in a given category. A manager who knows, for example, that his or her competition cannot drop prices below a certain level without losing money, can build up enough of a reserve fund to launch a one- or two-month campaign offering lower prices. Usually, the other business cannot meet the low price for such a long period of time, and, therefore, usually loses its business to the competitor. The important consideration for the competition is to know how low a price to charge and for how long. For most businesses, this information can be obtained from data contained in the computer.

Smaller businesses are the most vulnerable to this problem, not only from competition but also from suppliers. The small business usually cannot afford an in-house computer and will, therefore, turn to a computer time-sharing firm, which will accept raw data and turn the information into an understandable format. Although the time-sharing firm will give each client a code that will "open" the client's file in the computer, there are times when dishonest employees will "sell" this code to competitors, who will thus have complete access to the information and can then determine the financial position and strength of the company.

Suppliers are also interested in detailed information about a small business. Some suppliers will obtain inside information about firms through the use of a computer. With this information, the supplier will know, on a regional basis, the amount of merchandise the business can safely purchase, as well as the required profit margin. The supplier can estimate the price at which the company will buy the merchandise that will return a marginal but accepted profit by the company.

The computer files of a business should be treated with the same care that the manager uses when dealing with money. Information contained in computer time-sharing companies is an easy target for a computer thief. Unless the time-sharing company has tight security, the computer thief can usually work at his or her own pace without the fear of being caught since the business manager whose file is contained in the computer is usually miles away and will rarely, if ever, see the facilities of the time-sharing company. And even if the business manager does make an appearance at the computer location, there is an excellent chance that he or she will not realize what the computer thief is doing.

Although most computer thieves are trained in computer programming or engineering, computer technology today has grown to such a state of the art that even high-school and grammar-school children know how to program a computer. Computer manufacturers, seeking to capture more and more of the small business computer market, are designing computers that, with a few days training, can be operated and programmed by a store clerk. With the ease of instructing computers and of changing existing instructions already programmed into the computer, the small business manager must be on the alert for the computer thief, who will usually use three conditions to commit his or her crime in complete confidence. The business person (1) trusts the computer operator/programmer, (2) does not know how the computer operator/programmer instructs the computer, and (3) assumes that everything that is delivered from the computer is accurate and above question.

HOW TO IDENTIFY A COMPUTER THIEF

The small business manager can feel totally lost when confronted by the possibility that a thief may be attempting to steal information or in other ways manipulate the business's computer information system. Since crime involving computers is usually committed in subtle ways, catching a thief can be extremely difficult. Some larger firms, especially banks, may realize that funds are being illegally manipulated by computer thieves; however, knowing of and proving the crime are two different things. Many firms in such a position try to institute computer security controls. These procedures are usually less than completely criminal proof. For most of these businesses, management just hopes that such crimes do not exceed a reasonable level of the gross receipts. As long as this level is not exceeded, management simply considers the occurrence of computer crime as an expense of doing business.

The luxury of charging the cost of computer crime to the earnings of the business is usually not customary or feasible for medium- and small-sized businesses. A loss of, say, 2% of gross sales does not have the same impact on a large corporation as the same percentage of loss for a small business. The small business operator must account for and use every dollar earned by the business. Therefore, he or she must take an active interest in combatting computer crime.

Who is a Computer Thief?

A prime position for the small business manager to take regarding computer crime is for the manager to spot the thief before the crime occurs. Once the manager can identify a suspicious person, he or she can keep an eye on that person's movements and performance. But unfortunately for the small business operator, computer crime is unlike other crimes that affect a small business. Through the assistance of local and federal law enforcement agencies, the small business manager can construct a profile of a burglar or robber; however, computer crime involves a different breed of criminal. With the more street-oriented crimes, the criminal is usually out to steal money or other valuables. The person may come from an environment that did not supply a reasonable amount of financial security. The computer criminal, however, is drastically different.

For many computer thieves, the prime motivation for committing computer crime is not for personal financial gain but to see how, through their computer talents, they can "beat the system." Monetary reward is usually a secondary reason or even a byproduct of the criminal's efforts. The computer criminal usually comes from a rather financially secure environment. He or she usually has a college degree or at least advanced training in computer programming or related disciplines. Since the demand for computer-knowledgeable employees is higher than the number of such employees in the work force, the computer thief is usually in a position to negotiate for a salary that would eliminate the need for money as a driving force in committing computer-related crimes.

There are exceptions to this rule, of course. Some computer criminals have been known to have expensive habits, such as gambling or alcohol or drug addiction. Others live beyond their means and require additional money beyond their salaries in order to support their standards of living. These requirements for additional funds have forced even the most honest employee to commit computer crimes.

The description outlined here of a computer criminal does not help the small business operator in detecting the thief before the crime has occurred, because the description usually fits everyone who works with the computer. Although there are difficulties in making such an identification, there are a few guidelines that a small business manager can follow in order to identify a computer criminal.

Guidelines

The initial step in the identification process occurs during the interview with a candidate for the position of computer expert. Regardless of the position for which the candidate is applying, the manager must determine the employee's financial position. The manager, through questioning and background checks, must determine whether the candidate has any expensive habits or debts that cannot logically be supported by the salary paid to the employee by the small business. The manager should also attempt to find out if the candidate is in a position where he or she could be blackmailed.

The purpose of this latter check can be illustrated by a case in Washington. A relatively small bank was transferring all the accounting and bookkeeping functions from manually machined postings to computer operations. In order to accomplish this task within a reasonable time frame, a computer expert as well as four or five other persons were hired to assist in the transference. The computer expert devised a system by which a special code was required to be typed into the computer before any major transactions could take place. The code consisted of two numbers, one given to the programmer or computer operator wanting to make the transaction and the other held in confidence by the computer expert. Every day, the computer would randomly assign two new numbers. Therefore, a person who had the two numbers could not use those numbers to gain access to the computer the following day. One of the persons hired was a secretary to the computer expert. The woman, about 35 years of age, was returning to work after raising her family. Immediately prior to joining the bank, she had been employed by a local manufacturing company. After she had worked for almost a year, the bank auditors found that unsupported transfers had been made to five accounts. These accounts were later closed after the funds were transferred. Through investigation by the federal government, the bank had learned that a pair of computer criminals had gained access to the computer and made the transfers. The pair posed as cleaning help and managed to acquire the entry number. The number was good until midnight of that day, after which the computer automatically issued a new code number. Further investigations revealed that the secretary to the computer expert was the inside employee who made the number available. The bank also learned that the secretary was being blackmailed by the thieves. Apparently the two criminals had found out that the secretary, when she was about 18 years of age, had worked as a topless waitress for a few years. The thieves managed to obtain photos of her while she was waiting on customers. They had threatened to send the photos to everyone in the bank unless she gave them the number.

Situations such as the one described can place a small business—or any business, for that matter—in a difficult position. Although it may be difficult, if not impossible at times, the small business manager must make every effort to determine whether there are any sensitive conditions in the background of an employee, especially if the employee will work in an area where tight security is required.

Once an employee is hired, the manager must observe the employee's movements during the first six months to a year of employment. After this period, spot-checks should be made. The purpose of this activity is to reassure the manager that the employee is not "sizing up" the computer system and the business. A computer criminal will require knowledge of the complete flow of paperwork and funds into and out of the computer. Since a computer thief will usually not attempt to commit a crime unless he or she knows the probability of being detected, the thief needs to know the system like the back of his or her hand.

A new employee will usually want to know how the system operates. As required by good management procedures, the employee should be given a tour of the facilities and the computer. However, the manager, when describing the operation, should do so in only the most general manner, giving detailed information only about areas of the system with which the employee will be directly involved. For example, in a situation similar to the Washington case, if a new programmer was being introduced to the system, the manager should tell the programmer only that two code numbers are required to make any major transactions and that if the programmer needs to make such a transaction, he or she should contact the manager. The programmer need not know where the numbers are kept or when and how the computer generates the new numbers. In short, all information must be given on a "need-to-know" basis.

Once the need-to-know procedure has been established, the manager must then observe the new employee. Remember that a computer thief cannot commit a crime on general knowledge alone. He or she must have the complete details of the entire system. For the dishonest computer employee to obtain such information, he or she will usually have to ask detailed questions about the system or place him- or herself in a position to observe how the system operates. Many times, the questions and movements of the dishonest computer employee will give the manager reason to be suspicious. Once this suspicion has been developed, the manager should immediately transfer or dismiss the employee, making certain that the employee is not told of the actual reason for the change.

Whenever a new employee is hired for the computer area, the small business manager should pay careful attention to the information that is being developed by the computer. If the business has been operating smoothly, the information distributed by the computer will usually be consistent and will not vary from month to month or from the same period during the previous year by more than a few percentage points. Computer output from periods before the employee joined the company should be compared with the computer output several months after the employee began work. If there is any difference beyond the normal few percentage points, the business manager should become suspicious. If such a condition is detected, the manager should monitor all records being dispensed by the computer to see if a pattern of "mistakes" is developing. If the differences are related to the loss of funds or property, then the manager should transfer or dismiss the employee. Beware! Such a move may not change the situation; the move will only eliminate an obvious reason for the loss. Many times, older computer employees cause discrepancies to occur as a means of protecting their jobs from the new employee or even as a means of "getting" back at the employer for a procedural or monetary disagreement.

Unless these or similar guidelines are followed by a small business manager, the business is taking a great risk in assuming that all computer employees are honest. The only valid assumption is that most computer employees are honest.

WHAT SECURITY DEVICES TO ACQUIRE IN ORDER TO COMBAT COMPUTER CRIME

When computers were first introduced to business, management personnel handled the new electronic devices with kid gloves. Special rooms were designed specifically for the computers. The computer became a management "toy" that business leaders did not want everyone in the company to touch. Very careful procedures were established in order to ensure that only those employees required to use or operate the computer had access to the device.

Before long, through computer technology and the growth of computer usage by business, the computer became less of a toy and more of a work horse for the company. Computers have developed into the nerve centers of a corporation's existence. With this development, executives working with the computer relaxed the security surrounding the device. Special rooms were, of course, still required to house the computer, but fewer requirements were needed to control access to the computer. As part of the ever-growing learning period with computers, managers soon discovered that dishonest employees were using this freedom to alter corporate records and commit various other crimes.

Today, businesses using computers have instituted strict security procedures around the computer access areas of the building. Since the computer has truly developed into the activity center of the company, managers have realized that this nerve center could not only be the target of a criminal but also the object of industrial or employee sabotage. Few corporations could function efficiently today if the computer system malfunctioned. With this growing concern, special security measures must be taken in order to ensure that deterrents to computer crime do exist.

Areas of Vulnerability

The small business manager who is involved with computers will usually be at the beginning of the learning process regarding the use and protection of the computer and the computer records. In order to illustrate the problems and pitfalls of computer security that larger corporations have discovered, let's begin with acquiring the computer. The small business manager first recognizes a need that the computer can fill. This need may include bookkeeping, inventory control, and the like. After studying the various computer systems that are available, he or she purchases a computer. The manager must, after receiving the computer, instruct the computer on how the device can assist him or her to manage his or her business better. Usually, the manager will hire a programmer or use "canned" programs supplied by manufacturers of computer software. Once the instructions are placed in the computer, the manager or one of his or her assistants will then key the raw data into the computer. Following the input of information, the manager can, at any point, ask the computer for the reorganized information package.

Whether the company is large or small, the same basic procedures exist. Several segments of the typical computer system will leave the small business manager vulnerable to a security breach. The first problem arises when the manager hires the programmer to instruct the computer. As previously stated, the manager must trust the programmer's honesty. A dishonest programmer can tell the computer to "steal" and then to "lie" about the crime. In order to combat this security risk, many businesses use the services of either an outside programming company, which will devise the instruction, turn the results over to the manager, and then never touch the program again, or hire a free-lance programmer to perform the same task. The purpose behind the use of nonemployee help is that after the program is in operation, the programmer is no longer with the company. Therefore, although the programmer may be able to instruct the computer to "steal," he or she will not have the opportunity to instruct the computer when to "steal." Since the programmer is usually on the premises, if at all, only for a few months, he or she usually does not have time to develop a relationship that could compromise both him- or herself and the business.

Along the same lines, a business, after having a program developed by an outside source, may hire another firm or person to place the program in the computer. Although there is a limited variety of hardware on the market, which results in many firms having the same computer, the method of gaining entrance to the computer differs from company to company. As we have seen, methods of gaining access to a computer can differ from day to day. In order to prevent the method of gaining access from falling into the wrong hands, some companies break up the programming procedure into steps: a nonemployee to devise the program instruction, another nonemployee to place the instruction into the computer. Once the program is in the computer, the program should contain a special code that, when keyed into the computer, will permit the person operating the computer to change the program instruction. In the security procedure outlined here, only the computer manager and the outside programmer who placed the program in the computer actually know the code. Without the code, an employee programmer or a computer operator cannot modify the computer instruction.

After the computer program has been placed in the computer, the manager can then permit an employee programmer or computer operator to feed in the raw information and handle other matters dealing with the computer. The manager can usually be sure that, in order for a person to "break into" such a security system, he or she would have to know who developed the program as well as the details of the instruction. The person would also have to know who placed the program in the computer and the computer code required to change the program. In addition, the person would have to gain access to a computer terminal. The more steps required

187

by a criminal to commit a crime, the greater the risk for the criminal and, therefore, the less likely it is that the crime will occur.

The next part of the computer system that is vulnerable is the computer terminal. Although an employee, under the security procedures described above, will find it difficult to acquire all the information needed to alter the program, a crime can still occur by gaining access to the computer terminal. In order to control who can and who cannot use the computer, some companies have instituted computer codes for each of the programmers or terminal operators. Before a person can use a computer terminal, that person should be required to key in a personal code. Such a code can be a single number or letter, or it can be more elaborate. There are companies that, because of tight security requirements, have a terminal operator key in a code number and letter. The operator then waits for a few seconds, and when the computer asks the operator for a ''passowrd,'' something out of an old War War II movie, he or she must reply within a minute and a half. If no response is received, the computer, with the question remaining on the screen, will signal security personnel that someone is attempting to make an illegal entry into the computer. The security staff then investiates the situation.

Although security codes can be something out of a James Bond movie, most businesses do not require such an elaborate system. There should, however, be a requirement that all those who use the terminals have some form of code. The code, if properly programmed into the computer, can give the manager valuable information on how the computer is being used. As long as the computer will record the use of the terminal, the manager will be able to find out who uses the terminal and the purpose of the access. For example, if a dishonest employee is making illegal transfers of funds by keying wrong account numbers into the computer, the computer, if properly programmed, will indicate who the programmer or operator is. Although others in the firm could acquire an operator's code, by knowing the code, investigators would at least have a starting point when investigating computer crime.

Protecting the Tape Library

A key area of any computer system is the program and data base library. No matter how much money is spent on the purchase of a computer and on a computer access security system, the system and the computer are valueless without the program and data base library remaining intact.

Years ago, when a computer expert conducted a security survey of a major New York City stock brokerage firm, he remarked that if a fire destroyed the computer library, not only would the company be in near bankruptcy but the entire stock market would be as well, since a major portion of the records of all stock transactions was contained solely in this single room. A less drastic but also serious condition could occur in the case of a small business unless proper security measures are taken to protect the computer tape library.

The tape library is open to attack from several sources. First, an employee or other individual can leave the building with a computer tape—simply stealing the tape. Since computer tapes are magnetically sensitive, the tapes could be destroyed by sabotage by passing a powerful magnet over them. Tapes can also be subject to fire. Knowing the problems that could exist with computer tapes, the manager must develop security procedures that will prevent such losses.

The first step in protecting computer tapes is always to make a duplicate of the tape. The duplicate, if possible, should be in the form of a computer disc rather than a tape, since the disc is less vulnerable to magnetic attack. The duplicate tape or disc should not be kept in the same building as the computer or the other tapes. Many businesses use the service of a secured warehouse in which the tapes or discs are properly stored. If a tape is destroyed or stolen, the duplicate tape or disc should be available within an hour of discovering the crime.

Careful sign-in and sign-out procedures should be established in the computer library (see sample sign-out sheet in Figure 9–1). If possible, one person should be in charge of the library. Not only should that person distribute the tapes, but he or she should also monitor which tapes are used by each operator. Typically, highly security conscious firms will only permit each computer operator or programmer to use selected tapes. The more confidential tapes are not permitted to be distributed except when a specially authorized individual physically takes possession of the tapes. Usually, the tape library manager will not give such tapes to persons he or she does not recognize. No tape should be given to agents of the authorized person. This will exclude a manager who is authorized to handle the tape from asking a secretary, clerk, or assistant to obtain the tape from the library. Before closing the library for the day, the libary manager should collect the tapes and make an accounting for each tape. When confidential tapes are used, the manager should place a time limit on when the tapes are to be returned to the library. Of course, the time limit can be extended, but

COMPUTER TAPE ASSIGNMENT CHART

TAPE NO.	TAPE NAME	SIGNED OUT BY	DATE & TIME	SIGNED IN BY	DATE & TIME

Figure 9-1
Sample of computer tape sign-in sheet.

the purpose of having a limit, such as an hour or so, is so that both the person using the tape and the manager of the library develop a feeling for the confidential nature of the information contained on the tape.

The problem of computer sabotage, especially where computer tapes are involved, can be a serious security consideration. Any person having access to a tape can cause serious damage to the material. The damage will usually not be discovered until the tape is used again. Managers of tape libraries obviously do not check the condition of each tape that is returned. There is really no positive security measure that can be taken that will completely protect the computer tape from being sabotaged. Only two considerations can lessen the chances of such a crime: duplicating the tape and locating it in a different place. With a tight control on who uses a tape, any sabotage will be detected within a short period of time, and the person committing the act will usually be the last person using the tape.

Tapes can obviously be destroyed by fire, caused intentionally or by accident. In order to remove the threat of fire from the computer tape area, where possible, a special structure should be built to house the tapes. Some firms, for example, keep the tapes in a large room-sized vault. If fire should cause the building to collapse, the vault and the tapes would remain intact. When designing such a room, the manager must take into consideration what is required in order for a fire to occur—oxygen and fuel. It is extremely difficult and expensive for any business manager to construct a room in which, when the door is closed, no movement of air into or out of the room occurs. Therefore, the only control the manager can have when dealing with the threat of fire is to remove all material in the library room that can burn easily. The ideal situation is to have a room completely free from paper and similar products. Instead of wooden tape holders, the room should be outfitted with metal shelves. No one should be permitted to smoke in the tape room. There should be no windows in the room. All paint and ceiling material should be fire retardant. The room should also be outfitted with a smoke detector that will sound at the slightest clue of fire. All wastepaper baskets and the like should be kept outside the tape room. In short, by lowering the amount of fuel in the room, the manager is also lowering the chance that a fire could start and spread in the room.

Most security devices, outside of those used to protect a building or a room from burglary, are contained in the computer program itself. If properly programmed, the computer can actually inform the small business manager who the criminal or dishonest employee is. But when planning such a system, consider the importance of the information contained on the tapes and the true need for extremely tight security procedures. There is no need, for example, for a small business to have a security system similar to that of a firm handling a top secret government project.

Tips on Software Security

1. Duplicate all computer tapes and discs.
2. Store duplicate sets in a secured place off the premises.
3. Sign-in and sign-out procedures should be established.
4. All tapes must be returned at the end of every day.
5. Tapes and discs must be stored in a fireproof location.

WHAT TO DO IF YOUR COMPUTER SECURITY IS VIOLATED

There will be occasions when computer criminals will defeat even the best security system. When such a violation is detected, the small business manager is forced to react to the situation. Unfortunately, few managers have established guidelines and procedures to follow when a computer crime is first discovered. In order to protect computer security, the small business manager should develop such a policy.

The nature of computer crimes, as we have seen, is one in which detection of the crime is difficult and, at times, impossible. Some of the most famous computer crimes have been revealed only through a mistake by a computer criminal or by a criminal later admitting to the crime. Unlike many street-hardened criminals, the more intelligent computer criminal, whose sole purpose is to outwit the system, has been known to admit to "beating the system." Usually, such a criminal will be smart enough to negotiate an equitable settlement before he or she admits to the crime.

When the Crime is Admitted

Since there are several computer crime situations in which the small business manager will find him- or herself, our discussion should begin with the employee who admits to committing a computer crime. Since most computer crimes are committed by individuals who possess a high degree of technical skill, the manager is usually placed at a severe disadvantage. He or she usually does not have the required skills to detect and to understand how the computer criminal is stealing from the company. For that matter, many computer experts as well as law enforcement officials are in a similar situation. Law enforcement officials must not only discover the crime but also prove to a court that the defendant actually committed the crime.

The intelligent computer criminal who may feel that he or she has proven a point and has beaten the system also realizes that at some point in time his or her criminal actions may reappear. Later, when the manager and the law enforcement officials catch up with the computer criminal, he or she will lose an important advantage that he or she has while the crime is being committed—the knowledge of how the system can be defeated. These facts are usually not known to either the manager or the law enforcement officials. There have been numerous computer criminals who, through an attorney, have reached an agreement with the victim and the authorities. The computer criminal admits to the crime and tells how he or she defeated the system. In return, the manager and the law enforcement officials promise not to press charges. Usually, in the case of a dishonest employee, the employee agrees to leave the company in exchange for a good, general recommendation from the company to anyone who might wish to perform a background check on the employee.

In these early years of computer crime, most managers and law enforcement officials usually quickly agree to such terms. Many times, the computer criminal is required to return any funds or goods that were stolen through his or her efforts. A few computer criminals have even received a settlement without being required to return the stolen property. Law officials and managers seem to feel that such a settlement is equitable, since it is difficult to prove charges against the computer criminal, even though the criminal admits to the crime. But at least the knowledge gained from the settlement permits both the officials and the manager to devise a better security system.

Guidelines

When the small business manager first discovers the crime, through the thief admitting the situation, he or she must first determine all the facts in the case. The manager must know what was stolen and for what length of time the computer criminal has been stealing. The manager must also determine, preferably without the help of the criminal, how the crime occurred. The method used to commit the crime should be formulated in complete detail. Just the knowledge that the criminal used the computer to steal money from the firm is not enough for the manager to act on. The manager must, for example, know each step the criminal used to steal the

193

money. If the manager can ascertain this information without the assistance of the criminal, then no negotiations with the criminal should be conducted, because the manager and the company will not benefit by any information the criminal might barter in return for a promise not to prosecute. The entire matter should be turned over to law enforcement officials for disposition. On the other hand, if the manager cannot, with the aid of other computer-knowledgeable persons, re-enact the crime, then the manager must seriously consider such negotiations. This is especially important if the crime involved the removal of either large quantities of material or money at one time or small amounts over a long period of time. Even the latter condition could have a major impact on the performance and existence of the business. Therefore, the manager may, in fact, have to reach such a settlement just to prevent even larger amounts of money or goods from being stolen in the future.

Business managers will also be confronted with discovering that computer tapes have either been stolen or destroyed. If such a discovery is made relatively close to the time the crime occurred, then the manager should follow a procedure similar to that outlined in Chapter 7 on burglary. Usually, such a discovery takes place in the morning when the computer room is opened. As in the case of a burglary, upon discovery of the crime scene, the room should not be entered and should be sealed from employees and outsiders. The police should be notified immediately. When the police arrive, they will usually perform a thorough investigation. After the police leave the scene, the manager should take an inventory of the room and should also assist the police in creating a list of employees and other persons who would normally have access to the room—even those who may be only remotely connected with the computer area should be listed. The police will usually require the manager to help in determining the identity of the last employee or person to leave the room. All this information and any other details the manager may provide will give the authorities a greater chance to identify the criminal.

Many times, a missing tape will not be noticed for days or, in some cases, for weeks after the tape is missing. A professional thief, as you will remember, plans his or her crime in complete detail and will find a method of removing items such as a computer tape without causing anything to appear to be out of order. When the manager discovers that a tape is missing under these conditions, there is no need for the manager to preserve the crime scene. The manager should, however, call the police and prepare a list of employees and outside personnel who would have had access to the room and the tape. Employees should be questioned, either by the manager or by the police. These interviews must be conducted privately, with only one person interviewed at a time. The manager should try to determine whether any particular person showed an interest in the missing tape before the crime occurred. There will be times when the criminal will ask questions about a tape that, to experienced employees, may appear puzzling and outside the normal routine of the computer operations. Such information can be derived from interviews with those employees who would normally come in contact with the missing tape.

Over the years, business managers have developed a general list of the prime candidates who are likely to steal or destroy computer tapes. These suspects include those employees who have received some form of rejection by the manager, by his or her immediate superiors, or even by peers within the company. Also included are those former employees who have recently been dismissed or, on occasions, those who have left the company of their own accord. Likewise, employees of vendors who have either been fired or admonished because of complaints made by the manager should also be suspect. Such vendors include office cleaning help and security guards.

When a crime is discovered, the small business manager must think before he or she reacts to the situation. There have been occasions when a manager, upon discovering a computer crime, has immediately dismissed the computer tape librarian without cause. The manager must remember that he or she has an obligation not only to the business but also to the employees. The manager should, upon discovering a computer crime, first secure the crime scene if necessary and then notify the police. The manager must then make an inventory and determine which items have been stolen. He or she must also provide the police with a list of employees and other personnel who normally have access to the room, as well as a list of those persons who have recently been dismissed or admonished.

Computers can be useful tools, and they may be secured from a thief as long as the manager follows guidelines similar to those presented here.

Steps to Take Following a Computer Security Violation

1. Seal the computer tape room.
2. Call the police.
3. Determine what tapes are missing.
4. Create a list of persons who have access to the room.
5. Create a list of employees and former employees who have either been admonished or dismissed recently.

195

What you need to know about business and organized crime 10

WHAT IS ORGANIZED CRIME?

Newspaper stories and television movies have placed organized crime clearly in the minds of the public. Just mention the words "organized crime," and most small business managers will conjure up the image of a hood of Italian descent placing a "contract" out on another hood. Such an image brings to mind pictures of Al Capone or one of the latest dons being tracked down and eavesdropped on by the federal government. Organized crime is often thought of in terms of "murder incorporated" and gambling syndicates.

Although the descriptions mentioned here do illustrate some aspects of organized crime, they do not incorporate all the types of organized crime that small business operators may face. According to law enforcement officials, organized crime is defined as a group of criminals who plan and commit crimes. Besides the Mafia, organized crime can involve a group of politicians who force businesses to kick back funds either to the politicians themselves or to the political party. Motorcycle gangs who plan and commit crimes are also part of organized crime, as are business leaders who enlist the services of others in undertaking corporate espionage. For that matter, a group of high-school students involved in a drug-selling system can be and have been classified as part of organized crime. The business manager must not be misled by the term organized crime. There is no single national or international body to which every member of organized crime belongs. The high-school gang who has a small local network of drug sales is not a member of the Mafia, but it is a part of organized crime. The group of politicians who shake down local business operators may not be part of the Mafia, but they are, in the eyes of the law enforcement community, still a part of organized crime.

Not all organized crime groups attract the attention of the national news media. A group of high-school students selling drugs in Connecticut is of little interest to persons residing in Florida. In these times, groups of high-school students from almost every state have been known to organize and sell drugs at school, and therefore, the news media usually play down such stories. This type of organized crime, at least to those who operate the national press, is commonplace today. The local news media, on the other hand, will usually announce such occurrences. But because of the lack of nationwide attention for small groups of organized crime, most business operators will rarely think of organized crime as any group other than the Mafia.

Because of this situation, many small business operators are unaware of the many areas in which all forms of organized crime can and do affect a business. In this chaper, we will look at the whole spectrum of organized crime, from the noted national crime figures to the smaller, localized forms of organized crime. Many times, those involved in organized crime on all levels use similar techniques, although the more experienced and better financed crime groups will usually have a more professional touch than the local amateur groups. These groups frequently use shake-downs, forced take-overs, and forced purchase contracts, as well as other techniques, to encourage the business manager to patronize the crime group.

The Mafia

The most widely known form of organized crime is, of course, the Mafia, a highly organized group of men who have switched their concerns from small hood-like crimes, such as shake-downs and protection, to more businesslike enterprises. This organized crime group has designed nearly foolproof methods of cornering illegal markets in gambling, prostitution, drugs, and hijackings; they have also entered legitimate businesses. Law enforcement officials have noted the presence of the Mafia in such businesses as franchises, car dealerships, and, to some extent, in funeral homes. Industries noted for Mafia involvement include the restaurant business, laundry operations, and garbage removal. Although it is difficult to prove conclusively in a court of law, law enforcement officials have indicated that some smaller banking and savings and loan operations are controlled by the Mafia. Not everyone in these industries, however, is Mafia-associated. Many honest business operators in these industries are competitors to the Mafia-controlled businesses.

Most of the Mafia operations have been concentrated on large dollar-producing businesses. In rare cases, for example, will a single restaurant be owned and operated by organized crime. The Mafia organization directs its attention to the supplier level of retail businesses. The influence of the Mafia is usually felt when retailers in certain businesses deal with wholesalers, since the Mafia has gained control of some businesses at the wholesale level. For example, say that a restaurant requires linens to be cleaned and replaced and food supplies to be delivered. The Mafia have been known to operate such distribution systems, even without many retailers realizing that such a situation exists.

The wholesale level of the business distribution system provides the operators of the business with less risk and a broader potential market. An established territory of the Mafia will have many of the same business surroundings as the areas where no Mafia influence is present. Small retail business operators will usually find it rather easy to open shop and conduct business. When the shop operator seeks out wholesale suppliers, usually only one supplier will cover the location of the business. In a pure economic sense, the retail business manager does not have a choice. The manager must deal with the wholesaler who is the most economical.

In a developing Mafia territory, retailers will see more obvious signs of the Mafia. The movie and television dramas developed most of their background information for their scripts from such circumstances. "Salesmen" from the reputed Mafia wholesaler may persuade the small business manager to stop purchasing supplies from the traditional source and to turn the purchases over to the new wholesale operation. Such a visit will only occur if the existing supplier has decided to fight the new competition. When the Mafia moves into a territory, they usually force the wholesaler to sell his or her business to them. Such an arrangement is more in keeping with the relatively new business approach the Mafia has taken.

Once the territory has been clearly identified to potential competitors, an unwritten and unmentioned code is then enforced: "You don't bother me; I won't bother you." It is this code that can force a small business operator to use a Mafia-controlled supplier. The Mafia do not use guns; rather, the retailer is economically and legally forced to use the Mafia supplier.

The Mafia has also entered legitimate business, using it as an investment. As previously mentioned, law enforcement officials have indicated that several franchises, such as car dealerships, are actually owned by the Mafia. These businesses are operated without any outward sign that the business is in any way connected with organized crime. In fact, the Mafia runs such a business according to common business practices and standards. The purpose of such a business is twofold: It both provides a method of filtering dirty money and acts simply as a good investment that earns money.

Mafia members, like all members of organized crime, have a major single problem that is difficult to resolve—the Internal Revenue Service (IRS). Although members of organized crime can obtain large sums of money illegally, they find it difficult to spend the money. This statement may sound unbelievable, but people, regardless of their connections with organized crime, have a serious problem explaining unaccounted-for expensive merchandise and money to the IRS. For example, when an IRS agent investigates or audits a person in detail, the agent lists all the person's property and income. A person showing $20,000 a year in salary will have a difficult time explaining how he or she can afford a house worth $500,000 and a car valued at $35,000.

Organized crime members have hired teams of lawyers and accountants to devise schemes that will permit members to spend large sums of money on expensive merchandise without showing any income. Many times, the answer to this problem involves legitimate businesses. A member, for example, might purchase a franchise for an equitable price, although on paper and in legal documents the member's investment is rather modest and will usually be justified when compared with previously reported income. The franchise will obviously return large sums of money to the member and will give him or her the outward justification for living in a high and expensive lifestyle. Since there is no obvious imbalance of income compared with net worth, the IRS many times cannot find a legal reason to conduct the kind of thorough investigation that, unless certain accounting measures have been taken, would reveal an inconsistency between income and net worth.

As previously indicated, small business managers who deal with the

Mafia may not actually know that such an association exists. From outward indications, dealings with a Mafia supplier will many times be conducted in the same manner as dealings with a non-Mafia-connected supplier. The economic cost of using a Mafia supplier will, of course, be present. Prices will usually be higher than those of a non-Mafia-connected supplier. Although there will be such differences, their economic impact often seems to blend in with the total economic conditions of the business and of inflation.

Politics

Small business managers are usually more vulnerable to the effects of non-Mafia forms of organized crime. Many times, smaller communities elect political leaders who have more at stake than to direct the affairs of local government honestly. In smaller communities, members of local government have enormous powers over the lives of community residents and small business operators. Typically, local leaders will determine who receives retail business licenses and what the design of a shop interior must be. There are all types of regulations imposed on the local residents and small business operators that are enforced at the local level. These normally include health codes, building codes, and site variances from zoning laws. The list is almost endless.

There are also occasions when not only the enforcement of such laws but also their adjudication is determined by local officials. In order to fight charges and legal findings, the small business operator and residents need to hire an attorney and press the matter in court. Such an expense for a legal action that the defendant may eventually lose is usually prohibitive and unjustified.

A case in New Jersey illustrates a typical organized crime–political corruption situation. The town was actually operated by four political leaders—an attorney, the mayor, a real estate broker, and a member of the town council. In this community, the local government controlled the approval of liquor license transfers, the enforcement of liquor laws, and the adjudication of violations of these laws. The community also controlled the health regulations of all structures and of health-related businesses. All investigations were made under the control of the local leaders, and the municipal judge adjudicated the charges. All construction was also controlled by the local leaders in the same fashion. Within a limited scope, the local leaders could create criminal laws and had discretion as to which of all the laws were enforced.

A group of four persons would find it difficult to conduct investigations and later charge any "violators" with the crime. These leaders, however, did have their power of appointment. Everyone employed by the community, including the judge, the inspectors, and every member of the police department was hired and remained employed because of the help of these four men. Legally, only the six members of the town council and the mayor could make such appointments; however, through the selection process in the local political party, the council members were also indebted to these four men. Through years of effort, these four leaders developed a high following in the community for the mayor. The four were always willing to perform any favor for the voters, including paying all parking tickets; having criminal charges lowered or even dropped; and, in the more difficult cases where a son or daughter of a local resident was sent to jail, the mayor would arrange to have the youngster housed in the best of conditions and available for release as soon as possible. One of the prime patronage instruments used by the mayor was to make anyone who asked to be one an "official" of the local government. The mayor and council created and distributed badges of office for positions, such as sheriff, marshals, special police, and a host of other assistants to local officeholders. It was once estimated that everyone in the community had a badge and title of some kind.

With such a tight control on the community, these four men required business operators to pay kick-backs and protection money on a regular basis. Whenever a business operator wanted to have a variance to a certain law, all the operator had to do was to make a payment—indirectly, of course—to the four men. An outsider who wanted to install cable television in the community approached the attorney, who was also the municipal attorney, to propose such a move. The first words out of the attorney's mouth were, "What's in it for us?" If a business operator did not cooperate with the required payments, various inspectors would investigate the small business to be sure that all the regulations were in compliance with the law. Few, if any, businesses could undergo such an inspection without being charged for a violation or two. Many business people in the community simply complied and did not make any waves. Even the local newspaper was indebted to these men, since the paper needed the legal ads from the local government in order to survive.

In this community, the conditions for local business managers were worse than if the most extreme movie version of the Mafia were actually in power and placing pressure on every business person. Business leaders who depended on the community were afraid to speak out. A few leaders who did try to fight the system in this community found few sympathetic ears. Residents in the community ''knew'' the mayor as a person who did them all kinds of favors. The mayor even attended church on Sunday. When similar remarks about the condition in the town reached state political leaders, those leaders took two positions. First, like the local residents, they knew the mayor and could not believe that such a condition existed in the town. The other position involved an unwritten and unmentioned rule in politics: Unless a condition threatens the life and safety of the community, all matters are to be handled on the local level; only in extreme conditions does an authority outside the local level ever consider overruling a local decision. In short, the state officials did not make waves for the local officials, and, in return, the local officials provided local support to the state officials at election time. There were one or two local business managers who were able to ask the federal government to investigate the situation. The federal government sent agents in to determine the status of the complaint. Unfortunately, besides these one or two business managers, there were no witnesses who would step forward. Many business operators who, in the past, had complied with the local leaders' financial requests were confronted by two problems: First, reprisals from the local leaders and, second, if they did admit to receiving payments, the local business managers would be admitting that they had committed a crime.

When federal investigators asked community residents about the leaders, investigators received only good comments from apparently unbiased residents of fine character. Finally, the federal investigators concluded that if the charges made by the business operators were true, the crime was occurring at a lower level of government, such as, say, from the actions of a local inspector. Since the condition appeared to be an isolated case that was not as widespread as the managers had suggested, the agents concluded that it should be handled by local or state authorities.

Cases similar to this are not unusual in other locations in the United States. Political leaders, may times under the direction of four or five actual participants in the crime, can have a life or death control over small businesses. Most of the time, these leaders are in a position to bring pressures and charges against the local business operator—all in the name of the law—if the operator does not comply with the leader's requirements. Although such political corruption is usually reported by the news media as corruption, it is actually a form of organized crime.

To a lesser degree, the small business manager will be confronted by another type of organized crime—the typical youth gang. Much in the manner depicted in many hood movies, youth gangs usually use the threat of force or the destruction of property as means to encourage the small business manager to comply with requests, usually for protection money. Such youth gangs may ride motorcycles and wear identifying jackets, or they may not have any form of identification. They may show force in the form of chains, knives, sticks, and the like, or they may just use verbal threats. In any case, the small business manager must be alert to the existence of this form of organized crime.

WHAT TECHNIQUES ORGANIZED CRIME USES

Regardless of the nature and size of a form of organized crime, there are several basic methods that members of these groups use to persuade honest business operators to go along with the criminal's idea. Even though the Mafia has now developed into a less physical organization, when the organization was initially making inroads into various operations, the same basic street tactics were used as are used today by the less refined groups of organized crime. Most small business operators have never had a confrontation with organized crime; however, with the growth of organized crime, more and more small business managers will be facing such confrontations in the future. The small business manager needs to be alert to the more common techniques used by organized crime.

The Take-over

A major growth area where the business manager may, in fact, be confronted by Mafia-connected organized crime groups is the business take-over scheme. Many Mafia-connected organized crime groups will seek out wholesale supply operations and, on occasions, important restaurants and night clubs. As any business manager will agree, when entering a new business, an operator is usually better off taking over an existing company under favorable terms rather than beginning from scratch, and members of organized crime are no exception. Therefore, when such a group is taking over a new territory by operating a wholesale business, for example, the organized crime group will usually seek to take over an existing operation. In such cases, a member of the group will make an offer to the manager of the business. The offer may be less than the market value of the business. Typically, the business operator rejects the idea, especially if he or she does not have any intentions of selling the business. Without warning, days or weeks after the offer has been rejected, the business operator usually realizes serious but unusual problems in conducting the business. Trucks may be hijacked or disabled due to unusual mechanical

204

failure. This often happens to the entire fleet. If employees are unionized, the operator may find workers walking off their jobs on a wild-cat strike. Customers may soon turn to another supplier for merchandise, and buildings or trucks may be burned.

The entire technique is designed to create accidents that will place the business operator in a financial squeeze. Before long, insurance companies may not write policies or will require such a large deductible that the business manager cannot afford the losses. Several times during this "bleeding" process, additional offers to buy out will be made by members of organized crime. Unless the manager is willing to fight, the deal is agreed upon, and the organized crime group begins to operate the business. On the other hand, if the manager wants to fight, additional "accidents" occur until, finally, members of the group physically force the operator into signing the sale agreement. There have been times when the organized crime group lowered the sale price of the business if the negotiations reached the stage where the owner had to be forced into signing the agreement.

This technique is extremely useful for members of organized crime. Regardless of whether the business manager calls the police or not, rarely will there ever be enough legal proof that such a take-over actually took place. The only proof that will exist is that a citizen offered to buy the business from another citizen. The person who owned the business, after rejecting the offer, had a stroke of bad luck. Usually, all the "accidents" that were created could only, in the eyes of the courts, be construed as freak accidents. After seeing that the business owner was having a period of bad times, the offer to buy the business was again made. Eventually, the owner signed the papers, turning the business over to the other citizen. Even if the owner was physically forced to sign the sale agreement, he or she would have to have witnesses to testify to the forced signing. Without such witnesses, it would be the owner's word against three or four other witnesses, who would swear that the owner sold of his or her own free will. Very few cases like this ever come to court, since most business operators are fearful for their lives and for the lives of their loved ones.

Hijacking

A technique that has gained popularity recently involves the hijacking of trucks carrying important cargo. A case in point involved the hijacking of a cargo of automobile owner's manuals and maintenance manuals. A group of unconnected organized crime members hijacked an entire shipment of manuals headed for the automobile assembly line. When

205

the theft was reported to the police and the FBI, very few officials became concerned. Most of the law enforcement officials thought that a hijacking team took pot luck in stealing a load and came up unlucky or that the group simply hijacked the wrong truck. After all, even Mafia-connected organized crime groups have been known to set out to hijack a truckload of television sets and to end up with a load of ashtrays. The only persons who did become extremely alarmed were the executives at the automotive company. The actual dollar value of the shipment was not substantial; however, according to regulations, the cars could not be delivered to the dealers without the two manuals present in the glove compartments of the vehicles. Without the manuals, the auto company would lose millions of dollars due to the two months delay that would occur if the manuals had to be reprinted. The hijackers knew this and hid the hijacked truck. The company was contacted by one of the hijackers and asked if the firm intended to pay a finder's fee to anyone who found the truckload of manuals. After consulting with corporate attorneys and executives, a representative of the company negotiated with one of the hijackers, and a settlement was made for a sum in excess of $100,000.

The important consideration in such a technique is that as long as the hijackers did not get caught until they hid the truck, there would be almost no chance that they would be arrested after the goods were hidden. Although there is a law that makes it a crime to extort money from anyone, legally, the hijackers did not extort anything from the company. According to the courts, a person approached the company and asked if a finder's fee was being offered for the discovery of the stolen goods. The company said "yes" and stated an amount. The person told the company where they could find the goods, and the company, after confirming the find, paid the money.

This technique is frequently used by more professional organized crime groups who are able to have someone on the inside to arrange the actual crime, persons to commit the crime, and another person far removed from the actual crime to negotiate not only with the company but also with the insurance company. When an important shipment is stolen, the insurance company usually stands to be out the dollar value of the loss. Many times, the insurance company is willing to pay a percentage of the total loss as a finder's fee rather than paying the complete dollar value of the loss.

Other Techniques

There are, of course, more crude techniques that each organized crime group uses during the early stages of its development. These include the protection shake-down, in which members of the group cause damage and injury around a retail store area. After a one- or two-week crime spree, a representative of the group approaches business managers and claims that the group can protect the store and the operator, as well as customers in the store, as long as the manager pays a certain weekly or monthly fee to the group. If the manager agrees, the crime spree stops. If the manager does not agree, the crime spree continues.

A less uniform approach to the protection technique is the shake-down of business operators. A group of organized crime members desires something from the business manager. At times, the request may be money; at other times, it may be certain types of action, such as dealing with a particular supplier. In either case, the request is usually one that the manager is not eager to comply with. Members of the group approach the manager with the request; they may show signs of force, or they may actually cause damage to the store in an effort to prove that their threats are real. Usually, the manager quickly complies. This is similar to the protection technique, except that the shake-down does not continue over a long period of time.

The crime techniques presented here are not the only ones used by organized groups—variations of these techniques are also used. And the underlying strategy of all the methods used by organized crime is fear—fear that someone will injure the manager's life or property. In the presence of a threat to life, the manager usually complies.

Techniques Used by Organized Crime

1. Take-overs of businesses.
2. Extortion.
3. Hijacking.
4. Unfair competition.
5. Union control.

WHAT ALTERNATIVES ARE OPEN TO SMALL BUSINESSMEN WHEN CONFRONTED BY ORGANIZED CRIME

Some knowledge of how the various types of organized crime operate will alert the small business manager as to whether such a confrontation is in the offing, but most small business managers don't know what direction to take when a meeting with organized crime does take place. Hollywood has

207

conditioned the public into responding to the statement, "I'll make you an offer you can't refuse," and has also impressed upon the public that organized crime is another term for the Mafia. Yet this is a misleading impression.

According to Hollywood, through which most business managers and the public learn how organized crime operates, most persons and business managers automatically go along with any request made by a member of organized crime. A few who fought back have found themselves and their loved ones injured or murdered. The Hollywood version of organized crime leaves the small business manager with only two alternatives when confronted by a request from organized crime—comply or die. Although most movie viewers realize that Hollywood presentations are several steps from reality, such movies have been enough to create confusion among those who, for the first time, must deal with real members of organized crime. Is it true that the only alternative available to the small business person in such a situation is to comply or die? Is it true that organized crime members have strong ties to political officials and heavy influence in the courts? Can one trust law enforcement officials not to reveal contacts with the police to organized crime members? Answers to these questions and others are required before the small business manager has sufficient information to be able to react to a confrontation with members of organized crime.

Before the manager can determine a course of action to take in such a situation, he or she must clearly identify what kind of organized crime group he or she is dealing with. These range from the Mafia to local hoods to street gangs, and each kind of confrontation faces the small business manager with different alternatives.

The Shake-down

A typical confrontation involves the protection shake-down. If, for example, the confrontation is between a manager and a street gang, the manager can usually assume that the gang has no influence over the local police or local political leaders. When such a confrontation does arise, the manager has three alternatives. First, he can comply with the request. Once this course is taken, members of organizeed crime realize that the manager will "give" members anything they request, and therefore, there may be no end to the requests. Secondly, the manager can call in the police. Usually, the police are more than willing to enter the case, and when they do, gang members will obviously be alerted to such an investigation. The actions of the police, rather than inside information from members of the department, inform the crime group members of police intervention. During the investigation period, the manager may be open for reprisals from gang members, although the police are usually more than agreeable to arranging special protection for the manager. But if the investigation results in no arrest, police protection may be removed or may become less active, depending on the needs of the local police department. And if an arrest does take place, usually only a few gang members are taken into custody. Rarely do the police have enough information to arrest the entire group. And if members of the gang are under the legal age of consent, there is an excellent chance that the courts will immediately release them to await trial. Also, after a conviction, most juvenile courts are only willing to place even the most hardened youth offender in custody for about a year. The manager will usually still have to deal with those gang members who have not been arrested.

As a third course of action, the manager can fight back without the aid of the police. There are several major problems with this alternative. First, the manager is usually not in good enough physical condition to deal with a group of youth criminals. Many members of such gangs are armed and have had training in the matrial arts, which puts them out of the league of the small business manager. Realizing that he or she is outnumbered and is in no shape to enter hand-to-hand combat with the gang members, some managers have taken to arming themselves—legally or illegally. Although he or she may have a gun on the premises, very few managers have had any training in how to use the gun; some may never have fired a gun at all. During a confrontation, the manager may draw the gun in an effort to hold gang members at a distance, and the gun may fire simply because of mishandling. If such a situation arises, and if a gang member is wounded or killed, there is an excellent chance that the manager will be charged by the police and will face criminal prosecution, including imprisonment. Although the gang members are violating the law by attempting to extort money from the small business manager, the manager does not have the right to shoot the gang member unless the gang member attempts to use deadly force, which has to be physical. Although a group of gang members confronting a manager can be mentally threatening, the manager is still, under the law, not permitted to use deadly force to ward off gang members. Some managers have been overcome by the gang members, who have later killed the manager with his or her own gun.

Although the alternatives in coping with a street gang shake-down racket are very limited, there are individual cases where each alternative

209

has been successful. The determining factor as to which alternative to select is the degree of professionalism of the organized crime group. A small street gang who is just starting to enter the shake-down scheme might be scared off by police intervention or by a show of force from the manager. But hardened youth gang members will not diminish their actions because of a show of force by either the police or the manager. Under such conditions, managers usually comply with the request and hope that within five or six years the gang will grow older and leave the community.

Politicians and the Mafia

When the small business manager is confronted by situations involving local hoods, such as politicians or the Mafia, there are four alternatives open. First, the manager can comply with the request. This is usually the least destructive alternative. Those members committing the crime are usually professionals and have considered every angle. Secondly, the manager can call the police or other authorities, but two problems will usually occur. First, there is an excellent chance that those members of the gang who confronted the manager have strong connections with the local authorities. In some cases, the members who are making the demands are superior to the local law enforcement agency. The other situation involves the legal requirements for an arrest and prosecution. Gang members will make sure that there is no evidence that a confrontation with the manager ever took place. And without evidence, even the Federal Bureau of Investigation cannot make an arrest.

Third, the small business manager can personally fight gang members; however, as we saw during the discussion of youth gangs, the manager may not be in a good position to enter combat. When dealing with professional organized crime groups, if the manager shows a gun or some other weapon, the member of the group will often simply call the police. There will usually be witnesses on the side of the organized crime figure who will testify that the manager drew a gun and threatened the gang member without any provocation. The manager may find him- or herself in jail. The final alternative that many small business managers have taken is to comply with the request and then sell the business or move to a new location that is beyond the grasp of the organized crime group.

A good rule to follow when confronted by organized crime is first to determine the type of crime group and the breadth of their operation. Then determine whether you have a "big enough stick" to resist the request. If you do not have such an advantage, then you should seriously consider selling the business and moving to a location that is not affected by organized crime groups.

WHAT LEGAL COURSES ARE OPEN WHEN DEALING WITH ORGANIZED CRIME

One of the alternatives that is open to the small business manager confronted by organized crime is calling the police for assistance. Doing this exposes the manager to the entire legal process that is designed to protect the innocent and to prosecute and punish the guilty. But the legal system does have many flaws, especially when dealing with organized crime. Many business managers who have experienced the legal system feel that the system protects the guilty and punishes the innocent.

The important point for the small business manager to remember is that the courts—in theory and, to a greater extent, in practice—act as a third party to any confrontation. The plaintiff—the person bringing the complaint—and the defendant—the person who is charged with a crime—start as equals before the court. Although the defendant may have a long criminal record and may have spent time behind bars, whenever the defendant is charged with a new crime, his or her past cannot be considered as a factor in whether or not he or she actually committed the crime he or she is charged with. In the eyes of the court, the defendant, regardless of his or her past, is as honest and innocent as the plaintiff. It is up to the prosecution—the lawyer for the plaintiff—to prove that the defendant, in fact, committed the crime against the plaintiff.

Such proof must be presented according to certain rules of court procedure. Although many of the rules are technical and require a lengthier discussion than is possible here, several rules are important to the business manager because they directly affect the prosection of charges against organized crime members.

The Arrest Process

In order to begin, let us consider the arrest process, which is the beginning of the legal alternatives open to the small business manager. The manager normally calls in the police and informs them of a shake-down or some similar organized crime technique. The first question the police will ask is whether the manager can identify the person who made the threat.

211

Many times, the manager has never seen the person before, nor can he or she give the police an adequate description of the suspects that would give them enough information to locate him or her. The next question the police will ask the manager is whether he or she, after the police arrest the suspect, will be willing to testify to the crime in a court of law. If the manager declines, the legal system comes to a halt, since the police officer did not see the suspect commit the crime and, therefore, has no evidence against the suspect. But if the manager gives an affirmative response, the police will usually begin to investigate.

The police investigation, assuming that the police are not influenced by the organized crime group, will usually position an undercover officer in the store or business to wait for the group to make another attempt to shake down the manager. If the police are Mafia-connected, the officers will usually ask the owner to call them the next time the crime group members come back to the store. Obviously, members of organized crime, in such a situation, will not stand by and let the manager call the police. Again, unless there is a good description of the suspect or unless the police actually see the suspect commit the crime, there is nothing they can do. If the police do plant an undercover officer in the business, officers may or may not use electronic surveillance devices to record the threat. In many circumstances, the police require a court order in order to conduct such a surveillance. Most members of organized crime, at least the more professional groups, will be extremely careful about where and how the threats are made. The initial threat may be made in the open, since the manager will rarely have any time to prepare for such a confrontation. The second confrontation will be made under special conditions. The professional group members will protect themselves from being "set up." Therefore, the police surveillance may continue for weeks or months, with actual contact between the member and the manager taking place outside of the surveillance area. Many times, the police will call off the surveillance if such a tactic is not fruitful within a reasonable period of time. When this happens, the manager is back to square one.

If the police do make an arrest as a result of electronic and undercover surveillance, there is still a long road ahead before the courts can find the defendant guilty and sentence him or her to jail. Remember that the courts can only find the defendant guilty if the evidence gathered by the police is presented in court. Although the police may have the evidence in custody, there is still a good chance that the evidence will not be available on the day of the trial. In a surveillance like the one described above, the only evidence available that can be presented to the court is the manager's testimony, the testimony of the undercover police officer, and the tapes of the conversation and the threat.

The Court Process

From the time the arrest is made to the time the evidence is presented in court, anywhere from six months to a year or more can pass. The police officer who witnessed the crime could have been transferred or even shot in the line of duty. Since he has handled hundreds of other cases during the delay, the officer may forget some of the details about the crime. The organized crime group may also be able to ''get'' the officer to change his or her testimony during this period. A key element in such a case would be the tapes. At the time of the arrest, the tapes are normally treated like gold and are carefully contained in the police department's property room. During the steps before the trial, which include the review of the evidence by several attorneys, the tapes are frequently moved from one location to another but are always returned to the property room after the review of the evidence has taken place. Once the prosecutor and the defense attorney have determined their individual strategies, the tapes, still contained in the property room, are usually forgotten until the trial comes closer. The same laxness often develops with everyone and with everything about the case. There have been times when certain organized crime groups have managed to have the tapes misplaced or lost during this lax period. Without the tapes, there is a good chance that the defense attorney can change the witnesses' testimony under cross-examination enough to give the court reasonable doubt that the defendant actually committed the crime.

A point to remember is that the court, besides looking at the defendant and the plaintiff as equally innocent, must be shown enough evidence against the defendant to find that there is no doubt in the mind of the court that the defendant actually committed the crime. ''Beyond a reasonable doubt'' is what many attorneys who represent organized crime figures set as their goal in defending the crime group member. For example, if a manager took the stand and stated without a doubt that the defendant threatened to kill him or her if he or she did not agree to buy merchandise from the defendant, the defense attorney could actually create a doubt in the mind of the court.

The attorney could ask the manager to give the court, word for word, the actual statement made to the manager by the defendant. The manager may have paraphrased the actual statement. If the defendant said to the manager, "Buy from me, or you'll be sorry," the defendent did not threaten to kill the manager, although the tone of voice and the implications of the statement could have conveyed such a meaning. If the manager states that the defendant used any words other than ". . . or I'll kill you," the court will probably find the verdict in favor of the defendant, based on reasonable doubt that the defendant actually meant that he or she would kill the manager.

Fixing the Judge

Although there are times when Hollywood and the newspapers depict an organized crime group having "fixed" the judge, there are enough legal requirements that must be met before a guilty verdict can be returned to be able to release the organized crime figure legally without any need for the organized crime group to place pressure on the judge. A classic example occurred in Los Angeles. A member of a youth gang was placed on trial for the actual assault and attempted murder of a store manager. The manager was the only witness in the case. During a preliminary hearing, the defense attorney and a person dressed in a fashion similar to that of members of the youth gang sat at the defense table. The judge, after the reading of the charges, asked if the defendant was present. The defense attorney stood and stated that the defendant was represented. The manager took the stand and stated that the man sitting at the defense table was the person who attacked him. The defense attorney repeatedly asked the manager if he was sure. The manager said, "yes." The defense attorney then revealed to the court that the person sitting at the defense table was not the person charged with the crime. In fact, the person at the table was a junior partner in the defense attorney's law firm. In this case, there was no need for pressure to be placed on the judge. Once the manager testified to the fact that another person and not the defendant attacked him, the case was dismissed.

When the small business manager is confronted with organized crime, he or she must clearly understand the nature of such a confrontation and the scope of the organized crime activities in the area. No rash decisions should be made until this complete analysis is performed. Confrontations with organized crime should be handled like any business problem—that is, investigate the situation, outline all the alternatives and the repercussions of each alternative, and then act. During this review, the small business operator should not assume anything. As we have seen, just because a suspect is arrested does not mean that the matter concludes favorably for the manager. Rarely will there ever be a quick, favorable solution that will completely satisfy the manager. Many managers, after making such a review, determine that it is better to find another location—losing the battle, perhaps, but eventually winning the war of survival.

MEANS OF PROTECTION III

What you need to know about security and the law **11**

In several chapters, we have looked briefly at the relationship between a crime victim and the law. Such a relationship is important for the manager to understand in greater detail. The interrelationship between protecting the rights of the business and rights of a criminal has become so complex that, at times, even law enforcement professionals find it difficult to keep up with the legal changes. Citizens who react to criminal situations without knowing some basic points of the legal rights of the criminal are taking a serious risk. Although the citizen may think that he or she is acting within his or her rights in protecting his or her property, the courts may view such actions as criminal in nature, and they could lead to the prosecution of not only the criminal, but also the victim.

The Laws

Laws do not stand still. Governing bodies create laws in order to rectify a particular problem affecting the community as a whole. The problem may be one that remains stable for years, such as murder, whereas others, such as laws regarding horses on city streets, may change with society. Changes also take place in the minds and attitudes of those officials who enforce and adjudicate the laws. Such a condition exists with marijuana laws and decisions. In the 1960s, anyone caught with the drug was treated as an enemy of the state. In the 1970s, a person carrying a small amount of the substance was treated in the same manner as a person who had violated a traffic law. What was a legal sentence for the crime in the 1960s would be declared illegal for the 1970s.

Changes in the attitudes of lawmakers and the courts have obviously had repercussions on the nature of crimes involving the small business manager and the home owner. More and more youngsters are finding out that if they challenge the system and commit a crime, the courts will almost always release them. Many times, the courts see the youngster as misguided, not as a criminal. The courts would rather give a youngster a second, third, and fourth chance before committing the youngster to some form of detention facility.

The small business manager who is the victim of a crime can only react in accordance with the laws that are presently enforced. Before the manager finds him- or herself in a situation that requires him to react to a criminal, the manager should consult with an attorney. The attorney should tell the manager about all the local laws governing the actions of a citizen who seeks to protect and defend his or her property. Although many of the laws throughout the United States have similar definitions, there are fine differences in the law that can make certain actions in one state illegal if the action took place in another state. But there are many similarities, and we will look at a few common points.

Confronting the Criminal

The actions a manager should take when he or she becomes the victim of a crime will, of course, depend on the nature of the crime and the relationship of the manager to the actual crime incident. A common situation a manager will find him- or herself in is one in which the manager confronts the criminal. Unless the crime is robbery, the manager will often surprise the criminal and catch him or her in the act of committing the crime.

Human instinct tells the manager to defend his or her property and rights. Usually, the manager's immediate reaction is to attack the criminal. Two conditions could exist during the confrontation. The criminal may be armed and may threaten the manager with a weapon, or the criminal may be unarmed and not threaten the manager. The manager's right to defend his or her property will differ drastically depending on which of the two conditions exists.

The Equal Force Rule

The general rule of law that applies to these situations comes under the heading of the equal force rule—that is, anyone involved in such a confrontation can use only an equal amount of force in order to defend him- or herself or his or her property. For example, if the criminal is unarmed, the manager is not justified in firing a gun at the criminal; he or she cannot attack the person unless the person shows some signs of violence. Typically, courts have permitted a manager to hold a criminal in custody at gun point as part of a citizen's arrest until the police arrive. Such permission is invalid, however, if the gun held by the manager is not legally registered. Courts have been known to punish the manager of a business who, under the conditions described, fires the gun at the unarmed criminal.

The only time a manager can use deadly force is if his or her life or the life of another is in immediate danger and is threatened by a criminal who intends to use deadly force. The equal force rule is difficult even for lawyers to understand completely. The manager and law enforcement officials, however, are often required to react to a situation on a moment's notice, based on this law. There are obviously many gray areas where a jury could interpret the use of equal force either for the defendant or the plaintiff. Unfortunately for the business person, he or she will not know which way the actions will be seen by the courts until it is too late. Such a situation could arise out of a condition where a manager, who is holding an unarmed criminal at gun point until the police arrive, is struck by a wooden box thrown by the criminal. After the box leaves the criminal's hands, the manager pulls the trigger, killing the suspect. The question for the courts to decide is whether the wooden box was, in fact, a deadly weapon used by the criminal. In the past, courts have decided similar cases, some in favor of the defendant and others in favor of the plaintiff.

In Immediate Danger

Another important rule that the manager should be aware of involves this phrase "The manager's life is in immediate danger." Remember that either the manager's life or the life of another must be threatened to the point where the criminal, at any second, may take that person's life. In any other situation that does not involve this condition, neither the manager nor anyone else can use deadly force. For example, if a manager confronts an armed criminal in the store and the criminal turns and runs toward an exit, the manager does not have the right to shoot the criminal. The manager's life was not in immediate danger, since the criminal was, in fact, leaving the building.

Many courts and lawmakers are of the opinion that the preservation of human life is more important than catching or injuring a criminal. The taking of a human life is therefore only justified if, based on the facts of the situation, the person taking the life has no other recourse than to kill or be killed. But, of course, it is up to the courts to determine whether the conditions relating to the shooting warranted such actions by the person who fired the gun. Rarely are there ever clear-cut situations where all those involved in law enforcement and the courts can agree on the same decision.

The manager should follow some basic guidelines when he or she is the victim of a crime. If the crime involves a confrontation with a criminal, then the manager should let the criminal go about his or her business and leave. Any confrontation can and usually does cause both the criminal and the manager to overreact to the situation. Although the manager may not make any threatening motions to the criminal, the criminal may assume that such threats are forthcoming and may, therefore, make the first move to attack the manager and then escape. Never corner a criminal; always give him or her room to escape. More often than not, the criminal is more interested in escaping than in attacking the manager. But the criminal will usually attack as a last resort.

If the manager discovers a crime scene, he or she should not enter the building or room. He or she should contact the police and wait on the street until the police arrive. Such actions will remove the chance of a confrontation between the criminal and the manager. When the police arrive, the officers, who are both prepared and well trained, will make the initial survey of the building. If the criminal is still present in the building, the police have both fire power and legal knowledge about when to use that force against the criminal.

The manager should always value life over property. Most businesses are—or should be—insured against loss of property. Therefore, the manager is foolish to enter into a confrontation with a criminal over the possession of property. In a confrontation, the manager has no indication as to what the criminal will do: He or she may simply escape or may attack the manager for the fun of it. Avoiding such a confrontation will also avoid unnecessary injury.

TIPS ON DESCRIBING THE THIEF

There will be times when the manager cannot avoid a confrontation with a criminal. This is especially true when the manager is the victim of a robbery. Typically, the manager and his or her employees are surprised by a criminal making demands and waving a gun or knife. No matter what the manager does, there is really no way for anyone to avoid a face-to-face meeting with the criminal. In previous chapters, we have suggested that the best procedure to follow in such a situation is to do nothing but to comply with the criminal's request. The more a manager and others in the store comply, the less likely it is that the criminal will use force to stimulate such compliance.

What You Can Do to Help

The manager and others in the store during the confrontation can and should do something that will later assist police in capturing a criminal—that is, they can take mental notes on the description of the criminal. More often than not, a crime victim will not be able to apprehend the criminal regardless of how hard he or she tries; however, many times, criminals are arrested within minutes following a crime because of a detailed description given to the police by the crime victim. If the victim spends less time during the commission of a crime determining how he or she can physically defend him- or herself or how he or she can capture the criminal and concentrates instead on the identification of the criminal, more criminals could be apprehended by police.

Line law enforcement officers know that descriptions given by crime victims are often of little use. There is a saying, "If you ask ten witnesses of an accident how the accident occurred, you will get ten different answers." There are numerous occasions in which law enforcement officials have accepted statements from witnesses only as a matter of normal procedure, knowing that such statements usually contradict each other and are therefore of little use to the police officer, who must re-create the incident.

Such a conflict occurs because of two major problems: The witness is usually taken by surprise by the incident and may well make certain assumptions that are given to authorities as fact. A victim of a robbery, for example, is not expecting to be robbed, and many thoughts will go through his or her mind during the crime, the least of which is obtaining a good description of the criminal. The victim will naturally be concerned about his or her safety more than about what the criminal looks like. The victim may, in fact, have seen the entire commission of the crime; however, his or her mind is usually not in a proper state to make and note the observation.

Be Sure of the Facts

Witnesses frequently give police officers more than the facts of the case when describing the event or the criminal. A typical accident involving two automobiles illustrates this point. Car "A" was entering an intersection when the traffic light was amber. Car "B" tried to get a jump on the changing of the red light to green and entered the intersection assuming that by the time the car was actually in the intersection, car "B" would have the green light and, therefore, the right of way. The cars obviously collided. Witnesses told police that car "A" failed to stop at the red light and was, therefore, the cause of the accident. What the witnesses saw, however, was slightly different from the account given by them to the police. The witnesses, in fact, did not look at the accident or the light until after they heard the crash. At the time of the crash, both cars were in the intersection, and the light showed red for car "A" and green for car "B". Witnesses who only noticed the situation after the collision assumed that car "A" did not have the right of way, since when they saw the car, the light had already turned red.

Many witnesses will look at a situation and assume that it could have been caused only by a certain action. Therefore, what the witness tells the police is not fact but the results of a mental assumption. For example, the witness will reason that if the car had an accident in the intersection and if, at the moment the witness heard the collison, the traffic light was red, the car had therefore failed to stop at the red light. The witness will only tell the police his or her conclusion—that the car failed to stop at the red light.

The manager who has become the victim of a crime should avoid making any assumptions about the event and the criminal. As in our example involving the accident, the witness may be wrong, even though he or she sincerely believes that what he or she is telling the police is true. When giving any information to the police, always give just the facts in the case, based on what you actually saw. Police will be able to take facts, not conclusions given by witnesses, and with additional investigation, arrive at a logical conclusion that takes into consideration all the possible outcomes to the event.

An example that clearly illustrates that what appears to be happening actually isn't happening involved the branch of a bank in New York City. The city was hit by a series of bank robberies. One day, a well-dressed, elderly man walked over to the customer's courtesy desk and filled out a withdrawal slip. He handed the slip over to the teller and waited. The teller looked at the slip and, for some unknown reason, turned the slip over. The back of the withdrawal slip contained a message: "Give me all the money if you value your life." Without missing a beat, the teller sounded the silent alarm and then stalled as she prepared the money for the elderly man. When the police arrived, the man was still waiting for his money. The police officers confirmed what the teller had seen. The withdrawal slip did, in fact, contain the note. Police asked the elderly man what he was doing. The man replied that he was making a withdrawal. The police officers laughed, placed the man in custody, and brought him down to police headquarters to be booked on charges of bank robbery.

In reality, although the teller and the bank guard both gave statements saying that the man wrote the note at the courtesy desk, some customer was playing a practical joke. The elderly man had no idea that there was a note on the back of the withdrawal slip. The teller and the bank guard told police that the elderly man wrote the note at the courtesy desk, but both these witnesses only saw the man writing on the slip at the desk—they had no idea what the man was writing. This slight difference could have saved this embarrassing situation from getting out of hand. It was fortunate that police handwriting experts could determine that the handwriting of the elderly man did not match the handwritten note on the back of the withdrawal slip.

What to Look For

The manager who is confronted with a criminal should make mental notes of the facts surrounding the incident as well as noting the description of the criminal. Always describe what you actually see. When two persons walk in the store at the same time, for example, and one of them pulls a gun, don't assume that both persons are criminals. Two people, unknown to each other, have been known to be in the same place at the same time. Their presence together does not always mean that they are associated with each other.

The manager should, of course, note several items in as much detail as possible: the type of weapon, the clothes the criminal is wearing, and the manner in which he or she conducts him- or herself during the crime. Police find it important to know whether the suspect walked with a limp or whether he or she had no visible handicap. Of course, a basic description of the suspect must include sex, height, weight, complexion, nationality, and any descriptive marks on the person's body or clothes.

The manager should, after the crime has occurred, try to determine whether there were any incidents that could have led up to the commission of the crime. For example, when the manager last looked out of the store, were there any suspicious situations, such as persons loitering in the area? Did the manager get a feeling that he or she was being followed? There are some criminals who actually plan the crime and will have a rehearsal, unbeknownst to the victims, before the actual crime occurs. Many times, this rehearsal will make the suspect appear to stand out from all the other customers. Such a condition could exist, for example, if the suspect spends too much time in one part of the store, longer than even the most undecided customer. If such incidents preceded the crime, the manager should make this information available to the police.

Everything a crime victim sees during the commission of a crime, including the means of the criminal's escape, is important for the manager to note. This information should, if possible, be communicated to the police as soon after the crime as possible—even over the telephone. Above all, the manager must relay only facts, not assumptions.

Ten Ways to Describe a Thief

1. Height.
2. Weight.
3. Complexion.
4. Color of eyes and hair.
5. Clothing.
6. Any defects.
7. Type of weapon.
8. Mannerisms during the crime.
9. Direction of escape.
10. Method of escape.

The statements given to police by the crime victim become the initial step in the apprehension and prosecution of the criminal. A timely and accurate statement can save the police a great deal of time in tracking down the suspect. Once the suspect has been apprehended, law enforcement officials will then try to prove to a court and jury that the suspect actually committed the crime. Such proof is based on the legal term evidence. Evidence constitutes the facts involving the nature of the crime and the suspect that would make a reasonable man believe, without a doubt, that the suspect actually committed the crime.

Sufficient Evidence

Crime victims are deeply involved with the rules of evidence even though most victims have no idea of the existence of such rules. Crime victims, without an exception, feel that since the police have arrested the suspect that the victim clearly identified as the person who committed the crime, the courts will automatically punish the criminal. But, as we pointed out in earlier chapters, the legal system is just not as cut and dried as most crime victims believe. The suspect, of course, is completely innocent of the charges until the state presents to the court enough evidence to alter this opinion. The road to convicting a suspect of a crime is long for both the suspect and the crime victim.

In recent years, the law enforcement community and those in the legal profession have set out to streamline the legal system, especially when the cases require a jury and a complete trial, which occurs frequently in criminal cases. In some states, this streamlining takes the form of steps in the legal process to be taken before the case comes before a judge, where authorities will determine whether there is enough evidence to warrant the time and money of the judicial system being spent on the case.

Experienced police officers have been through criminal proceedings time and time again. Officers know what degree of evidence is usually required before there is a reasonable chance of conviction. For example, if a person is seen by the manager running down the street near the store, and if the manager then realizes that the store has been burglarized, he or she may conclude that the person who was running committed the crime. Police, called by the manager, may apprehend the suspect. At this point, the police must determine whether there is sufficient evidence to warrant charging the suspect with the crime of burglary. In this case, the police and the courts would require one of the following: that the manager actually saw the suspect on the manager's property, that the suspect admitted committing the crime, or that the suspect was seen inside the store. Without such evidence, the suspect will not be convicted—even if charged with the crime. In this situation, the manager did not see the suspect on the property but only saw him running on the street near the property. The suspect did not admit the crime to the police, nor did he have any merchandise on his person when he was arrested by the police that would indicate that he was inside the manager's store. There were no signs inside the store demonstrating that the suspect had actually been inside the building. So, although the suspect may have actually committed the crime, there is not enough evidence available to prove the case in court.

At this point in the investigation, law enforcement authorities will often not press the charges and will try to discourage the manager from doing so. Authorities know from experience that such a case, based on the evidence at hand, would not be successfully prosecuted and that, therefore, the time and energy spent by authorities in bringing the suspect to trial would be wasted. Some law enforcement officials and experienced criminals look at the legal process as a type of game. Both the official and the criminal know the rules of evidence. For the criminal, the objective is to commit the crime without giving the authorities enough evidence to prosecute him or her if he or she is apprehended. For the police, the objective is to hope that they can enter the case soon enough to develop enough evidence against the criminal. Usually, the longer time there is between police intervention and the crime, the less likely it is that there will be enough evidence available to prosecute a suspect successfully.

To the crime victim, the standard police and judicial procedures of releasing a suspect whom the victim knows is guilty of a crime can disillusion the victim as to whether the legal system is protecting the criminal or the victim. The legal system and those officials who supervise the system are usually on the side of the victim; however, there are certain guidelines that, regardless of the feelings of law enforcement officials, everyone must abide by. There have been many cases in which law enforcement officers have known that the suspect has been guilty of the crime, but they have not been able to prove the case in a court of law.

Types of Evidence

There are two basic types of evidence that courts will accept—factual and direct evidence, such as a confession or a witness's testimony, and circumstantial evidence, such as two people being in a locked room with a gun on the table and one of the persons being found murdered from a gunshot wound. No one actually saw the murder, but the circumstances of the situation do not allow a reasonable man to believe anything except that the other person in the room committed the murder. Courts try to avoid convicting a suspect based on circumstantial evidence unless, as in this example, no other possibility could have existed.

The crime victim must understand that only direct evidence will usually bring about a guilty verdict, except in extreme cases. A case that illustrates this point occurred in New Jersey. A person was walking down a street at night. The light was very poor. A black man came from behind, placed a pointed instrument in the person's back, and stole the victim's wallet. The victim only noticed that the person was black and that he wore dark clothes. The victim lost sight of the attacker but did manage to tell officers in a passing patrol car in which direction the attacker had escaped. The victim and the police drove around the immediate area. Within seconds, the victim noticed a black man in dark clothes about a block or two away from where the attack took place. The victim quickly identified the person as the attacker, and the police brought both the suspect and the victim to police headquarters for questioning. A search of the suspect revealed that he was carrying a small pocket knife that was closed at the time of the arrest and that he had about ten dollars in his pocket.

The victim was more than willing to give the police a formal statement about what occurred. Police, on the other hand, were not at all quick to charge the suspect with the crime. The police had only circumstantial evidence in the case and very little direct evidence. The victim's only direct evidence was that the attacker had used a pointed object in the victim's back and had removed the victim's wallet and that the attacker was black and wore dark clothes.

On the other hand, the only evidence the police had about the suspect was that the suspect was black and wore dark clothes. The suspect was a few blocks away from the scene of the crime. The suspect did have a pointed instrument in his possession—the pocket knife. Although the suspect did not have the missing wallet in his possession, he did have ten dollars in his pocket.

The problem with the evidence police did have about the crime was that the suspect might have been the first black man in dark clothes that the victim saw. Because the attack was made from behind and in the dark, the victim never actually got a good look at the attacker. The description given to police could have fit thousands of men in the area. There was a good chance that if the police had driven in a different direction, the victim would have identified an entirely different black man as the suspect. The suspect did have a knife, but so do many people, especially when walking the street late at night. Besides, the victim did not know whether the attacker used a knife or just a finger. The evidence against the suspect was circumstantial and did not contain enough facts for the courts to be able to prosecute the suspect successfully. The key element that was missing in this case was the wallet. If the suspect had had the missing wallet on his person, the circumstantial evidence would have been supported by important and conclusive direct evidence. This is not to say that the suspect who was detained was not the attacker. The suspect could very well have been the attacker, but the evidence did not support such a claim.

The crime victim must understand that unless law enforcement officials and the courts have strong evidence against a suspect, the suspect will not be prosecuted further than the arrest. To a victim of a crime, such a release may give the appearance that the system does not care about the victim. In fact, the system does care and is trying not to waste everyone's time needlessly.

A VICTIM'S GUIDE TO THE COURTS

The courts are primarily designed to make a judgment as to the guilt or innocence of a defendant based on evidence presented by the prosecution. The purpose of the courts is simple, but how the courts carry out this purpose can appear complicated to the crime victim. As we have mentioned, the court system has recently been designed to speed up trials and halt unnecessary and unwarranted prosecutions. But before discussing the various mechanisms that have been established to streamline the court system, let us first take an overall look at the judicial system.

Classification of Laws

Each state has a modified version of the typical judicial system, but most states do have three general classifications of laws: disorderly persons, misdemeanors, and felonies. Every law falls into one of these three categories. The disorderly person category usually involves a lesser violation of the criminal code, such as barroom fights and traffic violations. Misdemeanors are crimes that are more serious than those labeled disorderly person complaints. These may include such crimes as assault with a motor vehicle or simple burglary. The most serious crimes fall into the felony classification. These include armed robbery and murder. The actual classification of a particular crime will, of course, differ in every state.

In order to deal with such violations, the judicial system is constructed in such a way as to have particular courts to handle the various classifications of crime. For example, only a county or state court would normally handle misdemeanors and felony charges, whereas disorderly person complaints are normally handled in municipal court. A person who is charged with murder, for example, would not appear in the same courtroom as the person involved in a simple barroom fight. The courts mentioned here are involved only in criminal actions and are totally divorced from civil actions, the most common of which are settled in small claims court.

The Judge and His Powers

Each court is, of course, operated by a judge, who is either elected by the community or appointed by political channels. The judge has very broad boundaries within which to operate his or her court. Whenever, during a trial, a rule of law can be interpreted in several ways, the judge's interpretation is the final decision on the question. The judge can allow or disallow witnesses and evidence during a hearing and has total power to force anyone in the courtroom, including onlookers, to behave in a certain manner. The judge alone can at will declare anyone in the courtroom in contempt of court and send that person to jail.

Because the powers of a judge have been loosely defined and interpreted, there have been cases in which judges have appeared to exceed the limits that a prudent man would normally define as the limitations of a judge's power. For example, a judge in New York City has been noted for his decisions on permitting hardened criminals who have long histories of violent crimes to be released without bail when they are charged with similar violent crimes. Although law enforcement officials, members of the legal professions, political leaders, and the public have publicly shown a dislike for the decisions made by this judge, legally, there is little anyone could or would do to curtail the judge's power to rule in his court. As long as a judge does not exceed his or her authority, no higher judicial body will ever step in to punish the judge or limit his or her effectiveness. There have been times, however, when unofficial reprimands have been voiced against those judges who overstep reasonable guidelines.

The Legal Process

The process that brings a criminal to trial starts when the police enter the case. Law enforcement officials must gather enough evidence against a suspect before the person can be formally charged with a crime. Once the evidence is developed, a superior officer of the police department will usually determine whether there is sufficient evidence to actually file criminal charges against the suspect. If there isn't, the suspect will be released. Usually, police can detain a suspect for 24 hours before law enforcement officers are required, by law, either to charge the suspect with a crime or to release him or her.

If it appears that enough evidence does exist, the suspect is then charged with the crime. His or her photograph is taken, and his or her fingerprints are checked against those of suspects wanted for other crimes. Following the procedural booking process, the police present the case to a representative from the local prosecutor's office, who again reviews the facts in the case and the evidence against the suspect. If the member of the prosecutor's staff agrees that there is enough evidence to proceed, the suspect is brought before a judge in what is called a bail hearing. It should be pointed out that if the prosecutor does not agree with the police as to the quantity of evidence against the suspect, the prosecutor can have the suspect released.

At a bail hearing, the suspect is brought before the judge, where the prosecutor informs the court of the charges and some of the evidence. The judge then determines whether or not the suspect, although still not guilty, should appear for the next step in the judicial process, called a preliminary hearing. If the judge feels that the suspect will not appear, the judge may require the suspect to post a high amount of bail. On the other hand, if the suspect is likely to appear at the hearing, the judge may not require any bail. After the bail hearing, the suspect is permitted to leave the court as long as the bail requirement, if any, has been satisfied.

At the preliminary hearing, another judge will hear the evidence presented by the prosecutor against the defendant. The defendant does have tne right to an attorney to represent him or her; however, the attorney cannot introduce any evidence that will negate the evidence presented by the prosecutor. The attorney's only means of "fighting" the charges at this point is to cross-examine those witnesses who testify for the prosecutor. The only purpose of a preliminary hearing is not to determine guilt or innocence but to determine first, that a crime did, in fact, occur and, second, that the defendant could have committed the crime. Usually,

232

preliminary hearings are used in cases more serious than a disorderly person crime classification. The judge at a preliminary hearing can only make one of two decisions. The judge can either find that a crime has occurred and that the defendant could have committed the crime or find that one of these two requirements has not been met; if the latter, the judge frees the defendant. If the judge continues the judicial process, the next step is usually the grand jury. Also, after the judge's decision, the defendant's bail arrangement can either be continued or altered.

The grand jury is a group of citizens who are selected according to a number of techniques used for jury selection in each state. These lay individuals sit as a panel behind closed doors and hear evidence presented by the prosecutor against the defendant. Usually, the defense attorney is not present during this hearing. Members of the jury can ask witnesses and the prosecutor questions about the case and can even ask for additional evidence before reaching a decision. The purpose of a grand jury is to prevent unnecessary criminal charges from taking up a court's time. Like that of the judge in a preliminary hearing, the grand jury's prime purpose is to hear the charges against the defendant as well as all the evidence in the case. If the grand jury feels that the defendant could have committed the crime, the panel votes an indictment, which is nothing more than a formal statement by the state saying that "we accuse the defendant of the crime."

An indictment is not a guilty verdict. Remember that only one side of the case has been presented. The defendant has not given his or her explanation of the charges. Grand juries have frequently been used by prosecutors who seek elected office. Since the prosecutor controls what is presented to a grand jury, the prosecutor will have almost total control over who is and who is not indicted. Usually, an indictment by a grand jury will draw newspaper headlines and publicity for the prosecutor. Even if there is really no conclusive evidence against a defendant, who is later found innocent by the courts, grand juries have been known to return an indictment.

The next step in the process is a pretrial hearing between the prosecutor and the defense attorney. Usually, all the evidence is presented in this informal meeting with the judge and lawyers. At this time, if the evidence warrants it, the prosecutor, trying to avoid a trial, will enter a plea-bargaining arrangement whereby the defendant pleads guilty to a lesser charge and receives a lesser sentence. If everyone agrees, the case is adjudicated. If there is no agreement, the case goes to trial, where the evidence is presented, and either a judge or a jury decides the verdict— guilty or not guilty.

Steps in the Judicial System

Disorderly Person	*Felony*
1. Arrest.	1. Arrest.
2. Booking.	2. Booking.
3. Bail hearing.	3. Bail hearing.
4. Trail.	4. Preliminary hearing.
	5. Grand jury hearing.
	6. Pretrial hearing.
	7. Trial.

A VICTIM'S GUIDE TO THE POLICE

Throughout the entire legal process, the crime victim is given a less important role than most victims feel is justified. The victim may testify briefly against the defendant at a preliminary hearing and then before a grand jury. If the case goes to trial, the victim will again be called upon to testify once more. Rarely will the victim ever be informed as to the outcome of such testimony. This is especially true in cases that do not attract attention of the news media. Many times, the only members of the legal system who appear somewhat compassionate are the police. Usually, the prosecutors are too busy with other cases to become personally involved with the victim of each case. Since the police are the first and possibly the most important contact the victim has with the legal system, potential victims should have a better understanding of how the police function.

Types of Police Departments

There are three types of police departments: the large city departments, the more common small departments, and the police departments depicted in the movies. The larger city police departments will be organized into smaller groups called precincts and into specialty groups, such as a major crime unit, a detective squad, and the like. The larger police department will usually be operated by a police commissioner, who is either elected or appointed. The commissioner is not a police officer and usually does not have any police powers himself, such as carrying a firearm, but the commissioner can give directives that all police officers must follow. If these directives are not followed, disciplinary actions, including dismissal from the force, could follow. Each unit is usually under the direction of a police captain, who is responsible for the personnel under his or her command as well as for the enforcement of the laws within the jurisdiction of the unit. Some large police departments are also organized into areas where an officer superior to a police captain is in command. The actual operation of a large police department is more in the style of the miliary or of large corporations. All matters that are part of the normal daily routine are handled on the lowest possible command level, such as the police captain. Only those matters that are exceptions to normal routine and require higher policy decisions are handled by police executives higher in command than a captain.

The smaller police department will be organized much differently than the city department. The head of the police department in a small community is usually the chief of police. The chief is responsible either to a town administrator or to local elected officials. Usually, the town administrator or elected officials do not have the power to order a police officer to perform a certain task. Many times, either the police chief or the governing body as a unit has this power. Of course, such power differs from location to location. Typically, the small town police department will have three divisions: the patrol division, the detective division, and the juvenile division. All the divisions except the patrol division will be made up of only one police officer. Most of the officers will be on patrol. The actual operation of the small police department will be more like a neighborhood business than a large corporation, more like a local unit of the National Guard than the U.S. Army.

The movie version of the police department, which, for most members of the public, is the only image of the police they have, is far from the real situation. On the screen, police are usually shown as being highly professional in their work and as following strict departmental policies covering almost every situation an officer can be called on to handle. In reality, such high professionalism is only seen, at best, in highly prestigious law enforcement agencies, such as the FBI and the Secret Service. Few police departments operate on well-defined policies. Many times, after an officer has undergone basic training, he or she is left to learn the ropes on the street with only a few guiding comments from experienced officers. In fact, there are some small police departments that do not give either new or experienced police officers any formal training in police work.

The actual day-to-day job of a police officer has been dramatized by screenwriters time and time again. If people were to believe what they see in the movies, police officers would be involved in gun battles almost every day. Nothing can be further from the truth. Most police officers have never drawn their guns more than twice in their law enforcement careers. In fact, most police officers have never fired their guns in the line of duty. Of course, in larger cities having a high crime rate, there will be more times when a police officer uses a gun in the line of duty, but there are relatively few large cities in the United States. Most police officers work for small police departments in communities with relatively low crime rates.

A typical day in the life of a member of a small police force begins as he or she reports for work at 8 A.M. After he or she signs on duty, the officer will patrol the streets of the town until about noontime. During this period, he or she will usually be asked directions several times, will write a few parking tickets, and will check that local businesses open without any problems. In the morning, security alarms at many of the local businesses often sound when the manager opens shop. As part of good police practice, the officer must check to make sure that the manager and not a criminal caused the alarm. After an hour for lunch, the officer will again drive through the streets of the community for another four hours. Frequently, the only calls the officer will have to respond to are a medical emergency, an investigation of strange noises around a resident's house, helping a stranded motorist, or investigating a suspicious person. On rare occasions, the officer will be called on to handle a fire, investigate a crime, or deal with a barroom fight

Motivation Problems

Considering that some communities are perhaps a mile square, police officers on patrol frequently find it difficult to keep attentive during a shift. The most important question that is usually asked by superior police officers is, ''How many times can an officer drive within a square mile during an eight-hour shift before he or she becomes bored?'' The answer to this question and the resulting solution to the problem are not easy to find. Usually, a new officer is self-motivated when starting his or her new job, but after five years on the job, this motivation is almost completely lost. The officer begins to look at the job as something he or she has to do—put in the eight hours and go home. Departments, especially smaller departments, will find that such a low morale problem may interfere with the few times the officer has to handle an important police function. The people in

LAW ENFORCEMENT OFFICERS KILLED
1969-1978

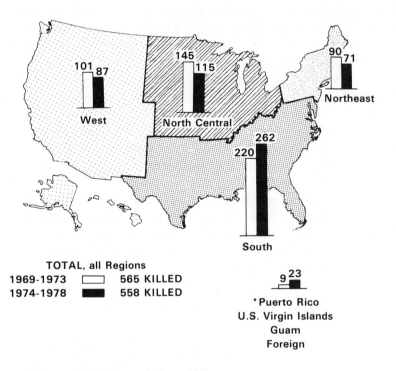

101 87
West

145 115
North Central

90 71
Northeast

262 220
South

TOTAL, all Regions
1969-1973 □ 565 KILLED
1974-1978 ■ 558 KILLED

9 23
*Puerto Rico
U.S. Virgin Islands
Guam
Foreign

*Data not available for years prior to 1971.

Figure 11-1
From *The Uniform Crime Report* (Washington: Federal Bureau of
Investigation, 1979).

the community usually become directly affected by a low morale problem
within the department.

Police department officials try to avoid this problem by shifting the
duties of each officer every five years. First, the officer is on patrol. When
boredom begins to set in, the officer is switched to the detective division.
After another five years, the officer is moved to the juvenile division.

237

Promotions within small police departments are not frequent. Some police officers must wait ten or more years before they receive their first promotion. The prime reason for such a policy is that there are not enough promotable positions available in the small department; any turnover in manpower is usually caused by illness or retirement.

The larger police department also faces the same motivation problems, but there are usually enough special units and promotable positions in the department to keep a police officer's interest high. Also, in the larger department, the actual daily routine of a police officer is different from that of the officer's counterpart in the small department. The officer on patrol in a large police department may have about the same area to cover as the officer in the smaller department, but usually the city police have more calls that involve the use of the officer's police training. In a large city, there is always a strong possibility that the officer will have to use his or her gun, whereas in the smaller town, such a likelihood is far removed from reality (see Figure 11–1 for statistics on police deaths).

There are many important points that the small business manager should consider regarding the security of his or her business and the law. The real environment that the business manager must contend with is drastically different from that shown in the newspapers and depicted on television. In reality, the police do not always catch the criminal. The law does protect the rights of the victim, but not at the risk of placing an innocent person behind bars. Crime, in fact, does pay as long as the criminal knows the ropes in the law that will permit freedom even if the criminal is caught.

Key facts about insurance 12

WHAT KIND OF PROTECTION YOU WILL NEED

In the old West, the only insurance a business manager needed was his or her trusty gun. As long as the gun was in working condition and the manager could shoot straight, all problems facing the manager could usually be handled successfully. Times have changed since a gun was the lifeline of a business manager. Today, however, some managers feel that the tide has come full circle and that the only insurance policy the manager requires is a gun at his or her side.

Guns as Insurance

Conditions for small business managers in the inner cities are, in fact, close to the situation that existed in the old West. As we have seen, the judicial system and law enforcement officers are working to protect the rights of the innocent crime victim. Such protection often appears almost nonexistent because of the various legal requirements that must be fulfilled before a criminal is found guilty. For the business manager in the inner city, the problem is like a double-edged sword. The legal system, for whatever reason, is not keeping the criminals off the streets and in the jails. Time and time again, the same store managers are victims—sometimes of the same criminals. Police may arrest the suspect, but before the officers are back on patrol, the suspect is on the streets.

The other problem with small business managers in the inner cities is that insurance companies are finding it harder and harder to write policies to cover people and businesses in high-crime neighborhoods. If lucky, shopkeepers, when dealing with insurance protection, are left with two alternatives. Either the manager will have to pay extremely high insurance premiums on policies that contain high deductibles or he or she will have to operate the business without insurance. There are some unlucky managers who cannot purchase insurance at any price. Under these conditions, many store operators have taken to the only protection that will not fail them—a gun.

Most small business managers will not have to go to such extremes to ensure the safe and continual operation of the business. Those who do face the alternative of insurance by sidearm should consider relocating the business. Using a gun as insurance is more dangerous than operating the business with no coverage at all. A business with no coverage will stand to lose property, whereas a business protected by a gun can lose both property and the life of the manager and customers.

Since most business managers do not face such alternatives and do have the availability of insurance coverage at a reasonable price, the most important question for the manager to decide is what kind of insurance protection is required. The variety of available insurance policies is almost endless. Insurance can sometimes be similar to having a car repaired: Never tell a mechanic to fix whatever is wrong with the car. Similarly, never tell an insurance agent to give you all the coverage you need. Only very large corporations can usually afford the price of complete insurance coverage from all possible occurrences.

Before contacting any insurance company, the business manager must make an inventory of the things that could happen that would have a serious impact on the continuous operation of the business. There are, of course, natural disasters that could cause anything from a long power failure to the destruction of the building. A power failure for a long period of time could have a serious effect on a business that requires its inventory to be frozen, for example. A great loss of such inventory could force the business into bankruptcy.

Events to Insure Against

The list of events that a business should be insured against is long and will differ from business to business. Since the major concern of this book is business security, there are few conditions that the manager must consider while taking this inventory. The small business should be covered by insurance for burglary. The policy must include repair of the damage caused by the burglar as well as payment for any goods stolen in the burglary. The manager must also be prepared for claims made by either the burglar or law enforcement officials who may have injured themselves through a condition existing in the building that was caused by the burglary. There have been strange cases where the victim of a crime has been successfully sued by the criminal over a negligent condition. The manager must also be covered for any claims made by customers. For example, if the business is involved in the printing of sales material for a client and the burglar, for some unknown reason, stole this material, the manager's contract with the client will still be enforced. Usually, clients will have schedules to meet, and if the manager does not deliver the goods on time, which causes the client to lose sales, the manager may be held liable for the client's loss. Therefore, any insurance policy should protect the client as well as the manager under such situations.

In the case of robbery, again there are certain events that could take place for which the manager may be held responsible. For example, some courts have held that customers who are injured by a robber on the property of the business can hold the business responsible for any damages to the customer. The manager must also have coverage in case he or she is injured in a robbery. Without question, any money or merchandise stolen in a robbery must also be covered. There have also been occasions when the robber, after leaving the business, has discovered that the manager is following him or her. The robber may fire a weapon, missing the manager but striking an onlooker. Some courts have held that such an action by the manager was negligent and have allowed the business to be sued by the onlooker.

There have been countless cases where the manager, depending on the opinion of a local insurance agent, has not been covered for these unseen events. The penalty for not having full coverage can be devastating for the small business. If the business requires the manager to be present

241

during operating hours, and if the manager is injured during a crime, the business could be out of business and not earning money until the manager is able to reopen it. Such a financial loss may not be recoverable.

When purchasing an insurance policy, never agree to a policy unless you know that every necessary item involving your business is covered. Logically, compare the inventory of events that could happen with the provisions of a typical insurance policy. There is a good chance that a few important items on the inventory list will not be included in the coverage supplied by the policy. Many times, additional riders and policies must be purchased in order to ensure proper coverage. If the policy is too expensive, the manager should consider whether the neighborhood has changed to the extent that the business should be relocated.

HOW TO DOCUMENT YOUR VALUABLES

The insurance business is like any other busiess: Its prime objective is to make money. The small business manager opens a business and risks the possibility that there is not enough of a market for the product to support the activity; the insurance company does almost the same thing. The insurance company weighs the probability of an occurrence and the impact of that occurrence against the premiums received for protection. Through careful analysis by insurance company executives, the premiums received for a certain type of coverage far exceed the probable expense to the insurance company when such an occurrence happens.

Most insurance company representatives are more than happy to visit a business manager and submit suggested policies and prices. Even when the business manager files a claim, the insurance company representative is again happy to assist the manager; however, the insurance company may then be a little less trusting of the manager. For some reason, when the manager takes out an insurance policy to cover valuables of a certain dollar amount, the insurance company rarely requires the manager to prove that these valuables exist. However, when the manager files a claim, the insurance company usually becomes interested in evidence to prove not only that valuables were taken from the building but also that they were there in the first place.

Many business managers and home owners have found themselves with very serious problems over insurance company claims. Few of these people could prove to the insurance company that valuables that were stolen had actually existed. Without such proof, insurance companies usually only pay the policyholder a token amount for the loss.

Steps to Take

Before the manager decides to purchase insurance coverage, there are a few steps that he or she should take in order to prepare for an insurance claim, should one arise. Similar to the inventory of events that could have a serious impact on the business, the manager should make an inventory of the items normally contained on the business property. Without question, most business managers can make a good accounting of inventory items and equipment frequently used in the business. However, there are other items—personal items belonging to employees and to the manager—that are not normally inventoried. For example, although a typewriter and a cash register will appear on the records of the business, rarely will a television set, a radio, a stereo, and the like—items that are of personal use to the staff—be listed anywhere on the records.

In particular, items that are not required to operate the business but that are present at the location of the business should be documented. Insurance company representatives may not question, for example, a waxer in a typesetting business, but they will question the loss of a stereo system and a television set from the typesetting business, even though the president or manager of the business may frequently use the entertainment system in his or her office. But before the insurance company would pay a claim that included the entertainment system, the company would require the manager to show evidence that the system did exist.

Insurance companies are usually more than willing to pay a claim that is supported by documentation. It is up to the manager to arrange for such documentation before the need arises. The documentation required by the insurance company need not be conclusive evidence. Insurance companies will usually give the manager who is making a claim the benefit of any doubt; however, more evidence than the manager's statement will be required in order to support a claim.

In preparing such documentation, the manager should develop a complete inventory list for the business. One is usually available from the accounting records. The list should include all items normally found on the business premises, including goods that are considered the niceties of a business, such as television sets. The inventory must indicate the type of good; the serial number, if available; the date the good was obtained; and the purhcase price of the item. Once the list is prepared, the manager will

243

know the dollar value of an insurance policy required to cover a total loss of property. The manager should make several copies of this inventory list. One copy should be given to the insurance company, another should be kept on the premises, and yet another should be given to the attorney for the business. Every quarter, the manager must update this list and redistribute copies to the appropriate parties.

The manager must also keep, in a secure location, receipts from purchases of each item on the inventory list. These receipts will serve as another piece of available documentation to the insurance company in case the manager files a claim. Besides documenting the existence of the item, the receipts also serve another purpose. Since the insurance company and the manager will have to settle on the value of the goods that were stolen or destroyed, the dollar value on the receipts will usually be the starting place for the insurance company when arriving at a settlement offer.

There will be times when the manager will be unable to furnish either an inventory list or receipts to the insurance company. But there is another method of documentation that the manager can prepare that can serve as proof that an item existed. The manager can take several photographs of the inside of the business and of each individual item in the building. A good clear photograph can be presented to an insurance company as documentation that the item did, in fact, exist in the store.

If possible, the photographs should also be sent to the insurance company soon after the policy is written, as well as to the attorney for the business. As we have seen, most insurance company representatives will give the manager the benefit of the doubt when settling a claim. If the insurance company is presented with the list of goods at the time the policy is written, the company representative will, many times, accept that list as proof. There will be times, however, when an insurance company representative will require that receipts be presented. This will usually be warranted when individual expensive items are reported stolen. Although the item may be on the inventory list filed with the insurance company, the company representative may spot-check the more expensive items on the list.

Without documentation, the business manager's recovery of the loss will be totally in the hands of the insurance company representative. Remember that the insurance company, although willing to pay a claim, is not in the business of giving money to policyholders unwisely. Some insurance companies have a policy that claims in amounts over a predetermined limit must be totally supported by documentation. Without documentation, the company will not pay more than a small percentage of the loss. Many times, even when managers take insurance companies to court, the judge requires documentation before ordering the insurance company to pay the claim.

Types of Property Documentation

1. Serial numbers.
2. Receipts.
3. Photographs.
4. Inventory list.

WHAT INFORMATION IS REQUIRED IN ORDER TO MAKE A SUCCESSFUL CLAIM

Although the report of a theft or robbery may be out of the normal routine of the business manager, for the police and the insurance companies, such claims are filed, investigated, and paid every day. Business managers have heard that every insurance company does not pay claims as speedily as the company representative had promised when the policy was written. Usually, the insurance company representative will tell the manager almost anything but an outright lie as long as the manager signs the policy contract. Most insurance companies do not purposely stall the payment of claims to policyholders, but there are a few insurance companies who delay payment for cash flow purposes.

Time Limits

In reality, claims are not paid as fast as some policyholders may want simply because the policyholder has failed to submit all the information required by the insurance company when a claim is filed. For those policyholders who provide the insurance company with the necessary data, payments are usually mailed within a few weeks after filing. To prevent the manager from giving insufficient information, there are several points that he or she should consider when making a claim to the insurance company.

First, the manager must contact the insurance company representative, who will list the various kinds of information that the company requires in order to process the claim. Although each insurance company will have different requirements, most companies require that the

245

policyholder give the company the policy number and the normal information about the name and address of the person and business making the claim. The insurance company usually requires a copy of the police report, which can be obtained at police headquarters after the police have concluded their preliminary investigation. The manager must remember that some insurance policies require that the policyholder making a crime-related claim must report the incident to the police within 24 hours after the crime has been discovered. Some business managers, not realizing that such a clause existed in their insurance policies, have lost all rights to protection supplied by the policy. Although major crime incidents will almost always be reported to the police, minor incidents can easily be overlooked by the manager and unreported to authorities.

Insurance Fraud

A few insurance companies also set a time limit as to how long, following an incident, a claim will be honored by the company. The purpose of such a regulation is to cut down the chances of insurance fraud. This is the same reason behind the 24-hour requirement on reporting a crime to the authorities. Forcing a policyholder to contact the police does more for the insurance company than provide hope that law enforcement officials may be able to track down a thief. Most states have a law that makes it a crime for a person to file a false police report. Many persons seeking to collect funds from an insurance company for losses that actually did not occur may think twice before telling the police about the alleged crime. This deterrent is more of a psychological obstacle placed before the policyholder by the insurance company than an effort to apprehend a person either on the grounds of making a false police report or on charges of insurance fraud.

Before leaving the topic of insurance fraud, the manager should be aware of another common clause in an insurance policy. Many policies require, in the case of a burglary, for example, evidence of definite signs of forced entry to the building. Such signs would include pry marks on the door or windows or a broken window with glass fragments present on the floor inside the building. An incident in Maine points out the importance of this statement. A store manager forgot to lock the back door of the shop overnight. It was just the manager's luck that a thief discovered that the door was unlocked and helped himself to the contents of the store. The manager, upon discovering the crime scene, realized that his insurance policy did not cover any burglary unless there was a sign of forced entry.

The manager was mad and so, without thinking, picked up a piece of wood in the store and broke the nearest window he could find.

The manager then quickly called the police to report the crime. When police arrived, they noticed that glass fragments covered the area under the window outside the building. The officers did not bring this point up during discussion with the manager. They just made note of the facts and placed the information in their report. The insurance company, after receiving the manager's claim and a copy of the report, was not so polite. They refused to pay the claim. The manager, who had suffered a material loss from the crime, brought legal action against the company. Unfortunately for the manager, once the insurance company brought out the fact that glass fragments were found outside the building, providing evidence that the window was broken from inside the building, the insurance company won the case.

Mistakes such as the one that occurred in this case are bound to happen to even the most careful manager. Many insurance companies also realize this weakness and have designed riders to policies that will cover the business and the manager in case of a loss regardless of whether the loss occurred when the building was locked or not. The rider, of course, will cost a few extra dollars, but it is well worth the protection.

What to Do if Payment Is Held Up

Although the manager may be prompt in filing the insurance claim form with a copy of the police report, he or she must be prepared to operate the business without the insurance claim payment for at least two to three months following the crime. There have been times when the normal system of filing, investigating, approving, and paying of claims has taken months to complete, even under the most favorable conditions. During this period, the manager must continue to operate the business. If the insurance company should challenge the manager's claim, there is a good chance that the delay between the filing of the claim and the final payment can be as long as a year or more.

Some businesses in such a situation may find it difficult to continue a smooth operation while waiting for payment. There are several alternatives that are open to most small business managers that should be considered under the worst of conditions. For example, if the insurance company has approved payment of the claim but the check is delayed, the manager may be able to use the forthcoming payment as collateral for a short-term loan. Usually, the bank will require a letter from the insurance company stating that there is a delay but that the claim will be honored. Some banks may require that the check from the insurance company be made out both in the bank's name and that of the manager's business. This will protect the bank from giving the loan and then having the manager cash the insurance check without repaying the money to the bank.

If the claim is being held up by the insurance company because a discrepancy was discovered during the insurance investigation, the manager can usually ask for two actions that will immediately release funds to the business. First, the manager can ask the insurance company to make partial payment on the claim for those items that have been approved. Usually, the manager can operate with partial payment. The second alternative is to negotiate with the insurance company. If the company is balking on payment for a certain loss, the manager may be able to settle with the insurance company for less than the amount originally requested. Of course, the manager must be an alert business person. Some insurance company representatives have been known to hold off on the payment of claims knowing that, as the business becomes tight on cash, the company will probably settle the claim for less than the full amount due the policyholder. The manager must determine whether a delay is caused by accident or design.

The Claim Form

On the claim form, the manager will be required to list the items that were lost as well as the value of those items. Such forms should not be made out in haste. Most insurance companies will give the policyholder at least ten days after the incident to file the claim. Once the manager has completed the claim form, it is usually difficult for him or her to add any items to the list of missing goods. Normally, there is always a question as to the value of missing merchandise. As the manager is aware, there are many different dollar values that can be given to the same item. There is the wholesale value and the retail value as well as an inflation value and a replacement value. Some items can depreciate, whereas others appreciate. Therefore, special attention must be given to this portion of the claim form.

The insurance company, of course, will try to value the goods as low as possible, whereas the policyholder will do the reverse. Most times, the insurance company will seek to value the goods at fair market value for the particular area of the country. Of course, the obvious question is, "What is fair market value?" Insurance companies and the courts will survey the manager's peers and determine an average sum for the goods. This will be the declared value for legal and insurance policy purposes. Some goods, however, cannot be easily valued by taking a simple survey. Usually the value of these goods, such as antiques, will be negotiated between the insurance company and the policyholder.

An important consideration that the manager must make is that of replacement cost. Most insurance policies will only cover the business for actual loss, not for replacement cost. For example, a firm in the typesetting business may have made final payment for expensive typesetting equipment. The $10,000 in payments may have been made over a three-year period. If the machine is stolen, the insurance company will only pay the depreciated value of the machine. If the machine had a five-year life, the insurance company may only pay $4,000 to the business. Of course, in order to replace the machine, the manager may have to pay $15,000. The true impact of the loss is not lessened by the fact that the business had insurance.

Insurance can save a business thousands of dollars when a loss occurs, but the business manager cannot purchase insurance in the same manner as he or she would order a case of soda. An insurance policy is an agreement in which nothing is assumed. If the policy does not mention a coverage that the manager needs, it is up to him or her to ask for such coverage before the contract is signed.

TIPS ON SELF-INSURANCE

One of the fastest growing areas of business management concerns the cost savings by a corporation that insures itself against the various losses frequent in its operation. Managers have taken a careful look at the cost of insurance policies compared with the actual amount of claims filed during a given period. For some businesses, the results of this investigation have proven very interesting. If a business has not filed many claims in the past for losses covered by insurance, then, according to some business managers, there is an excellent chance that the same condition will continue in the future. Money spent on insurance premiums can then be diverted into a more productive activity.

With more and more companies and municipalities confronted by increasing insurance costs, managers are seriously considering the concept of self-insurance as an alternative to the high expenses of the more common insurance policy. The determining factors that may lead a manager to select the self-insurance plan are very basic to any business manager and gam-

249

bler. The criteria that must be met before a manager can direct all efforts toward a self-insurance program are having the probability of the loss in the favor of the business and having the guts to gamble on the accuracy of that probability.

The Chances of Winning the Gamble

In short, the determining factor is whether or not the manager is willing to gamble that a loss will not occur, or, at least, that it will not occur until some time in the distant future. Although the concept of self-insurance does deal with the same considerations that a poker player faces when playing a hand, there are two important financial benefits that the business can realize if the business manager "wins" the hand. First of all, the manager will normally bet that the loss will occur within a very short time from when the insurance policy is written, whereas the insurance company is betting that the loss will not occur for a longer period. The insurance company accepts the money in the form of premiums and then invests the funds. The business manager, of course, does not have the availability of the funds to invest and also loses any interest on the money that would have been realized if the money had been stored in an interest-bearing account.

Over the years, if the insurance company "wins" the bet, the money received from the premiums plus gains on the funds from premiums previously paid over the years begin to amount to a sizable sum. The business manager, who has lost the bet through the years, will have been minus the money paid to the insurance company as well as minus any possible gain that he or she could have received from managing the funds properly. If the manager never files an insurance claim, there is a good chance that the money paid to the insurance company is a total loss to the business.

Of course, the question is "What would happen if the insurance company lost the bet and the manager won?" The insurance company's risk is not as severe as one might believe at first glance. If the insurance company lost a bet in the distant future, many times the company would have received enough money in premiums and gains from previously paid premiums to reduce the out-of-pocket cash loss to almost nothing. Remember that, on those claims the insurance company pays, the items covered by the policy are covered for depreciated value rather than for replacement cost. For example, a machine originally costing $10,000 with a life of five years would depreciate $2,000 per year. As long as the loss was realized three or four years after the purchase, the payment by the insurance company to the policyholder would be far less than the value of the machine when the device was new.

The real gamble that both the insurance company and the policyholder is taking is on how long the policy will be in effect before a loss is realized. The shorter the period, the better it is for the policyholder. The longer the period before a claim is filed, the better it is for the insurance company. The same gamble is taken when a business decides to develop a self-insurance plan. If the business realizes a loss shortly after the plan has started, then there can be serious repercussions for the business, depending on the nature of the loss. Of course, the longer the time from the start of the self-insurance plan before the loss occurs the more funds have been made available to pay for the loss.

Considering the Decision

For the small business manager, the decision to develop a self-insurance plan must not be made in haste. Many small business managers will find that although a self-insurance plan may save money for very large corporations, unless the risks are carefully reviewed, such a plan can cost the small business more than if a more common insurance policy had been purchased. For example, a large corporation with sales and profits in the high millions of dollars may find it very easy to pay a loss of $25,000 through a self-insurance plan, but the same will rarely hold true for a small business.

The important point for the manager to review very carefully involves the nature of the loss. Some insurance policies are, in essence, self-insurance policies where the policyholder pays an additional fee to the insurance company for the paperwork. This may sound confusing, but the following illustration will make the point clear. A manager of a small business purchased a health insurance policy to cover himself. Other employees were not covered by the plan. The policy stated that any emergency care would be paid by the insurance company as long as the amount was about $500. The manager studied the policy and learned that any long-term illness or care given outside the emergency room would not be covered. For this policy, the manager paid about $35 a month in premiums. The manager's accountant, who looked at the policy, told the manager that he would be better off developing his own self-insurance plan, at least for the coverage given by this policy.

According to the accountant, most, if not all, emergency room care can be received for less than $500. For those occasions when an extensive injury is incurred, treatment for such a condition is usually given outside the emergency room and, therefore, would not be covered by the insurance policy anyway. In essence, according to the accountant, the manager would have to pay for most, if not all, of any emergency room care out of the business funds and, on top of that, would have to pay the insurance company $35 a month for what appeared to be the privilege of not being covered for his most frequent losses.

The accountant then told the manager to cancel this insurance coverage and place $35 a month in the bank or in some other interest-bearing account. In a little over two years, the manager could have enough money in the account to cover most of the frequent losses occurring through emergency room care. Of course, the manager did continue a long-term medical insurance policy that he could not easily convert to a self-insurance plan.

The small business manager must carefully review all existing insurance policies in order to determine exactly what losses the business is covered for and the terms of that coverage. There will be times when such a review will indicate areas where the small business can convert to a self-insurance program; at other times, this will not be the case. The most important aspect to remember about self-insurance is that the manager must gamble in the same way the insurance company does. The only difference is that the insurance company can spread the loss over a wide number of policyholders who continue to pay premiums without filing claims. The small business does not have this advantage, nor does it have the capital position to support such losses from existing funds. For some small businesses, those in which the manager makes the wrong decision and selects the self-insurance alternative, the business may be forced into bankruptcy if the loss occurs early in the self-insurance plan.

Before leaving the topic of self-insurance, there is another point that the manager should consider about such a plan. Few, if any, lending institutions will honor any small business self-insurance plan. Many times, loans given to the business will require that certain insurance coverage be obtained and maintained. Usually, only policies from recognized insurance companies will fulfill this requirement.

A small business manager must meet certain requirements in order to file an insurance claim. Remember that an insurance policy is a contract and a gamble. Only those items listed in the policy are covered. No assumptions can or should be made. Insurance companies have carefully reviewed the probabilities of the bet and so should the business manager.

Index

253

Index